CLASSIFICATION AND COGNITION

OXFORD PSYCHOLOGY SERIES

Editors

Donald E. Broadbent

Nicholas J. Mackintosh

James L. McGaugh

Anne Treisman

Endel Tulving

Lawrence Weiskrantz

Classification and Cognition

W. K. Estes

Department of Psychology
Harvard University

OXFORD PSYCHOLOGY SERIES

NO. 22

New York   Oxford
OXFORD UNIVERSITY PRESS • CLARENDON PRESS
1994

Oxford University Press

Oxford   New York   Toronto
Delhi   Bombay   Calcutta   Madras   Karachi
Kuala Lumpur   Singapore   Hong Kong   Tokyo
Nairobi   Dar es Salaam   Cape Town
Melbourne   Auckland   Madrid
and associated companies in
Berlin   Ibadan

Published by Oxford University Press, Inc.,
200 Madison Avenue, New York, New York 10016

Oxford is a registered trademark of Oxford University Press

Library of Congress Cataloging-in-Publication Data
Estes, William Kaye.
Classification and cognition / W.K. Estes.
p.   cm.   (Oxford psychology series ; no. 22)
Includes bibliographical references and index.
ISBN 0-19-507335-5
1. Categorization (Psychology)   2. Recognition (Psychology)
3. Cognitive learning theory.   I. Title.   II. Series.
BF445.E88   1994
153'.012–dc20   93-13101

1 3 5 7 9 8 6 4 2

Printed in the United States of America
on acid-free paper

In memory of Gregory Walker Estes
1949–1985

The Fifth Paul M. Fitts Memorial Lectures
Delivered at the University of Michigan
Ann Arbor, Michigan
May, 1991

Preface

The invitation to give the Fifth Paul M. Fitts Lectures at the University of Michigan came at a highly opportune time for me. I had been intensively engaged in research on various aspects of classification for some 10 years and the the time was ripe for a concentrated effort to bring the strands together. This volume does not, however, give the results of that effort literally as I presented them in 1991. The reason is that giving the lectures in the very stimulating environment at Michigan constituted a highly effective learning experience for me, and it seemed only sensible to incorporate the products of that interaction into the chapters of this book.

What is presented here reflects a cooperative effort in still other senses, and I am indebted to many people for their contributions. Starting with the lectures, I appreciate the interest and patience of the audience at Michigan and the smooth orchestration of the logistics by Gary Olson. The numerous research results from my laboratory* that form the core of this presentation owe much to the work of my graduate assistants—Jane Campbell, Martha Gordon, Joshua Hurwitz, Todd Maddox, Robert Nosofsky, and Daniel Willingham. Several of these young people, in particular, Hurwitz, Maddox, and Nosofsky, developed closely related research interests of their own and their status shifted over a period of years from assistant to collaborator to independent investigator. Another Harvard graduate student, Eliott Mordkowitz, although never an assistant, was a stimulating member of our group.

My theoretical approach to classification has been strongly influenced by close and continuing interactions over many years with an "inner circle" of individuals engaged in closely related research—Douglas Medin, Ed (Edward E.) Smith, and Mark Gluck—and others not so much concerned with categorization and classification but sharing my interests in general problems of memory theory— Roger Ratcliff and Richard Shiffrin.

In the preparation of this book, I have benefited greatly from critiques of various sections by Evan Heit, Douglas Medin, Robert Nosofsky, and Ed Smith. As usual, countless slips and inelegancies of style were winnowed out of my manuscript by the patient efforts of my wife, Kay, who also prepared

* Much of the research reported, together with preparation of this volume, was supported by grants BNS 86-09232, 88-21029, and 90-09001 from the National Science Foundation. I especially appreciate the unflagging interest and cooperation of the Program Director, Joseph L. Young.

the index—and put up with all the solitary evenings during which I communed with my computer. Finally, I appreciate the friendly and perspicacious assistance of Editor Joan Bossert at Oxford University Press.

Cambridge, Massachusetts   W.K.E.
February 1993

Contents

CLASSIFICATION AND COGNITION

1. Introduction and basic concepts

The technology of the second half of the 20th century has given us machines that think, and in doing so has led us to hope that studying these machines may help us to understand the human mind and brain. The machines, most notably digital computers, acquire knowledge, solve problems that people find difficult, and in a primitive way recognize speech and comprehend language. I am not going to enter the debate about how closely computers may ultimately mimic human thinking. What I find more interesting is the vast difference between computers and human beings in one conspicuous respect: we know how computers achieve their results—how they are constructed, how their memories and cognitive mechanisms are organized, what algorithms they use to solve problems. We can usually predict what a computer will do in a problem situation, and we can explain its performance after the fact in terms of well-established principles. In contrast, we are usually mainly in the dark about the basis for human cognitive performance. We have a good knowledge of what people can do in familiar cases, but we have hardly a start toward a comprehensive picture of the mechanisms and processes responsible.

Because the enormity of the problem precludes any straightforward solution, many approaches compete for attention. Naturalistic observation of cognitive behaviors has its uses, but more for raising questions than for producing answers. The methods of experimental psychology, in contrast, enable us to analyze performance in a controlled fashion to discover the factors on which it depends. The combination of observation and experiment has made considerable progress toward a cataloguing of the diverse control processes—rules, strategies, heuristics—that people use to accomplish cognitive tasks. But I have been continually impressed by the very limited degree to which identifying these rules and heuristics helps explain how they evolve with experience, how they are represented in the cognitive system, and, why they sometimes succeed and at other times fail in application.* To go further toward the most challenging goal of cognitive science—understanding the unobservable mechanisms and processes that both enable adaptive thought and constrain it—a time-tested approach is to construct models based on the knowledge derived from experiments. These

---

* In the final chapter of this volume, I will return to these issues and propose a way of including rules and strategies within a general, memory-based, computational model for classification.

lectures portray the results of an interaction of models and experiments conducted over some 30 years in an effort to move toward that goal in the subdomain of human cognition comprising the many aspects of classification and their basis in memory.

1.1 Classification and cognition: an overview

We speak of memory as though it were a record of our experiences, with properties akin to those of a diary or an album of photographs. Not only everyday experience but much carefully conducted research assures us that, up to a point, this conception is well founded. If memory had only those properties, however, it would merely provide a basis for reminiscences. Situations never recur exactly, and therefore the record alone would be of no help to us in dealing with present problems or anticipating the future. Memory is essential to adaptive behavior because it is organized in ways that make information gained from past experience applicable to present situations. And the essence of memory organization is classification. Although we experience only individual events, we remember them and identify recurrences as instances of classes or categories.

I will not dwell at length on the importance of classification and categorization in the cognitive domain; how difficult our lives would be if we did not have classification skills; how many kinds of activities have classification at their heart. Suffice it to say that classification is basic to all of our intellectual activities. Appreciation of that obvious truth raises, but does not answer, the intriguing question of whether all forms of classificatory behavior can be explained in terms of the same mechanisms and processes. Presenting the answer to this question that seems most justifiable in the present state of research and theory is the main task of this volume.

1.1.1 Concepts and categories

The aspect of classification that has the longest history in the literature of philosophy and psychology and that, therefore, is the logical starting point for this enterprise is the problem of how we learn concepts and categories and how they come to be represented in our memory systems. The terms *concept* and *category* are often used interchangeably (e. g., in Smith and Medin 1981), as are *categorization* and *classification*, but I find it useful to make some distinctions. Starting with the latter two, classification implies only that a collection of objects is partitioned into groups, but categorization carries the further implication that knowledge of the category to which an object belongs tells us something about its properties. The fourth grade in a school may be subdivided into several classes, but a pupil's class assignment conveys no information about the pupil's personal characteristics. If the same pupils are categorized by means of a battery of aptitude tests, however, knowledge about the category a pupil belongs to may be quite informative. It might seem at first thought that in cognitive research we deal only with classification in the sense of categorization, but there are some conspicuous exceptions, perhaps most importantly recognition. In a typical recognition study, subjects view a sequence or collection of stimulus patterns, then are tested with a mix of previously seen and novel patterns with the task of classifying each as "old" or "new." Here, class membership carries no information about the properties of a stimulus (except time of occurrence), but otherwise the task is analogous to category learning. Historically, the study of recognition has been entirely distinct from the study of categorization with respect both to research methods and theory development. Whether, nonetheless, categorization and recognition depend on the same memory structures and cognitive processes is an issue that I shall address in some detail.

On the synonymity of *concept* and *category*, I again see reasons to make a distinction. In many instances the terms do seem to be interchangeable, as when the referent is a taxonomical term such as plant, metal, or noun. But other concepts, for example, monotonically increasing, elegant, or irregular, do not fit the mold. A formalist can construct a definition of such concepts in terms of categories, but these constructions appear awkward and remote from our ordinary understanding of the terms. It seems sensible to recognize that some concepts are most naturally expressed in the form of propositions, typically specifying the characteristic properties or best examples associated with the conceptual label (Smith, Osherson, Rips, and Keane 1988), and to be prepared to find that their interpretation involves aspects of memory beyond those essential to the interpretation of categorization. I proceed on the assumption that categorization is an important component of concept formation but not the whole of it. However, because nearly all research on concept formation actually deals with categorization, I will often follow the common practice of using the terms concept and category interchangeably.

1.1.2 Approaches to categorization: two theoretical traditions

Since the ground-breaking studies of the 1920s (Hull 1920; Heidbreder 1924), research on categorization has been polarized with respect to two principal motifs. These were labelled "active" and "passive" approaches by Heidbreder, the former identified with hypothesis testing and the latter with stimulus–response association. The labels have stuck, although the distinction between active and passive categorization has blurred since the emergence of the information-processing framework in the 1960s, and the distinction has shaded into one now better known as analytic versus nonanalytic cognition (Brooks 1978; Jacoby and Brooks 1984). A still more important distinction, to my mind, is between the types of research that have been associated with the two traditions.

(a) Hypothesis testing

In the hypothesis-testing approach, concept formation is treated, in effect, as a form of problem solving. The concepts studied experimentally in this approach are based on formal categories similar to many commonly met in school—for example, adjective/adverb, animate/inanimate, triangle/parallel-ogram—always definable in terms of critical features or properties common to all members of a category and both necessary and sufficient for category membership. The problem for the learner in such studies is to formulate hypotheses about the critical features and test the hypotheses against observations of a sequence of exemplars until an adequate hypothesis is discovered. The large body of research done in this tradition has given rise to a commensurately large body of theory, much of it taking the form of mathematical or computer models (Bruner, Goodnow, and Austin 1956; Bourne and Restle 1959; Hunt, Marin, and Stone 1966; Levine 1967; Trabasso and Bower 1968).

Solution of categorization problems by trial-and-error hypothesis testing seems to me quite characteristic of the kind of experience many of us have had on the occasion of acquiring a personal computer, a spreadsheet, a telephone answering system, or other complex device that comes to hand bristling with problems for the user that cannot be solved by reference to the typically cryptic instructions. The trial-and-error mode does not, however, typify most concept formation in school learning, where rules for categorization are usually communicated verbally or by example rather than being left to be discovered by the pupil. Hypothesis-testing models seem still less applicable to the learning of linguistic or natural categories in ordinary environments. The problem for a child learning to identify objects as members of "natural categories," such as plants, animal species, types of substances, or for an adult learning to respond categorically to the phonological units of a new language is not to test a set of hypotheses known a priori, but to acquire and process relevant information (Rosch 1973; Rosch and Mervis 1975). My view is that hypothesis testing is an important cognitive skill that merits study in its own right but that it has little to do with concept formation. My focus in this volume is on the more basic, or at any rate more general, processes of learning, memory, and cognitive processing that underly the formation of category representations and the use of categorical knowledge in problem solving and decision making.

(b) Category learning

What constitutes category learning? The answer depends, first of all, on the nature of the learning situation (Estes 1989b). Perhaps the most important distinction is between finite and infinite categories (Estes 1986*b*). The suits of an ordinary deck of playing cards constitute finite categories, since each suit has exactly 13 members. Siamese and Persian cats are examples of infinite categories, since it would be impossible to produce an exhaustive list of the members of either category. The distinction may sometimes be subtle but still important. The classification of digits into odd versus even, for example, requires only finite categories, but the same classification of integers requires infinite categories. When finite categories are small, mastering a categorization may seem trivially easy in that the task can be accomplished by rote memorization of the associations between exemplars and category labels (as is no doubt the case when a child learns the distinction between odd and even digits). But when finite categories are large, as in the classification of the citizens of a town, state, or country by ethnic origin, rote memorization does not suffice, and other processes must enter into one's ability to classify newly encountered exemplars with greater than chance accuracy. In fact, it would seem that the task demands of finite categorizations must shade into those of the infinite case as category size increases.

A second important aspect of category learning situations may be expressed as a distinction between taxonomic and statistical, or probabilistic, classifications. In taxonomic classifications (denoted "classical" by Smith and Medin 1981), category membership is definable in terms of a set of critical features or attribute values, and all objects having the same description belong to the same category. Familiar examples are classifications of: compounds as acid, base, or salt; animals by species; and speech sounds by phonemic categories. In probabilistic categorizations, no such definition is available, but there are statistical relations between features and categories with the property that possession of some features or feature combinations makes an object more likely to belong to one category than another. More formally, probabilistic category structures are defined in terms of probability distributions over featural descriptions. Probabilistic categorizations are learnable to the degree that the probability distributions differ between categories. In the case of judicial candidates, for example, review boards and executives responsible for appointment must make decisions on the basis of descriptions of the candidates that are generally only probabilistically related to ultimate classification as liberal or conservative. Similarly, some medical diagnostic categories (for example, varieties of schizophrenia) can be characterized only in terms of statistical relations between symptoms and categories. Whereas experimental research in the earlier, "classical" period of concentration on hypothesis testing was almost entirely limited to simple and clear-cut taxonomic categorizations, there has more recently been a shift of attention to the probabilistic case, partly on the supposition that it is more characteristic of category learning in ordinary life (Fried and Holyoak 1984; Estes 1986*b*; Gluck and Bower 1988*b*).

1.1.3 Categorization and induction

Categorization has been of interest for centuries mainly for its relevance to the problem of induction—how we derive generalized knowledge from specific past experiences. It seems that the most popular answer among laymen who think about such matters, as well as some philosophers and many psychologists, is that, having observed a number of members of a category, we form a mental representation in the form of an abstract image. The representation lacks the detail of a visual or auditory image but contains enough information to enable us to classify and respond appropriately to new instances of a category.

But, although intuitively appealing, the notion of abstract images of categories has often failed to stand up to close philosophical analysis or to gain support from empirical observations. As long ago as the early 18th century, the British philosopher Bishop Berkeley examined the evidence that had then been put forward in defense of a concept of abstract images and found it wanting. He concluded that abstractions are, rather, exclusively verbal in form (Berkeley 1710/1947). Some concepts are, however, fated to be continually reborn. The conception of an abstract image was revived and popularized by Sir Francis Galton (Galton 1878) in his studies of composite photographs, but again ran into hard going in early experimental researches, which firmly supported Berkeley (Stepanovich 1927; Fisher 1931). However, these experiments leaned mainly on evidence from introspection, which for most psychologists cannot stand alone as the basis for theoretically significant conclusions, so the way remained open for the very vigorous revival of the idea of abstract images, or, in more modern terms, *prototypes* of categories associated with the work of Posner and Keele (1968, 1970). Two decades later, we have a curious situation: Theoretical approaches to categorization based on a concept of prototype or abstract image must lead all others in terms of frequency of citation, but the central concept has had so little formal elaboration that it is difficult to test these approaches empirically. We evidently have yet another example of a situation common in science: a theory remains influential over a long period of time, not because of a continuing accrual of empirical support but because of the absence of competing theories.

Until recently, it may well have seemed inconceivable that generalization and induction could be explainable by any theory that did not assume the development of abstract representations of categories, the only question being whether these would prove to be verbal in form or more akin to sensory images. Advances in memory theory during the past two decades have, however, opened up other possibilities. In semantic memory research, for example, a live issue is whether the meaning of a concept is stored in some form in a memory network or is computed from more primitive ingredients when a judgment about meaning is called for (Smith 1978).

Analogously, we need to consider whether category judgments that seem to exhibit generalization or induction from past experience might depend, not on abstract representations of categories, but rather on computations performed, at the time of decision, on a store of memories for specific experiences. In similar vein, Jacoby and Brooks (1984) have marshalled a substantial amount of empirical evidence in support of the idea that many phenomena of perception, recognition, and categorization depend on memory for instances rather than on stored abstractions. However, qualitative arguments alone cannot settle the issue. We need demonstrations that an instance-based memory system can actually generate the specific kinds of performance that have seemed to require abstraction. An important part of the task I wish to accomplish in the following pages is a close examination of the degree to which present-day memory theory can meet this challenge.

My approach in this effort is not to compare and contrast the various published versions of the two approaches, but to ask what the more general theories of memory now available can tell us about structures and processes that must be implicated in all forms of classificatory behavior and what these in themselves enable us to predict about categorization. With this groundwork, we may be in a better position to see just what aspects of categorization require the assumption of more specialized mechanisms and whether or not a theory of categorization need be based on an assumption that generalization depends on stored abstract representations.

1.1.4 Remarks on theoretical style

The primary aim of the research discussed in this volume is to discover more about the processes and mechanisms underlying classification as it occurs in categorization, recognition, and other cognitive domains. I share the hope of many investigators that the kind of theory described here will prove useful in dealing with problems that arise outside the laboratory—in areas of education, health, business, and the like. A time-tested strategy is to draw on those areas for interesting and important practical problems that can be simulated to some degree in the laboratory, but to rely on experimental analyses in the controlled laboratory environment to guide the development and testing of theories. The degree to which the experimental simulations capture the essentials of the applied problems needs verification, which is not easy to obtain. However, an accumulation of relevant studies provides some encouragement in this respect (Bordage and Zacks 1984; Spiegelhalter and Knill-Jones 1984; Lesgold, Rubinson, Feltovich, Klopfer, Glaser, and Wang 1988; Collins, Brown, and Newman 1989; Elstein, Shulman, and Sprafka 1990; Brooks, Norman, and Allen 1991).

For perspective on my theoretical approach, it is useful to think in terms of the distinction between control and structural processes (Atkinson and

Shiffrin 1968). The former category includes the knowledge-based rules, strategies, tactics, and procedures we use in coping with cognitive tasks; in general, they describe or prescribe appropriate performance (rehearsal in a laboratory learning experiment, rules of syntax acquired when learning a new language, tactics that should be used in various positions in chess, and so on). The latter category comprises the processes, mechanisms, and structures that make it possible for us to acquire knowledge and apply learned rules and strategies but that at the same time limit what we can achieve with them.

I focus here on the second category, the cognitive machinery. The work presented has both short- and long-term objectives. My most immediate concern is to develop improved models that can serve as aids to research and provide links to the burgeoning results of neuroscience. But in the longer term, the models should prove useful in analyzing problems and guiding practice in situations that arise outside the laboratory, ranging from language learning to education to decision making in many arenas.

Because research on cognition has these multiple purposes, it is impossible to concentrate on every aspect simultaneously, and thus we run into the problem of tradeoffs. We want the models we develop to provide accurate descriptions of experimental data, to predict new phenomena, and to exhibit steadily increasing scope, that is, ability to address problems across the cognitive domain. Up to a point, descriptive power has to be our first concern in any line of research because models have to demonstrate the ability to describe observational facts before they can begin to qualify for other uses. The only hazard in this respect is losing sight of the fact that giving adequate quantitative descriptions of data is not an adequate goal in itself. It needs to be done as a part of a task with another objective. One important objective is to yield a measure of progress. Informal theories, however intuitively appealing, have the weakness that we generally cannot be sure of the full implications of the theoretical assumptions. When we embody our assumptions about a set of phenomena in a mathematical or computer model, we can "run the model" to discover what the implications actually are and to determine whether the model is sufficient to account for the phenomena.

A perhaps still more important reason for fitting models to data is that our most time-tested way of progressing beyond speculation about the processes that underlie observed phenomena is to use models as frameworks for testing hypotheses. A standard, and very powerful, procedure that is available once we have a model that provides a good fit to a set of data is to augment the model by adding one additional mechanism or process of interest (often, but not necessarily, accomplished by adding one free parameter) and then to compare, statistically when possible, the fits of the augmented and the "nested" original model, taking a significant difference in fit as evidence that the added mechanism or process pays its way and should be retained (Wickens 1982; Estes 1991*c*). It is hard to overestimate the power of this technique for gaining evidence about mechanisms and processes that cannot be directly observed.

But here we run into a tradeoff between prediction and description. When making a start in any new domain, one often finds it quite easy at first to get some very good descriptions. It is those happy events that bring some people into the game of trying to generate descriptions of behavior from models. A notable example is the burst of remarkable descriptions of some forms of paired-associate learning and concept identification by simple all-or-none learning models of the stimulus-sampling family in the early 1960s (Bower 1961; Atkinson, Bower, and Crothers 1965). It inevitably turns out, however, that as a model is applied to variations on the original experiments, its descriptions begin to fail. Then the natural tendency is to augment the model with additional processes, additional mechanisms, and additional parameters so as to improve the descriptions. But the improvement occurs at the cost of genuine predictions. In the nature of things, one cannot use a model to anticipate what is likely to happen in a new situation if predictions can be generated only after data from the new situation are available to enable estimates of many free parameters.

The answer to this tradeoff problem, in my view, is to treat description and prediction as distinct, if not entirely independent, goals and to give serious attention to both. Thus, in the following chapters, I will follow the standard practice of using fits of models to data as a basis for testing hypotheses about component processes, but also I will continually raise the question of what a model enables us to predict a priori about the outcome of an experiment. Often it turns out that the model that yields the best description of a set of data must be greatly simplified in order to yield a conceptual tool that can help us anticipate the outcomes of experiments in advance and interpret data in instructive ways.

Pursuing concurrently the goals of description and prediction seems, in my experience, to lead to a hierarchical organization of theory. For a given domain, in this case cognition, the top level comprises collections of phenomena that have been analyzed experimentally in various subdomains, for example, categorization, identification, recognition, and short- and long-term recall. At a middle level are principles or models developed more or less independently in the various subdomains. At the bottom level is a set of core concepts or principles. The core model alone can yield non-trivial predictions for all of the subdomains; and, in combination with local principles, it can supply rigorous descriptions of specific phenomena. Finally, but perhaps most importantly, the core model can be a useful aid to the interpretation of research results in all of the subdomains.

The most ambitious goal I have in mind for this volume is to give as concrete a demonstration as I can of the progress made in the last few years toward a core body of theory that realizes these objectives. The theory combines a general framework, which I have termed for brevity the *array model* (Estes 1986*b*, 1991*b*), and a core set of concepts that can be used to help analyze situations in any of the cognitive subdomains.

1.2 The array model framework

Just as even the most complex natural objects can be understood as resulting from the combining of a small number of basic particles in an almost infinite variety of ways, human mental activity can be seen as a compounding of a small number of mental operations. Pre-eminent among these are representation, selection, and comparison.

1.2.1 Representation: attributes, dimensions, and features

The basis for all mental activity is a memory in which representations of previous experiences are recorded. We have no way of getting directly at the nature of these representations, but a great deal of indirect evidence from research on memory supports the idea that they are encoded in terms of attributes of objects or events (Bower 1967; Underwood 1969; Spear 1976). Thus in the cognitive architecture assumed in my approach to memory, the contents of memory can be viewed as an array of vectors, each vector constituting a list of the attributes of some object or event (Estes 1986*a*, 1991*b*).

The attributes may be values on stimulus dimensions—e. g., brightness, pitch, length—or they may be qualitative features recorded only as present or absent—e. g., feathered, rusty, plastic. The coding is assumed to be accomplished by units in the sensory processing system familiar under such labels as analyzers or feature detectors. The neural bases of these units must, of course, be very different at different levels of the cognitive system. At the level of the visual cortex, even single cells function as detectors. For example, a particular cell may remain quiet as the organism inspects a scene till a sharp edge between light and shadow comes into view, then spring into activity (Hubel and Wiesel 1962). At a somewhat higher level, analyzers that must be supposed to comprise ensembles of cells generate outputs when information is being processed from stimuli that vary along simple sensory dimensions. This conception has become standard in domains as far apart as animal learning (Sutherland and Mackintosh 1971) and coding in human visual processing (Uttal 1973; Levine and Shefner 1981). In speech perception, a listener is assumed to analyze speech input in terms of binary-valued "distinctive features" (Jakobson, Fant, and Halle 1952)—for example, a small part of a table presenting the standard phonological encodings of English consonants takes the form:

Feature	Consonant
	p b m
Nasal/oral	– – +
Tense/lax	+ –
Uninterrupted/interrupted	– – +

In each case a record of the output of the detector or analyzer is an element of the coded representation of the stimulus in memory. The same concept has been extended to still higher levels, where one speaks of detection of semantic features, with no implications about the associated neural machinery but with the expectation that the functional properties will be very similar to those at lower levels (Smith, Shoben, and Rips 1974). When we speak of an organism, subhuman or human, detecting features or encoding attribute values in memory, we do not imply that objects or scenes in the environment should be viewed as comprising bundles of features or attributes—only that the enormously rich information coming into the sensory system from the environment is encoded in a less rich but more manageable form in memory in terms of the outputs of detectors or analyzers.

In the literature on attribute representations, there have been suggestions of a qualitative distinction between dimensional values and on/off features (Smith and Medin 1881; Garner 1976). It seems clear, however, that a feature, even though recorded in an all-or-none manner by an investigator, can generally be seen to vary in the degree to which it is present. Antlers on a deer may be defined as a qualitative feature, but antlers are present on a particular deer to differing degrees depending on age of the animal and time of year. And similar observations can be made about other commonly listed features such as living, feathered, rigid, wooden, and so on. My view is that the terms dimension and feature simply denote modes of coding attribute information from the environment. Depending on many conditions, the processing system may store in memory graded representations of attribute values or may apply a criterion and store only an indicator of whether the criterion is met in a given case. For theoretical, and perhaps sometimes practical, purposes, it is important to know which mode of coding is being used. We rarely have any direct knowledge on the issue, however, and it is one of the prime functions of models to help us test relevant hypotheses. In one study of categorization, for example, the investigators wanted to determine whether information about medical symptoms presented to experimental subjects would be encoded in terms of on/off features or binary-valued dimensions (Estes, Campbell, Hatsopoulis, and Hurwitz 1989). They fitted their categorization data with two models that differed only with respect to the coding assumption and obtained a significantly better fit for the on/off feature version. The result may or may not generalize to other apparently similar situations, but that question, too, can be answered by further applications of the same method.

1.2.2 The problem of access to memory

(a) Access by strength of association

Once memories have been stored, how can they be accessed when needed for some current purpose? In the century-old literature of memory research, there have been three principal answers. The oldest is that of association psychology: items stored in memory, or their connections with responses, have different strengths by virtue of differences in frequency and recency of activation and the rewarding or nonrewarding consequences of associated responses, and these strengths determine current availability. When memory is probed, as by presentation of a stimulus in a recognition or recall test, the most strongly associated item in memory is the one most likely to be activated (Carr 1931; Robinson 1932). A richly elaborated modern version of association theory, which has many features in common with the theory I will present, is the SAM model of Raaijmakers and Shiffrin (1981).

(b) Access by search and retrieval

Beginning about 1960, association theory was displaced from its long-standing position of prime influence in memory theory by concepts of information processing—storage, search, and retrieval (Atkinson and Shiffrin 1968; Rumelhart Lindsay and Norman 1972; Anderson and Bower 1973). The now highly familiar mode of speaking about retrieval from memory by analogy with the retrieval of books from a library or bits of information from the memory of a digital computer has a good deal of heuristic value, but for most investigators (with the notable exclusion of Anderson 1990, 1991) has not seemed to provide a sufficient basis for interpreting the wide variety of phenomena of memory, as witness the flourishing of hybrid models that combine concepts of information processing with concepts of spreading activation in networks (Collins and Loftus 1975; Anderson 1976; Posner 1978; Dell 1986).

(c) Access by similarity and resonance

The third answer to the problem of access, and the one assumed in my proposal for a core theory of memory, is based on similarity. In much the same vein as Ratcliff (1978), I assume that a perceived stimulus pattern resonates with stored patterns in somewhat the same way that a tone sounded on a musical instrument resonates with a set of tuning forks, activating vectors in the memory array in direct relation to similarity of the perceived to the stored patterns. My specific way of conceptualizing and measuring similarity derives from the work of Medin and his associates (Medin 1975; Medin and Schaffer 1978) and will be fully explicated in the next section.

1.2.3 Comparison and similarity

Of the basic concepts that need close attention before we can begin to look at full models and applications, perhaps the highest priority goes to similarity, which to my mind is at the very heart of theory of cognition and memory. It is because of the ability of organisms like ourselves to make positive use of similarity that the past is relevant to the present. Remembering accurately events that happened in the past would help our present activities very little if we were unable to judge the similarities between past events and present situations so as to have a basis for deciding on the relevance of things remembered for present tasks.

Because of the central role of similarity, one of the prime tasks that we have to keep coming back to again and again is looking for the best models of similarity. What we need is a model that captures the notion of similarity as it appears to our intuitions and that also has the formal properties essential to make it an effective tool in the development of mathematical and computer models and the analysis of data. None of the efforts that have been made in the past have been entirely adequate to meet these desiderata but, because of the importance of the concept, the efforts continue. In my own research history, I have had to come back more often and try harder than anyone else I know of because the historical setting when I entered the field of learning research all but compelled a strong attachment to a then popular model whose limitations only very slowly became apparent to me.

(a) Similarity and commonality

The historical setting I refer to is the common elements theory of generalization, first set forth clearly by Thorndike (1913) near the beginning of this century, though he was building on a tradition of thinking going back to John Locke and David Hume. Thorndike assumed that the similarity between any two situations is measurable in terms of the proportion of common elements and that similarity, so defined, is the basis for generalization, or transfer of learning, between tasks practiced in school and situations outside the schoolroom for which pupils are preparing. In my earliest formal theory (Estes 1950), which came to be known as a *stimulus sampling model* for learning and behavior, I simply incorporated the notion of common elements into a model that could generate quantitative predictions about transfer of training.

In stimulus sampling theory it is assumed that we do not always perceive situations all of a piece, but may take in only information about fragments, or aspects of them. Usually only samples of all the possible components are available to us on any particular occasion, and only the sampled components enter into learned associations with response alternatives or with events that we might be trying to predict. Relative probabilities of any two responses in a situation are assumed to be in the ratio of the proportions of components of the situation that are associated with them.

These notions can be conveniently illustrated in terms of a very small scale experiment that was done long ago in my laboratory (cited in Atkinson and Estes 1963, p. 193), with the design summarized in Table 1.1. After learning to associate Response 1 with stimulus components denoted a, b, and c and Response 2 with d, e, and f, the subjects were tested with a new display made up of some elements from the first set and some elements from the second. The prediction from the model is that the probability of making Response 1 is equal to the proportion of these elements that were associated with it, and the accuracy of the prediction was gratifyingly close.

The gratification, however, proved double edged. This success and a number of related ones had the unfortunate consequence of wedding me and my associates of that period so strongly to the idea of generalization via the proportionality rule that, even though some severe limitations were soon manifest, we took a very long time weaning ourselves from it. One of the most conspicuous limitations had to do with the tradeoff between discrimination and generalization. If the situation of Table 1.1 were just slightly modified so that subjects had the task of learning a discrimination between two overlapping sets of components (e.g., abd indicating that Response 1 was correct and bcd that Response 2 was correct), it must be predicted from the stimulus sampling model that the kind of generalization shown in Table 1.1 would continue to occur and thus the learner would continue to make errors indefinitely. However, both everyday experience and formal experiments (Uhl 1964; Robbins 1970) assure us that people can readily learn perfect discriminations in such tasks. Over a period of years there were numerous efforts to solve the "overlap problem," but all were constrained by the premise of generalization via commonality and none yielded fully satisfactory solutions (Bush and Mosteller 1951; Restle 1955, 1961; Estes and Hopkins 1961).

Table 1.1   Transfer via common elements in stimulus sampling model (SSM)

Training	Stimulus	Response	
	a b c	1	
	d e f	2	
Test	*Stimulus*	*Probability of response 1*	
		SSM	*Observed*
	b c d	0.667	0.669
	c d e	0.333	0.332

A deeper problem with the model was a lack of richness in the representation assumptions that made it difficult to address tasks requiring response to multidimensional stimuli. Other approaches to the conceptualization of similarity appeared during that period, perhaps the most ultimately fruitful one being that of Shepard (1958), but they were not immediately brought to bear on the overlap problem. It was not until the mid-1970s that a combination of new influences shook me out of a mental rut and led me to take a genuinely new look at the problem of conceptualizing similarity.

(b) Context, hierarchical organization, and the product rule

In retrospect, the transition from the treatment of similarity that once seemed inescapable as the basis for models of classification to the one that I now find far superior required an incredibly long time and illustrates how difficult it is for investigators to get away from old ways of thinking even in the face of an accumulation of evidence pointing to the need for change. The way the transition occurred revolves around the role of context. By the time I entered upon research on behavior in the 1940s, experimental psychologists had established to the point of a truism that performance of any learned act, including retrieval of information from memory, depends on reinstatement of the context in which learning occurred. In studies of human memory, recall of material learned in a particular practice session is impaired if the test is given in a different room or at a different time of day (Thorndike 1913, 1931; McGeoch 1942). Similarly, in studies of animal learning, a conditioned stimulus may fail to evoke a conditioned response if the experimental chamber, the experimenter, or other source of background stimulation is changed (Pavlov 1927).

During the early development of stimulus sampling theory, I was well aware of the importance of context, and, in fact, formulated a model for the function of drives in animal behavior based on the conception that the effective stimulating situation for any behavior includes internally generated stimuli, for example, those arising from stomach contractions in a hungry animal or from a dry throat in a thirsty one, as well as stimuli from external sources—discriminative cues, conditioned stimuli, or whatever (Estes 1958). On the standard assumption of stimulus sampling theory that stimuli combine additively, it was possible to account for such phenomena as changes in performance levels of learned responses with shifts in drive states. It was not until a decade later, when I became familiar with the extensive summarization of relevant research by Konorski (1967), that I began to realize that the effects of changes in context, internal or external, are often too large to be accounted for by the additive model. Consider a typical conditioning situation in which a response has been conditioned to a stimulus, S, in the presence of a set of contextual cues, X. The number, or "weight," of stimulus elements in X must be assumed to be fairly small relative to those in S, or it would not be possible for the animal to learn to make the conditioned response to $X+S$ but not to X alone. On that assumption, changing the context between conditioning and a test of retention could have only a small effect on probability of the conditioned response, but work cited by Konorski made it clear that actually a change in context often suffices to reduce probability of a conditioned response to zero. And still later, research showed that shifts in context can have nearly as drastic effects on recall of verbal material by human subjects (Baddeley 1976).

Once the insufficiency of the additive combination rule had become clear, I modified my model by assuming that stimulation from discriminative cues and background context (whether external or internal) combine in the manner of an AND gate in an electrical network, as illustrated in Fig. 1.1 (Estes 1972, 1973). In the example of the preceding paragraph, once response R has been conditioned to cue S in context X, evocation of R by S requires the simultaneous activation of elements of S and elements of X. The extreme sensitivity of conditioned responses to shifts in context can now be accounted for, because regardless of the strength of association of the learned ("conditioned") response to S, the probability of occurrence of the response is reduced to zero if the context changes sufficiently from learning to test that presentation of S in the test context, X', activates no elements of X. The new assumption has the additional attractive property that the mechanism of an AND gate provides a convenient basis for the development of hierarchical organization in memory (Estes 1972).

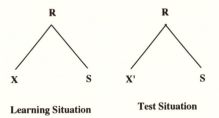

Learning Situation   **Test Situation**

Fig. 1.1 Multiplicative combination of cue and context following learning in which stimulus S has become associated with response R in context X. The converging paths leading to R in each panel express   the assumption that the strengths of activation (tendencies to evoke R) associated with the two paths must be multiplied to determine response probability. If, in a test situation, the context has changed from X to X', then the strength of activation in the path from context to response is reduced; specifically, the probability of R in the new situation is proportional to the similarity between X and X', dropping to zero if X and X' are sufficiently dissimilar.

In this new formulation, cue and context are said to combine *multiplicatively* rather than *additively*. To explain why, I will need to fill out the assumptions of the revised model. When, in the conditioning example, the cue S (termed a "conditioned stimulus") occurs in the new context, X', the probability of evocation of the conditioned response is assumed to be equal to the similarity between the total test situation $(S + X')$ and the total learning situation $(S + X)$. The similarity of S to itself is assumed to have a value of unity and the similarity of X' to X some value s, whose value falls between 0 and 1. The similarity between the two situations is assumed to be given by the product of the constituent similarities, in this case the product of 1 and s, which is simply s. Obviously, if X and X' are sufficiently different that s is equal to 0, the probability of the conditioned response is equal to 0. Thus the model, so revised, readily accounts for shifts of context.

Just one nagging question marred my pleasure with the successes of the revised model. Namely, why should discriminative cues combine additively with each other but multiplicatively with context? I was too constrained by habitual modes of classification to see any satisfactory answer, but the same was not true of Douglas Medin, a faculty associate at Rockefeller University, where these developments were occurring in the early 1970s. It was Medin who produced an elegant solution. The multiplicative combination of cue and context is simply a special case of a *product rule* that holds in general for the dependence of behavior on stimulus similarity relationships. Whenever learning occurs in one situation and a test for retention is given in another, response probability on the test is a function of the similarity of the training and test situations, computed as follows. We compare the two situations (which may, but need not, include contextual components), feature by feature, applying a similarity coefficient of unity if the features match and a coefficient with some smaller value, s, if they differ. The measure of similarity is the product of these coefficients. Simple as this idea appears, it laid the groundwork for a new model of animal discrimination learning (Medin 1975), and then, with only slight elaboration, for the first effective formalization of the concept of instance-based categorization learning (Medin and Schaffer 1978). Turning now from the historical account of this development, I will begin a portrayal of its consequences for categorization theory with a systematic discussion of the treatment of similarity by means of the product rule.

1.2.4 The product rule for patterns of binary-valued attributes

For simplicity of exposition, I will illustrate the product rule in this section only for binary-valued attributes, including on/off features, but the extension to continuous dimensions is direct, as will be shown in a later section.

Table 1.2   Computation of pattern similarity

	Feature					
	1	2	3	4	5	6
Starling	+	+	−	+	+	+
Sandpiper	+	+	+	+	−	+
Feature similarity	1	1	s	1	s	1
Pattern similarity =	$1 \times 1 \times s \times 1 \times s \times 1 = s^2$					

A first example of the application of the product rule to patterns of on/off features is shown in Table 1.2. We assume that two birds, starling and sandpiper, are represented for a particular observer in terms of six features, an entry of + in the table denoting presence of a given feature and an entry of − representing its absence . We start the similarity computation by determining the similarity between the two birds on each individual feature, entering a 1 for a match (presence of a given feature in both patterns or absence of a given feature in both patterns) and the parameter s for a mismatch, as shown in the row labelled "Feature similarity." Application of the product rule then yields the expression s^2 for the pattern similarity, as shown in the bottom row of Table 1.2. It will be readily seen that, more generally, the similarity of any two patterns, i and j, generated from a set of N features must be given by

$$\text{Sim } (i,j) = s^{N-k}, \tag{1.1}$$

where k denotes the number of matches between the two patterns. One obvious implication of Equation 1.1 is that, so long as s is less than unity, the pattern similarity tends to zero as the number of mismatches increases. To enable quantitative predictions, the parameter s must be assigned a numerical value in the range 0 to 1, either by an a priori assumption or by statistical estimation from data.

In a more general version of the product rule than will be considered in this chapter, we might assign different similarity parameters to mismatches on different attributes, i. e., s_i for a mismatch on attibute i, as illustrated in Table 1.3. Once the feature similarities are entered, as in the Feature. Similarity row of Table 1.3, the pattern similarity is computed just as in the simpler case of Table 1.2. The right side of Equation 1.1 would now be replaced by the product of the values of s_i for the $N-k$ mismatching attributes.

In most laboratory experiments on categorization, the instructions specify the set of attributes or features on which comparisons should be made, and application of the product rule is then straightforward. In some experiments, however, and often outside the laboratory, the specification is ambiguous or

Table 1.3 Computation of pattern similarity with mismatch similarities varying over attributes

	Feature					
	1	2	3	4	5	6
Starling	+	+	−	+	+	+
Sandpiper	+	+	+	+	−	+
Feature similarity	1	1	s_3	1	s_5	1
Pattern similarity =	$1 \times 1 \times s_3 \times 1 \times s_5 \times 1 = s_3 s_5$					

lacking, and before applying the product rule to compute similarity between patterns, one must decide what set of features will enter into the comparison. There is no body of formal theory available to predict what features individuals will attend to in ambiguous situations, so we have to fall back on guidelines suggested by general theory, experience, and intuition. The customary default procedure, applied when there is no apparent reason to do otherwise, is to use what I will term the *union rule*. The procedure is to list all of the features belonging to either of the objects being compared and then compute a product in which the value 1 is entered for each feature in the list that belongs to both objects and the quantity *s* is entered for each feature that is in only one of the two objects, as done for the comparison of two birds in Table 1.2. Suppose, however, that an individual with the memory representation of starling shown in Table 1.2 encountered a new bird (actually a sandpiper) and was in a position to perceive only that it had features 1, 2, and 3. If we wished to predict whether the individual would categorize the new bird as a starling, we would base our prediction on a computation of similarity using what I will term the *intersection rule*. That is, we would assume that the individual would focus attention on features 1, 2, and 3, and would compute the similarity between the new bird and starling on only these features, obtaining $1 \times 1 \times s = s$ for the pattern similarity, in contrast to the value s^2 obtained with the union rule. This problem of selection of the comparison set is discussed further in Appendix 1.1.

(a) Storage versus computation of pattern information

Some simple but very useful properties of the product rule are responsible for its widespread appearance in models for classification. One of these has to do with capturing relational information and can be illustrated as follows. Suppose that a lifelong city dweller on a first visit to a rural area observes a number of birds that are new to her and, with the help of friends native to the area, tries to learn to identify the birds. A series of observations generates the following memory array:

Feature pattern	Bird category
Red with crest	Cardinal
Red with no crest	Tanager
Blue with crest	Bluejay
Blue with no crest	Bluebird

That is, she learns that a bird with a crest is either a cardinal or a bluejay, that a red bird is either a cardinal or a scarlet tanager, and so on. But in order to identify birds correctly, she must use relational facts, for example, that only the combination of red and crest signifies a cardinal, only the combination of blue and crest signifies a bluejay. Must we, then, assume that not only joint occurrences of features and category labels but also information about relations between features is stored in memory? That assumption has, in fact been made in some theories. For example, Hayes-Roth and Hayes-Roth (1977) assumed that each combination of perceived features is registered in memory as a higher-order unit, so that in the example the combination of red and crest would be stored in memory as a unit that occurred only in conjunction with the label "cardinal;" and much the same assumption has been incorporated into the "configural cue" model of Gluck, Bower, and Hee (1989). I will not try to evaluate that type of model here except to note that the assumption of relational storage requires the further assumption of mechanisms for detecting and encoding joint occurrences of features and faces the difficulty that, unless the number of features is very small, the number of higher order units that must be processed becomes very large.

The critical point I do want to make is that in the case of the array model, there is no need for any special mechanism for storage of relational information. It is assumed that the only units of storage are features, or attribute values, and that the work of taking account of relations among features is accomplished by application of the product rule at the time when memory is probed. In the example of the birds, if the individual were shown a red bird with a crest, its similarity to the stored representation of cardinal would be $1 \times 1 = 1$, its similarity to tanager $1 \times s = s$, its similarity to bluejay $s \times 1 = s$, and to bluebird, $s \times s = s^2$. Thus, providing only that s had a value less than unity, there would be a clear basis for identifying the test bird correctly as a cardinal.

(b) Weighting of matches in similarity computations

As the product rule has most often been used in models of categorization, the similarity parameter s has been assumed equal to unity for matches on attribute values and allowed to take on differing values for mismatches on different attributes (e. g., Medin and Schaffer 1978; Nosofsky 1984, 1986). For my purposes in this volume, I will nearly always simplify the standard treatment in one respect, by assuming that the value of *s* is the same for mismatches with respect to all features or binary-valued dimensions that occur in any situation considered. However, I will generalize the standard treatment by allowing the possibility that the similarity value for a match can have a value greater than unity. The expression for similarity of two *N*-feature patterns (Equation 1.1) then becomes

$$\text{Sim } (i,j) = ts^{N-k}, \tag{1.2}$$

where *t* represents the similarity value of a match and *s* the similarity value of a mismatch on any one attribute.

The rule for computing pattern similarity for patterns defined by on/off features or binary-valued dimensions is, then: (1) compare two patterns feature-by-feature and (2) enter the feature similarities, *t* for a match and *s* for a mismatch, into a product. The parameter *s* has a value in the range $0 \leq s \leq 1$ and in nearly all applications is assumed or estimated to be less than 1, in which case higher powers of *s* denote smaller values of pattern similarity. The value of the parameter *t* falls in the range $0 \leq \infty$. In the literature involving the product rule, *t* has customarily been tacitly assumed equal to 1 (as in Equation 1.1 above) and thus has not appeared in expressions for pattern similarity. Except where otherwise specified, I will follow the same practice. Sometimes, however, it is desirable to allow for other values, as is brought out by the following illustration.

In the same-different task much studied in experimental cognitive psychology, a subject is shown on any trial two brief visual displays, usually strings of digits or letters, for example,

A B

A E

and quickly makes a judgment as to whether they are the same or different, reaction time or accuracy being used as the performance measure. If we compute the similarity of the two strings from the general form of the product rule, we obtain the value *ts*. If, instead, the pair of strings to be compared were

A B C D

A E C D

then the similarity would be t^3s. If we assumed that *t* was equal to 1, the result would be simply *s* in both cases, and a model based on the product rule could predict no difference in performance. However, it seems intuitively obvious that enlarging the patterns being compared by adding elements that are common to both should increase the pattern similarity. This intuition can be accommodated by the product rule with t greater than 1. If, say, t were equal to 2, then the computed similarity between AB and AE in the first example above would be $2s$, and the similarity between ABCD and AECD would be $8s$. Thus, only the general form of the product rule, incorporating the parameter t, can accommodate the many reported experiments on same-different judgments, in which the data uniformly show both reaction time and error frequencies to be increasing functions of the number of elements common to two patterns being compared (Bamber 1969; Silverman 1973; Krueger 1978).

Under precisely what conditions the inclusion of the powers of t will change predictions about similarity judgments or other responses depends on considerations that we are not ready to take up at this point.* Suffice it to say that in some cases the inclusion of t as a free parameter does affect predictions; in applications of the model to many sets of data on categorization and recognition, including a study of concurrent categorization discussed in Chapter 4, I have in some instances obtained estimates of t that differ from unity, usually being greater than unity and sometimes substantially so.

(c) Sensitivity to small differences

A concern one sometimes hears expressed about the product rule is that it may be excessively sensitive to minor differences between patterns. Suppose that a skeptic describes a hypothetical situation in which a judgment of similarity is to be made between two photos of the same person, taken in the same setting and with the person identically dressed on the two occasions except for the presence or absence of spectacles. On the assumption that presence versus absence of spectacles must imply a similarity near zero on that attribute, the skeptic claims that application of the product rule must predict that the persons in the two photos would be judged to be different despite the almost innumerable points of similarity. However, the problem is not as simple as it looks. An obvious complication is that the premise of a zero value of the similarity parameter s for presence versus absence of spectacles might not be satisfied in real life. We could only find out by conducting an appropriate experiment. A second complication is that a near zero value of s on one attribute implies a near zero similarity between two patterns only for the special case of the model in which the similarity parameter t for a match on any attribute is set equal to 1. In the general model, the parameter t is not fixed and it is the ratio of s to t that measures similarity; thus a near zero value of s could be compensated by a very small value of t.

---

* Sometimes the terms in t do and sometimes they do not divide out of ratios that are formed in the computation of response probabilities.

A deeper problem is that the skeptic's claim cannot be evaluated unless the conditions for testing it are specified. Let us consider one plausible test procedure. We show an observer two pictures of an individual A, one without and one with glasses, one picture of another individual B without glasses and one of a third individual C with glasses. Letting x denote the feature "glasses present" and a, b, and c the other features of A, B, and C, the observer's memory array will be:

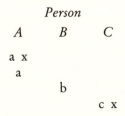

Now, if we test the observer on individual A with glasses (feature pattern ax), similarity to A will be $1+s$; if we test on A without glasses (feature pattern a), similarity to A is again $1+s$. And the similarity of A, with or without glasses, to B and C added together is s^2+s. So long as the value of s is less than unity, we predict that the observer will be more likely to judge either a or ax to represent A than to represent anyone else. The skeptic's supposition that, if s approached zero, the observer would fail to identify A with or without glasses as the same person is actually not an implication of the model. As so often happens, the apparent force of an intuitive objection to a model dissolves when we look closely at the question of how it could be tested.

(d) Attention to relevant attributes

In situations calling for identification or classification of objects, we often find that many, or even most, of the attributes of the events and context are irrelevant, that is, wholly uninformative. For an extreme illustration, imagine a pair of identical twins who match so closely on virtually all perceptual features that they can be distinguished only by the fact that one twin has a small scar on her left wrist. With the set of features common to the two twins denoted by f and the scar by f', we might find that a series of observations of the twins (plus information about the correct identities) would give rise to the following memory array:

Twin

1	2
f f'	
	f
	f
f	

That is, on two observations of Twin 1, the observer happened to perceive the scar on only the first, but on two observations of Twin 2 necessarily perceived only the common features, f. On a subsequent test with Twin 1, if the scar is noticed, so that the stimulus pattern is ff'', the similarity to column 1 of the array will be $1+s$ and to Column 2, $2s$; and if s is small, there will be a large difference in favor of Column 1, providing the basis for a correct identification.* If, however, the scar is not noticed, these similarities will be $1+s$ and 2; and, if s is small, there will be a large difference in favor of Column 2, which would tend to produce an erroneous identification. In general, if the scar is noticed on a proportion p of such tests, the average similarities to Columns 1 and 2 will be $1+s$ and $2(ps+1-p)$, respectively. When s is equal to 0, yielding maximal discriminability, these similarities are 1 and $2(1-p)$, respectively, and it is clear that identification can be accurate only if p approaches unity.

In the model developed up to this point, there is no mechanism to ensure that p will approach unity over a series of trials. The model can, however, be augmented with an attentional learning process that will do so. One way of achieving this end is discussed in Appendix 1.2.

(e) Memory size and the problem of selection

The memory of an adult human being must be almost unimaginably enormous, and, since transmission in neural circuits is very slow compared to that in computers, it seems clear that only a relatively small subregion of memory can be accessed during any one cognitive task. I assume that the essential selectivity is automatically accomplished by the similarity-based mode of access. Each stored vector includes features, such as category labels or aspects of the context in which a learning experience occurred. Thus, by a mechanism that will be discussed in detail in the next section, a group of memories that share a categorical or contextual feature that is present in a memory probe (i.e., in a perceived stimulus) has on that account an increased similarity to the probe relative to other groups and therefore the constituent memories can be selected and activated together. When interpreting experiments, one always deals with only a subregion of memory, and, for simplicity, the contextual features are omitted from the description of a hypothesized memory array unless there is some specific reason to refer to them.

(f) Memory and action

The theories that have developed in the information-processing approach to cognition impress many people as being somewhat "cold," or dehumanized in that storage and retrieval of memories are assumed to be accomplished by

---

* The formalities of going from similarity differences to identification probabilities will be taken up in Chapter 2.

processes that run off more or less mechanistically, without reference to motives or goals of the individual. I can empathize with this reaction, because long before the term "information processing" had even appeared in psychology, I had spent many years in research related to theories of learning in which motives, incentives, and feedback mechanisms were always major players. The model that will be the focus of most attention in this volume, a combination of the array architecture and memory access by similarity computations, falls squarely in the information-processing tradition. In contrast, an approach to learning and categorization developed by Gluck and Bower (1988*a,b*), termed an adaptive network model, interprets memory storage as the result of a process in which the weights with which memory traces enter into cognitive operations are continually adjusted during learning so as to reduce disparities between the actual consequences and the desired consequences of actions. Proceeding from that work, I have made some progress toward formulation of a "similarity-network" model that combines aspects of the two approaches. This model has two main components: (1) the array architecture, in which memory interfaces with perception by means of a mechanism based on similarity, and (2) a network in which strengths of associations between memory and action systems are modifiable by an error-correcting learning process. Thus, we separate two aspects of cognition that have been fused in earlier approaches. Access to an item in memory that may be relevant to a current situation depends only on its similarity to a component of the current situation that serves as a memory probe; but the selection of the response to be made on the basis of the retrieved memory depends on strengths (technically, *weights*) of connections in the network that reflect frequency, recency, and outcomes of previous activations. The system is designed so that, when it is working well, one remembers what actually occurred in an earlier situation rather than what one might prefer to remember, yet one's choice of actions based on the memory may adaptively take account of the payoffs and penalties experienced on previous occasions.

Because I have developed the information-processing model more fully and with many more applications, I will take it as the starting point in each of the treatments of specific problems of classification and cognition to be presented in this volume. As a secondary, though not necessarily minor, theme, I will develop the similarity-network model in parallel and discuss both comparisons between these models and possibilities of achieving some kind of unification.

1.2.5 The core model for classification

Henceforth I will refer to the combination of the array framework and the product rule as the *core model for classification* (sometimes, alternatively, the *array-similarity model*). It will become apparent in the following chapters that even this very limited theoretical machinery can be useful in the analysis of a variety of problems of classification and can even generate non-trivial a priori predictions for some situations. Most often, the core model will have to be augmented with some additional assumptions in order to yield quantitative accounts of experimental data. In the next two chapters, we will proceed through a series of applications with the objective of discovering the minimal set of augmentations needed to give us a useful model for category learning.

Appendix 1.1 Union and intersection rules for computation of pattern similarity

Before proceeding with applications of the product rule, we need to address in a preliminary way the problem of attribute alignment, that is, how the attributes of a complex perceived pattern such as a visual scene are set in correspondence to attributes of a representation in memory (Goldstone and Medin, in press). For the kinds of situations considered in this volume, the problem comes down to that of selecting the attributes on which the percept and the stored representation will be compared. When we are dealing with multidimensional stimulus representations, the standard way of handling alignment seems entirely satisfactory. If, for example, a comparison is between two stimuli, I and I', each of which has a value on each of N dimensions—

Stimulus	*Dimension*
	1 2 3 ... N
I	v_1 v_2 v_3 ... v_N
I'	v_1' $v2$ v_3' ... v_N'

—then we compute similarities between the two stimuli on each dimension separately, $s_{II'(1)}, s_{II'(2)}, \ldots s_{II'(N)}$, and multiply these terms to obtain overall pattern similarity, $S_{II'}$.

When we are dealing with on/off feature representations, however, there is no standard procedure, and I will consider two principal cases. The first, leading to what I will term the *union rule*, is a direct extension of the standard procedure. Suppose that stimulus I comprises features f_1, f_2, and f_3, and stimulus I' comprises f_1 and f_4. Then we can use an alignment analogous to the one for multidimensional stimuli:

Stimulus	*Feature*
	1 2 3 4
I	+ + + −
I'	+ − − +

We compute the similarity between I and I' with respect to each feature, normally by assigning a value 1 for a match and a value *s* for a mismatch, and multiply these values to obtain the pattern similarity. Thus the general procedure for the union rule is, in effect, to define a "slot" for each dimension on which two stimuli vary, or for each feature that appears in either stimulus, then to apply Equation 1.1 of the text,

$$\text{Sim}(i,i') = s^{N-k},$$

with *N* denoting the number of slots and *k* the number of matches. Roughly speaking, the union rule is applicable whenever the task is simply to judge the overall similarity of two patterns, as is nearly always the case during category learning.

The second alignment procedure, which I term the *intersection rule*, arises most often when transfer tests are given following category learning, the transfer stimuli often having different numbers of features than the training exemplars and the instruction to the subject is to estimate the probability of a category in the presence of only those features shown in the test pattern (as was the case, for example, in Experiment 1 of Estes, Campbell, Hatsopoulis, and Hurwitz 1989). More generally, this rule is applicable whenever task orientation implies that similarity between a perceived pattern (a "probe," in the terminology of memory research) and a remembered pattern is to be judged only with respect to the features present in the probe. The procedure, then, is to compute similarities only for the features represented in the probe. In the example above, if I is the stored pattern and I' the probe, then similarity would be computed only on features 1 and 4, yielding a pattern similarity of $1 \times s = s$, rather than the value $1 \times s \times s \times s = s^3$ that results from application of the union rule.

Appendix 1.2 Attentional learning in the exemplar model

Augmentation of the basic exemplar model with an attentional learning process will be illustrated in terms of the twins example discussed in the text (p. 25). Again, we denote the perceptual features common to the pair of identical twins by f and the scar on Twin 1 by f'. The learning problem set by a series of occasions on which an observer tries to identify the twins can be represented as

Features		*Twin 1*	*Twin 2*
Presented	*Perceived*		
f+f'	f+f'	*p*	0
f+f'	f	1−*p*	0
f	f	0	1

We will assume that the twins are observed equally often, and that when Twin 1 is observed, the scar is perceived with probability p and not perceived with probability $1-p$. The same table can be taken to represent the expected memory array after any number, n, of trials on which the twins are each observed $n/2$ times. (Technically, each entry in the table should be multiplied by $n/2$; however, this factor will divide out of all similarity ratios and can be neglected for simplicity.) Our assumption about the process of learning to attend to the scar is that on each trial when the scar is perceived, the difference between the attentional probability, p, and the probability of a correct identification given perception of the scar is reduced by a fraction β, in accord with the function

$$p' = p + 0.5p\beta(P_1 - p), \tag{A1.1}$$

where p on the right and p' on the left of the equal sign denote attentional probabilities at the beginning and end of a given trial, respectively, and P_1 denotes probability of a correct identification of Twin 1 when the scar is perceived. Clearly, if learning starts with P_1 greater than p, then p will increase on each trial, and if learning starts with P_1 less than p, then p will decrease on each trial; and in each case p will approach equality to P_1 asymptotically.

Given the current value of p, we can obtain the similarities of test percepts to the memory arrays for the twins in the usual way: on a test with $f+f'$, similarities to the Twin 1 and Twin 2 arrays are $Sim1 = p+(1-p)s$ and $Sim2 = s$, respectively; and on a test with f alone, the similarities are $Sim1 = 1-p+ps$ and $Sim2 = 1$, respectively.

Now, for a first illustration of the learning process, let us assume $\beta = 1$ and $s = 0.1$ and start the process with $p = 0.5$. The value of p will not change on the first trial, since p and P_1 are equal. At the end of the trial, substitution of $p = 0.5$ and $s = 0.1$ in the similarity expressions yields:

For observation of $f+x$,

$$Sim1 = 0.550, Sim2 = 0.100, \text{ and } P_1 = 0.85,$$

and for observation of x,

$$Sim1 = 0.550, Sim2 = 1, \text{ and } P_2 = 0.35,$$

where P_2 denotes probability of identifying f alone as Twin 1. The response probabilities are computed from the appropriate similarity ratios, $Sim1/(Sim1+Sim2)$, and, of course, the probability of identifying f alone as Twin2 is $1-P_2 = 1-0.35 = 0.65$. Now we can compute the new value of p at the end of trial 2 by entering the parameter values together with the value of P_1 in Equation A1.1, obtaining

$$p' = 0.5 + 0.5(0.5)(0.85-0.50) = 0.5875.$$

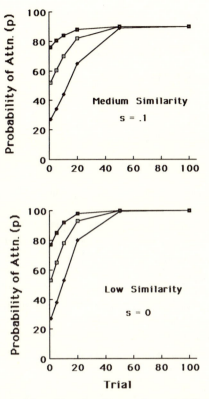

Fig. 1.A1 Theoretical functions for changes in probability (p) of attending (Attn.) to a uniquely valid cue during categorization learning.

Continuing the process (with a computer program doing the calculations!), leads to the asymptotic expressions $P_1 = 0.91$, $P_2 = 0.09$, and $p = 1$. Since, at asymptote, the scar is always perceived, Twin 1 is correctly identified with probability 0.91, as is Twin 2. Smaller values of s would yield better discriminability: As s approaches 0, P_1 approaches 1 and P_2 approaches 0, so that both twins are always identified correctly.

The way p changes over trials is illustrated in Fig. 1.A1. It will be noted in particular that for any value of the similarity parameter, s, the attentional probability, p, goes to the same asymptote regardless of its initial value.

2. Category structures and categorization

2.1 Similarity in theories of classification

2.1.1 The core model applied to a natural category

Investigators of categorization have been divided on the advantages of studying artificial versus natural categories. Artificial categories have the advantages of simplicity and tractability for experimental purposes and of avoiding the contamination of learning occurring in an experiment by the knowledge the subject brings to the experimental situation. Natural categories have the advantage of more directly sampling processes known to occur outside the laboratory. It has been essential to rely mostly on artificial or semi-artificial categories in the research I will be describing, but to show that the basic concepts of the models under development are not restricted to the artificial case, I will illustrate how the concepts discussed up to this point can be applied to research on the representation and interpretation of natural categories.

Developing, testing, and applying models of categorization entails knowing what attributes of stimulus materials will be encoded in memory by the people we study. There are basically three ways available to us for achieving this objective. The most common in experimental research is to make use of the fact that experimenters, like subjects, are people and to assume that subjects will encode stimuli in the way that seems natural to the experimenter. In some instances, however, the validity of this assumption may come into question; the standard resource then is to have groups of subjects make similarity judgments about samples of the stimuli to be used and to employ multidimensional scaling of the data to obtain evidence about the number and nature of the attributes on which the judgments are based (Shepard 1974; Nosofsky 1986, 1992). The third approach, useful either to obtain converging evidence on the validity of the first two or to deal with situations where they are inapplicable or inconvenient, has become familiar in the work of Eleanor Rosch and her associates on natural categories (Rosch 1973; Rosch and Mervis 1975).

Rosch opened up a new phase in the study of categorization and category learning with the observation that, even in naturalistic situations where one has no control over stimulus attributes, there is an incredibly easy way of finding out something about the dimensions or features that people use in encoding the stimuli. The strategem is to present subjects with a set of

Table 2.1   Feature List for Birds (after Smith, 1990)

Exemplar	Feature					
	Flies	Sings	Lays eggs	Small	Nests in trees	Eats insects
Robin	+	+	+	+	+	+
Bluebird	+	+	+	+	+	+
Swallow	+	+	+	+	+	+
Starling	+	+	−	+	+	+
Vulture	+	−	−	−	+	−
Sandpiper	+	+	+	+	−	+
Chicken	−	−	+	−	−	−
Flamingo	−	−	−	−	−	−
Penguin	−	−	+	−	−	−

natural objects, or names of objects, and the question: "what features come to mind when these objects are presented to you?" This procedure can be conveniently illustrated by a classic study of Rosch, Simpson, and Miller (1976) in which the stimulus material, a set of names of birds, was presented to their subjects with the instruction, "Name as many features of each bird as come to mind and write them down." The experimenters recorded the features in a table together with their frequencies of mention. Table 2.1 is adapted from Smith (1990), who, for expository purposes, presented a simplified analysis of a portion of the Rosch, et al study. The table includes a subset of birds with the features that were named most often listed across the top; a plus mark in the table indicates that, by the criterion used by the investigators, that feature characterizes the particular bird. Thus, the top three birds in the table are characterized by all of the listed features, and as we run down the table to the bottom we encounter birds that have only one or two of them. More precisely, it should be said, not that a particular bird, such as a penguin or a flamingo, has only one or two of the features, but rather that for these birds, only one or two of the features came readily to mind when the subjects were producing their feature lists.

(a) Family resemblance

Rosch and her associates recognized that, in ordinary life, people find it adaptive to learn to classify objects— animals, plants, tools, all of the things that we encounter continually. For the most part this learning evidently occurs without any trial-by-trial feedback from a teacher. Rather, the learning seems to be supported by the learner's observations of the usefulness of classifying together things that have significant properties in common. Perhaps most importantly, once a person has formed a mental representation of a category, discovering that a new object or event belongs to the category immediately conveys information about features that may not be directly perceptible. Being told over the telephone, for example, that my rental auto agency has a "compact car" available immediately gives me a good deal of useful information about the particular automobile. Being told that a book is an encyclopedia conveys information about the nature and format of its contents. The categories that are formed in our minds as we learn to deal with such things are not usually defined by simple rules, like those defining a triangle; they are simply characterized by a vague principle that we tend to classify together things that are similar to each other. From this observation, backed up by research on children and on people of various cultures in naturalistic, anthropological settings, Rosch and Mervis (1975) developed a very strong case for the idea that family resemblance is the basis for forming most categories in ordinary life. That insight, in turn, was the background for a more formal model for the learning of "fuzzy" categories that was developed by Medin and Schaffer (1978), and which is the immediate progenitor of one of the two principal kinds of models to be developed, compared, and integrated in the following chapters.

A key observation made by Rosch and Mervis (1975) is that the objects within a set like the one shown in Table 2.1, vary greatly in the number of pluses they receive. Some seem to be central to the category because they have many of the features of the category in common, whereas others are more peripheral. Starting from that observation, Rosch and her associates formed a measure of family resemblance, computed for any member of a category by summing the frequency with which its features occur in other members. This measure is widely used as a link between features and categories. For example, Rosch and Mervis (1975) found family resemblance scores for members of categories to be highly correlated with subjects' ratings of typicality (the degree to which the member is typical of the category). I will not discuss the quantitative details of the family resemblance measures that have appeared in the literature because they lack the simple, tractable, mathematical and computational properties that would make them useful in formal models of categorization and category learning. Starting with the product rule, however, it is straightforward to derive a way of measuring family resemblance that is close in spirit to the one used by Rosch and her associates but that has more desirable formal properties.

(b) Computing family resemblance from pattern similarity

The first step toward the desired measure is to compute similarities between category exemplars, as illustrated in Table 1.2 and discussed in a previous section. To proceed from inter-pair similarity to family resemblance, we take each member of the category in turn, compute its similarity to each of the others, and sum these values to obtain a measure of its similarity to the category. To illustrate, the nine birds whose features are shown in Table 2.1

Table 2.2 Computation of similarity to category

Exemplar	R	B	Sw	St	V	S	C	F	P	Similarity to category
Robin	1	1	1	s	s^4	s	s^5	s^6	s^5	$3+2s+s^4+2s^5+s^6$
Bluebird	1	1	1	s	s^4	s	s^5	s^6	s^5	$3+2s+s^4+2s^5+s^6$
Swallow	1	1	1	s	s^4	s	s^5	s^6	s^5	$3+2s+s^4+2s^5+s^6$
Starling	s	s	s	1	s^3	s^2	s^6	s^5	s^6	$1+3s+s^2+s^3+s^5+2s^6$
Vulture	s^4	s^4	s^4	s^3	1	s^5	s^3	s^2	s^3	$1+s^2+3s^3+3s^4+s^5$
Sandpiper	s	s	s	s^2	s^5	1	s^4	s^5	s^4	$1+3s+s^2+2s^4+2s^5$
Chicken	s^5	s^5	s^5	s^6	s^3	s^4	1	s	1	$2+s+s^3+s^4+3s^5+s^6$
Flamingo	s^6	s^6	s^6	s^5	s^2	s^5	s	1	s	$1+2s+s^2+2s^5+3s^6$
Penguin	s^5	s^5	s^5	s^6	s^3	s^4	1	s	1	$2+s+s^3+s^4+3s^5+s^6$

are entered in a matrix in Table 2.2, each cell entry being the similarity between the two birds listed for that row and column (e. g., the entry at the intersection of the row for starling and the column for sandpiper being s^2, as calculated in Table 1.2). The sum of the similarities in each row will be seen to be the Similarity to Category (SimCat) value entered at the right. If the parameter s is given any value between zero and one, the result is what one would intuitively expect—highly familiar birds, like robin and bluebird, having high values of SimCat and less familiar ones, like vulture and penguin, lower values. As anticipated, the values of SimCat correspond quite well to the family resemblance scores that can be calculated for the same birds (using the procedure of Rosch and Mervis 1975), the rank correlation being 0.89.

(c) Relative typicality

A substantial portion of recent research on natural categories makes use of subjects' ratings of typicality of category exemplars. These ratings are used to locate exemplars that are highly typical and therefore may serve as reference points when individuals are carrying out mental operations on categories (Rosch 1973) and are the basis for studies of conceptual combination (Smith 1990). Yet there has been almost no work on the problem of relating these ratings to theoretically significant quantities that appear in models for categorization. The task I wish now to address is how to treat typicality in models based on the product rule for similarity.

As suggested earlier, once application of the product rule has produced measures of similarity to category for a set of exemplars, as those shown for a set of birds in Table 2.2, it is a reasonable hypothesis that these measures relate directly to typicality. We cannot expect them to map directly onto typicality ratings, however, because when an individual is asked to rate the

Table 2.3   Computation of relative typicality

Exemplar	Similarity to category	Relative typicality
Bluebird	4.14	4.14/8.78 = 0.472
Penguin	2.80	2.80/8.78 = 0.319
Vulture	1.84	1.84/8.78 = 0.210
	8.78	

typicality of an exemplar and produces a number within some specified range, there is no reason to suppose that the absolute value of the rating has any simple measurement properties. However, much experience with judgments of other attributes, such as sensory properties and similarities, suggests that we might make progress by using ratios rather than absolute values.

The approach to be explored, then, is to assume that relative typicality is predicted by ratios of values of similarity to category (SimCat). To illustrate, consider Table 2.3, in which are presented the SimCat values for three of the birds included in Table 2.2. To deal with questions about the relative typicalities of the three birds, we divide the SimCat value for each bird by the sum of the values for the set of three, obtaining the quantities 0.472, 0.319, and 0.210 listed at the right under Relative typicality. An interesting and valuable property of this ratio measure is that the relative typicality of any two of the birds is independent of the size of the subset in which they are included. If, for example, the initial question had referred only to the relative typicality of bluebird with respect to penguin, we could have computed directly

$$4.14/(4.14+2.80) = 0.60, \qquad (2.1)$$

and similarly the relative typicality of penguin with respect to bluebird is

$$2.80/(4.14+2.80) = 0.40; \qquad (2.2)$$

that is, the ratio of typicalities of bluebird to penguin is 0.60/0.40. However, we obtain the same result if we take the ratio of the relative typicalities of bluebird and penguin within the set of three—referring to Table 2.3,

$$0.472/0.319 = 0.60/0.40. \qquad (2.3)$$

Thus, the relative typicality measure has the property termed "independence of irrelevant alternatives" (Luce 1963), meaning that the relative typicality computed for any two exemplars of a category is independent of the size of the subset in which they are presented for rating. This property is generally

Table 2.4   Relative typicality in a reduced category

Exemplar	Similarity to category*	Relative typicality
Bluebird	2.09	0.316
Starling	2.09	0.316
Penguin	1.19	0.180
Vulture	1.25	0.189
	6.62	

*Computed for the reduced category.

considered a desirable characteristic of a measure of choice behavior, since it facilitates many kinds of predictions.

It should be mentioned, however, that for relative typicalities based on the total similarity-to-category measure, independence of irrelevant alternatives (sometimes called the "constant ratio rule") holds only with reference to subsets of the master set on which the similarity values have been computed. Suppose, for example, we had started with the set of only four birds shown in Table 2.4 and computed total similarity values for the birds relative to this set only. If we, then, asked which is the more typical bird, bluebird or penguin, we would obtain for the relative typicality of bluebird

$$2.09/(2.09+1.19) = 0.64, \qquad (2.4)$$

compared to the value 0.60 obtained when we started with the larger set shown in Table 2.2.

(d) Derived categories

A problem of considerable interest with respect to natural categories is how people generate new categories by combining or subdividing ones already learned. A solution that has seemed natural to some investigators who approach the problem from the standpoint of formal logic is to regard a category derived by combination, for example, small bird, as the intersection (common portion) of the two categories "bird" and "small objects" (Oden 1977). Implementation of this idea in terms of either classical or fuzzy logic, however, raises issues that continue to be matters of debate (Osherson and Smith 1981; Hampton 1988), and current research is framed in terms of other approaches.

In the extensive recent literature on "conceptual combination" (reviewed by Hampton 1988; Smith, Osherton, Rips, and Keane 1988), a combined category is formed by conjoining an adjective, or a noun functioning as an adjective, to a noun that names a category, producing, for example, red apple, typewriter table; and the question most often asked is how the typicality of instances of a combined concept can be predicted from knowledge about the constituents. One finding that has received considerable attention is the "conjunction effect," referring to the observation by Smith and Osherson (1984) and Hampton (1988), among others, that rated typicality of an instance of a combined concept (a particular red apple as an instance of the category "red apple") may exceed its rated typicality with respect to the base category (the same red apple as an instance of "apple").

There must be many determinants of performance on typicality rating tasks, and several of these, including salience and diagnosticity of attribute values, are included in a model developed by Smith and his associates that has shown descriptive value with respect to relations between typicality ratings for basic and compound categories (Smith and Osherson 1984; Smith, Osherton, Rips, and Keane 1988). I will not go into the combination problem in detail, but I will illustrate the way in which it can be addressed in the array framework and the kinds of predictions that can be generated solely on the basis of similarity relations.

Starting from the model of similarity developed in the preceding sections, the direct approach seems to be to regard composition and decomposition of categories as resulting from the imposing or relaxing of restrictions on attribute values. For the set of birds shown in Table 2.1, for example, we obtain the two derived categories of small birds and large birds, displayed in Table 2.5, by setting the feature small to the value + or –, respectively. If we had started with the separate categories, small birds and large birds, we could of course obtain the combined category birds simply by taking their union. We would expect to base predictions about typicality ratings on relations among the total similarity values already obtained for the full category, birds, and those that can be computed for the two derived categories. Both sets of values are shown in Table 2.5, and, as would be expected, the values for each bird are different in the original and derived categories. The rank

Table 2.5 Similarity-to-category values for derived categories

	Derived category				
Small birds			Large birds		
Exemplar	Typicality		Exemplar	Typicality	
	Bird	Small bird		Bird	Large bird
Robin	4.14	4.00	Vulture	1.84	1.50
Bluebird	4.14	4.00	Chicken	2.80	2.62
Swallow	4.14	4.00	Flamingo	2.36	2.25
Starling	2.94	2.00	Penguin	2.80	2.62
Sandpiper	2.94	2.00			

Table 2.6 Hypothetical situation illustrating computation of similarity-to-category values for basic and derived categories

| Subcategory | Exemplar | Feature | | | | | Similarity† | |
		f_1	f_2	f_3*	f_4	f_5	To category	To subcategory
1	1	+	−	+	+	−	2.38	2.00
1	2	+	−	+	+	+	2.50	1.75
1	3	+	−	+	−	−	1.94	1.75
2	4	−	−	−	+	+	1.94	1.50
2	5	+	−	−	+	+	2.38	1.50

* Value of f_3 distinguishes subcategories 1 and 2.
† Similarities computed with s equal to 0.5.

orders are unchanged, however, raising the question of whether the relative SimCat values for any two exemplars are in general the same in both the original and the derived categories. For the data in Table 2.5, inequalities between total similarity values for two birds within a subcategory in all cases take the same direction as for the values computed within the combined category. However, it is easy to construct an example in which reversals occur, as shown in Table 2.6. Five exemplars of a hypothetical category, each defined by values on five features, are subdivided into derived categories 1 and 2 on the basis of their values on feature f_3. Similarities of each exemplar to the category and to its subcategory, computed with s equal to 0.5, are shown at the right. Here we do see a reversal in that exemplar 2 has higher similarity than exemplar 1 to the category but lower similarity to the subcategory. And, on the assumption that typicality ratings should be monotonically related to total similarity values, we would predict a corresponding reversal in typicality ratings for these exemplars. To predict whether reversals should be expected in real research situations, we would of course need empirically obtained feature lists, like the one illustrated in Table 2.1, as a basis for computing similarities.

A problem with using similarity to category as a measure of typicality for purposes that go beyond predictions of ordinal relationships is that its magnitude tends to be directly related to the size of the category or subcategory. As a consequence, total similarity values computed within derived categories, like small birds or large birds in Table 2.5, are necessarily smaller than the values for the same birds in the base category. Thus, the testing of quantitative predictions about category composition and decomposition from models based on the product rule will have to wait on research that is needed to determine the best way of mapping similarity-to-category values onto the scale used for typicality ratings.

2.1.2 From similarity to response probability

It having been demonstrated that some behavioral measures, e. g., the order in which individuals list exemplars of categories, are correlated with typicality ratings (Rosch 1973; Rosch and Mervis 1975), one might wonder whether relative typicalities computed from similarity-to-category values could simply be interpreted as predicted probabilities of categorization responses. Consider, for example, Table 2.7, in which the second column contains the SimCat expressions reproduced from Table 2.2 and the third column their values when s is equal to 1/2, and suppose subjects were asked, "given the category bird as a stimulus, what bird comes more quickly to your mind as a response—bluebird or penguin?" Dividing 4.14 by (4.14+2.80) would yield 0.60 for the theoretical probability of responding "bluebird." This prediction seems implausibly low, as do those we would compute in the same way for robin over vulture and starling over sandpiper. Further, there are good theoretical reasons for believing that relative similarities computed from relationships among stimuli cannot provide the sole basis for response probabilities. What is being left out of account is that an individual's response must be based on his or her memory array, in which different birds would have been entered with different frequencies, robin and bluebird much more often than vulture and penguin, for example, rather than on a canonical category representation in which each exemplar appears exactly once. I know of no studies that have addressed the problem of how often people encounter robins vs. bluebirds vs. penguins in ordinary life, so to illustrate the way in which I propose that we should go from SimCat measures to categorization probabilities, I have filled in the "Relative frequency" column of Table 2.7 with imaginary relative frequencies of occurrence that seem to have some plausibility. We would expect that the

Table 2.7   Computation of weighted similarity to category

Examplar	Similarity		Relative frequency	Weighted similarity
	General formula	$s = 1/2$		
Robin	$3+2s+s^4+2s^5+s^6$	4.14	0.30	1.24
Bluebird	$3+2s+s^4+2s^5+s^6$	4.14	0.20	0.83
Swallow	$3+2s+s^4+2s^5+s^6$	4.14	0.10	0.41
Starling	$1+3s+s^2+s^3+s^5+2s^6$	2.94	0.15	0.44
Vulture	$1+s^2+3s^3+3s^4+s^5$	1.84	0.02	0.04
Sandpiper	$1+3s+s^2+2s^4+2s^5$	2.94	0.05	0.15
Chicken	$2+s+s^3+s^4+3s^5+s^6$	2.80	0.15	0.42
Flamingo	$1+2s+s^2+2s^5+3s^6$	2.36	0.01	0.02
Penguin	$2+s+s^3+s^4+3s^5+s^6$	2.80	0.02	0.06

relative frequency with which a person has encountered robins and bluebirds would be high and the relative frequency of flamingos and penguins would be low, and so on. Now we can weight each of the SimCat values by its associated relative frequency, obtaining the Weighted SimCat values listed in the right hand column. Then, to answer the question posed about the probability that the person would initially recall bluebird rather than penguin given bird as a stimulus, we would use the weighted similarities, obtaining $0.83/(0.83+0.06) = 0.93$ and the intuitively more satisfactory prediction that bluebird would be the overwhelmingly more likely response. This assumption about frequency weighting has been supported by category learning experiments designed specifically to test it against the alternative assumption that response probabilities should be computed directly from SimCat values in canonical representations like the one in Table 2.2 (Nosofsky 1988*a*).

2.1.3 An alternative measure of similarity: the contrast model

Before proceeding with further applications of the product rule, I will discuss briefly the most popular alternative model for the computation of a measure of similarity between any two category exemplars or, more generally, between any two objects, namely, the *contrast model* (Tversky 1977). The contrast model in its present formulation is applicable only to objects with representations in terms of discrete features. The central idea is that similarity depends directly on the number of features two objects have in common and inversely on the number of features belonging to one but not the other. Formally, the contrast measure of similarity takes the form

$$\text{Contrast Sim}_{12} = af(F_{12}) - bf(F_1) - cf(F_2), \tag{2.5}$$

where F_{12} is the set of features common to objects 1 and 2, F_1 is the set of features in object 1 but not object 2, F_2 is the set of features in object 2 but not object 1, and a, b, and c are constants. The function $f()$ is defined on an interval scale so that, denoting the union of any two feature sets by F_i+F_j, the equation $f(F_i+F_j) = f(F_i)+f(F_j)$ is satisfied. In practice, applications of the contrast model that have appeared in the literature are limited to the special case in which $f(F)$ simply denotes the number of features in F. Thus I will illustrate the model only in the form

$$\text{Contrast Sim}_{12} = an_{12} - bn_1 - cn_2, \tag{2.6}$$

where n_{12}, n_1, and n_2 denote the numbers of features common to objects 1 and 2, unique to object 1, and unique to object 2, respectively.

The model can be conveniently illustrated in terms of the same example used in Table 1.2 for the product rule, as shown in Table 2.8. Substitution of the numbers of common and unique features for the pair of birds into Equation 2.6 yields the similarity function shown in Table 2.8, and

Table 2.8 Computation of similarity in the contrast model

	Feature					
Examplar	1	2	3	4	5	6
1 Starling	+	+	−	+	+	+
2 Sandpiper	+	+	+	+	−	+

Feature type	Number
In both starling and sandpiper	4
In starling only	1
In sandpiper only	1

$$\text{Similarity} = a(n_{12}) - b(n_1) - c(n_2)$$
$$= a(4) - b(1) - c(1)$$

If $a = 1$, $b = 0.5$, $c = 0.25$,

then similarity = 3.25

substitution of particular values for a, b, and c (the values used by Smith (1990) for interpretation of the birds data) produces the numerical value 3.25 for pattern similarity. Comparison of this particular value with the one computed for the product rule in Table 1.2 would be meaningless, but computation of similarity to category with the measure defined in Equation 2.6 yields an ordering of the birds in Table 2.1 very close to the ordering shown in the Relative frequency column of Table 2.7 for the product rule.

The product-rule measure of similarity and the contrast model measure are commonly thought to differ in two ways. The first is that it is generally believed that the contrast model is unique among the currently available models of similarity in taking account separately of common features and unique features of the objects being compared. In fact, the two models are actually very similar in this respect, and the important difference between them has to do with an entirely different property. To elucidate this point, we can conveniently start with the example of a comparison between the feature representations of two birds, of the kind illustrated in Tables 1.2 and 2.8. Letting n_{12} denote the number of matches between the two feature lists being compared, n_1 the number of features present only in list 1 and n_2 the number only in list 2, we obtain by application of the product rule (entering the parameter t into the product once for each match and s once for each mismatch)

$$\text{Sim}_{12} = t^{n_{12}} s^{n_1 + n_2} = t^{n_{12}} s^{n_1} s^{n_2}. \tag{2.7}$$

Now, taking the logarithm of the last expression yields

$$\log(\text{Sim}_{12}) = n_{12}\log(n_{12}) + n_1\log(s) + n_2\log(s)$$

$$= a(n_{12}) + b(n_1) + c(n_2), \tag{1.3}$$

where we have let $a = \log(n_{12})$, $b = \log(s)$, and $c = \log(s)$. The expression on the right is seen to be identical in form to the right side of Equation 2.6. It happens that $b = c$ in the example, but in a more general form of the product rule the mismatch parameter might have different values on different dimensions, say s and s' in the example, and then b and c could be unequal. Further, the mismatch parameter generally has a value smaller than 1 so that its log is negative. Thus, in the more general case, Equation 2.8 becomes

$$\log(\text{Sim}_{12}) = a(n_{12}) - b(n_1) - c(n_2), \tag{2.9}$$

and we see that the version of contrast similarity considered and the log of product similarity depend in exactly the same way on numbers of common and unique features. The essential and general difference between the models—that it is the log of product similarity that yields the linear dependence on numbers of common and unique features—is extremely important, however. It will be shown in a later section that this property makes the difference between being able or unable to capture correlational relationships between feature values of category exemplars.

A second way in which the product rule and contrast models have been thought to differ is that the product-rule measure is necessarily symmetrical whereas the contrast measure is not. Actually, that impression is half true and half false. If we consider only similarity on a single attribute, then it is true. The similarity between presence and absence of a feature or between two values on a dimension computed from the product rule is always symmetric. But for similarities between objects or patterns, symmetry does not necessarily hold. This point can be illlustrated by means of an example taken from Tversky (1977). In one of a series of ingenious experiments on similarity relations, subjects were asked to rate the similarity of North Korea to Communist China and other subjects were asked to rate the similarity of Communist China to North Korea. One might think it would not matter at all which country is mentioned first, but in fact the similarity rating proved to be higher on the average in the former case than in the latter.

Application of the product-rule model to this situation is illustrated in Table 2.9. The left-hand part of the table represents the first case, with China taking on the role of a representation in memory and North Korea the role of a memory probe. Using the intersection rule* for computation of

---

* Discussed in Chapter 1, Appendix 1.1.

Table 2.9   Illustration of asymmetic product rule similarity

Similarity of North Korea to China			Similarity of China to North Korea		
Probe	Memory	Similarity	Probe	Memory	Similarity
Korea	China		China	N. Korea	
f_1	f_1	1	f_1	f_1	1
f_2	f	1	f_2	f_2	1
	f_3		f_3		s
	f_4		f_4		s
Pattern similarity		1			s^2

similarity, we obtain a value of 1.0. On the other hand, if we reverse the order so that North Korea corresponds to the memory representation and Commmunist China to the probe, the similarity computed the same way is s^2. If s is less than 1, as it usually is, then of course, the similarity on the right is less than the similarity on the left (just as Tversky predicted from the contrast model with an appropriate choice of values for the parameters a, b, and c). If all of the features of both countries, rather than only those of the probe, were chosen as the basis for computing product similarity, the result would be symmetry, e. g., the value obtained would be the same (s^2) in both cases. I think that the procedure assumed is the appropriate one here since the subjects would presumably have interpreted the instructions to mean that they should judge how similar the two countries are in some respects, not how close they are to being identical. However, the point I wish to make is only that pattern similarity computed with the product rule is not necessarily symmetrical and that the prediction of symmetry or asymmetry is determined by one's assumptions about the processing strategy adopted by the subjects rather than by the values assigned to free parameters.

2.2 Predicting categorization performance

With some basic ideas about memory storage, memory access, and similarity computation in hand, we are ready to go on to models for the accomplishment of categorization tasks. These models in turn provide the framework for addressing questions about the nature of abstraction.

Because much of the research on categorization from the mid-1970s to the mid-1980s focussed on performance with respect to well-learned natural categories or performance at the asymptote of learning in experimental studies, it is natural that models emerging from this research, like many others in the information-processing tradition, were relatively static in character. That is, they dealt mainly with relationships between an individual's current state of memory and performance on transfer tasks, almost to the exclusion of the mechanisms of learning or its adaptive character. The theoretical formulations have been labelled as instance-based, exemplar-memory, exemplar-similarity, or context models by different investigators. I generally use the term *exemplar model*, which combines brevity with mnemonic value. For clarity, I will first develop the common core of this family of models as it has taken form in my own thinking and then distinguish as appropriate among subvarieties that have been prominent in the work of other investigators. The common core will be seen to include not only assumptions about the architecture of exemplar models but also shared goals and general strategies.

An important goal is a theory that can account for learning of different types of categorizations, whether based on explicit rules, family resemblance, or probability distributions, in terms of the same basic structures and processes. A prime strategy is to see how far we can go toward the interpretation of categorization on the basis of concepts already established in more general theories of memory.

The development of exemplar models within this common framework from the ground-breaking study of Medin and Schaffer (1978) to the present has taken us further toward the goal of quantitative prediction of categorization performance than might well have been hoped for in such a short period. However, in the late 1980s it became apparent that these models do have definite limitations with respect to accounting for some details of the category learning process. Aspects of learning that have to do with dynamics seem to be more naturally addressed in terms of network models that are currently migrating into categorization research from the newly active area of "connectionism." This latter development will be the subject of the next chapter.

2.2.1 The simplest categorization model in the array framework

(a) An introductory example

The assumptions discussed in Chapter 1 concerning array storage of stimulus information, the computation of featural similarity, the product rule for pattern similarity, and the function relating categorization probability to summed similarity give us the basic machinery for a minimal, stripped-down model of categorization. In a typical category learning experiment, subjects have the task of assigning members of a set of stimulus patterns to alternative categories (for example, symptom patterns to alternative diseases). On each of a sequence of trials, a subject is shown a pattern (a category exemplar), chooses a category, and receives informative feedback (usually the display of the correct category label). We assume that at the end of each trial, a featural representation of the exemplar is stored in the memory array, together with the correct category label (for example, a list of symptoms characterizing a patient together with a disease category). At the beginning of each trial after the first, the subject computes the similarity of the exemplar presented to each member of the current memory array, sums its similarity to all of the members associated with each category, computes the probability of each category, and generates a response based on these probabilities. It is not, of course, assumed that the individual carries out these calculations as a computer would do, only that the processing system accomplishes in some manner a set of computations leading to the same response probabilities as those produced by a computer programmed to simulate the model.

The basics of coding a memory representation of a simple categorization and applying the product rule to compute similarities and categorization probabilities can be conveniently illustrated in terms of the minimal problem illustrated in Fig. 2.1. The stimuli are white and black triangles and squares, assigned to categories in such a way that black triangles and squares occur only in Category A and white triangles and squares occur only in Category B. The subjects see these stimuli singly in a random sequence with a display of the correct category label following the subject's response on each trial. For convenience in representing tasks of this kind, I follow the standard

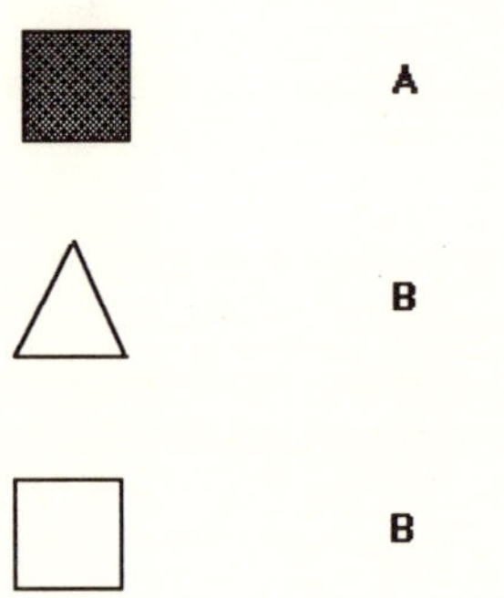

Fig. 2.1 Stimuli for a minimal categorization task. Dark figures, regardless of form occur only in Category A and light figures in Category B.

Table 2.10 Feature coding for minimal categorization problem

Training pattern	Coded representation*
Dark triangle	1 1
Dark square	1 2
Light triangle	2 1
Light square	2 2

* The entries in the first column refer to brightness, those in the second column to form.

practice of coding the attribute values as shown in Table 2.10. The entries 1 and 2 in the first column under Coded representation denote attribute values dark and light, respectively, and 1 and 2 in the second column triangle and square.

Now we are ready to exhibit the memory array we would expect to be formed after a subject had seen each of the four exemplar patterns once. The patterns are listed at the left in Table 2.11, and the entries 1 and 0 under Category indicate that patterns 11 and 12 have been stored in the A column and patterns 21 and 22 in the B column. As the basis for predicting categorization probabilities on tests given at this point in learning, we will start by computing the similarity of the first pattern, Pattern 11, to both of the items in Category A, the result being $(1+s)$ since the similarity of the pattern to itself is 1 and its similarity to the other pattern in Category A is s. The summed similarity of Pattern 11 to the entries in Category B is $s + s^2$, and, therefore, our prediction of the probability of a correct response, given

Table 2.11 Category similarities (product rule) for minimal categorization problem

Training pattern	Category		Sim A	Sim B
	A	B		
1 1	1	0	$1 + s$	$s + s^2$
1 2	1	0	$1 + s$	$s + s^2$
2 1	0	1	$s + s^2$	$1 + s$
2 2	0	1	$s + s^2$	$1 + s$

Correct response probability $= (1 + s)/((1+s)+(s + s^2))$
$$= 1/(1+s)$$

by the summed similarity to Category A divided by the summed similarities to both categories, is

$$P_{11}(A) = (1+s)/(1+2s+s^2) = 1/(1+s), \qquad (2.10)$$

which can easily be shown to be the probability of a correct response to each of the other patterns in this simple case. Thus, our prediction is that, unless s is equal to unity, the probability of a correct response will be greater than 1/2, and if s is equal to zero the probability correct will be unity.

(b) The XOR problem

We can point up the capability of even the simplest exemplar model to handle what is termed "relational" information by moving from the trivially easy categorization problem just illustrated to one that is slightly more difficult and a great deal more interesting, namely the "exclusive or," or XOR, problem made famous in many quarters by the fact that Minsky and Papert showed some 30 years ago that a single-layered connectionist network, a *perceptron*, in the terminology of that time, could not learn the problem (Minsky and Papert 1969). The term "exclusive or" in logic applies when one or the other, but not both, of two propositions is true. We can convert the simple categorization problem of Table 2.10 into an instance of the XOR problem simply by changing the way patterns are assigned to categories. Table 2.12 illustrates one such reassignment, the feedback rule now being that a pattern belongs to Category A if both features have value 1 or if both features have value 2, and otherwise to Category B. The reason that a perceptron cannot learn the new problem is that its network represents only individual features and each of the features taken by itself is wholly uninformative.—Each feature value occurs with the same probability in each category, so learning is possible only if the learner (human or model) is able to use information about combinations of feature values.

Applying the product rule to the array in Table 2.12, we compute the similarity of each stored pattern to each item that appears in its category and

Table 2.12 Category similarities for XOR problem computed from the product rule

Training pattern	Category A	B	Sim A	Sim B
1 1	1	0	$1 + s^2$	$2s$
1 2	0	1	$2s$	$1 + s^2$
2 1	0	1	$2s$	$1 + s^2$
2 2	1	0	$1 + s^2$	$2s$

Probability correct $= (1 + s^2)/(1 + s)$

to each item in the other category—obtaining the similarities that are labelled Sim A and Sim B in the table—and calculate the probability of a correct response in the same way as done for the preceding problem. The resulting formula for probability of a correct response proves to be the same for all four exemplar patterns. Examining the formula, we see that, as in the preceding problem, the probability of being correct is greater than chance for all values of s less than unity and as s approaches zero, the probability of being correct approaches unity, the result we should expect for adult subjects run in such an experiment.

(c) A research application of the minimal exemplar model

It is clear that the minimal categorization model based on the product rule can exhibit learning of simple problems, but one may wonder whether it learns them in the way people do. Can we, for example, predict anything in advance about the relative difficulty of different categorization problems, given only the minimal model defined above with no parameters evaluated from data? To obtain a preliminary answer, I will apply the model to a pioneering study of categorization in relation to problem difficulty reported by Shepard, Hovland, and Jenkins (1961).[*] Those investigators had subjects learn six different categorization problems, constructed so as to represent several levels of complexity in the logical structure of the categories. Several different sets of stimulus materials were used in different problems, but the formal structures were the same and can be conveniently illustrated in terms of a case in which the stimuli were constructed by combining two types of form with two levels of brightness and two levels of size. The assignments of stimuli to categories are illlustrated for three of the problems in Fig. 2.2. The simplest logical structure is that of Problem I, in which all dark figures are to be assigned to Category A and all light figures to Category B. The structure of Problem II involves logical conjunctions, dark triangles and light squares belonging to Category A, light triangles and dark squares to Category B. Problem VI, intended to be the most difficult, defies any simple characterization in terms of logical structure. Our purpose in this exercise is to see whether the theoretical error probabilities reflect the ordering of the observed error frequencies over the six problems.

In order to apply the model, we have to choose a value for the similarity parameter, s, and since we are not trying actually to fit the data, I have simply set s equal to the intermediate value 0.5. To generate the desired predictions, we can, for each problem, compute the pairwise similarities for all eight stimuli and then the summed similarity of each stimulus to all four stored in Category A and to all four stored in Category B, and finally the

---

[*] In this application, I am following the lead of Nosofsky (1984), who showed that the study is admirably suited to this purpose.

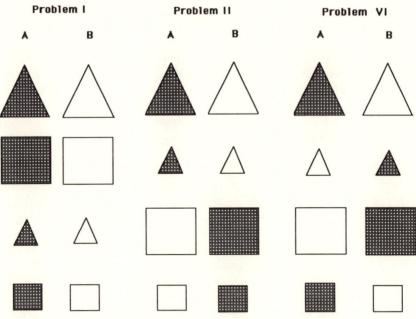

Fig. 2.2 Assignments of exemplars to categories in three problems studied by Shepard, Hovland, and Jenkins (1961).

probability of each category in the presence of each stimulus, just as was done for the illustrative example. Starting with the large, dark triangle shown under Category A for Problem I in Fig. 2.2: Its similarity to itself is 1, to the large, dark square s, to the small, dark triangle s, to the small, dark square s^2, and its summed similarity to the members of the A category is $1+2s+s^2$; and so on for the other stimuli in each column.

Now, on the assumption that both categories and all stimuli within each category occurred equally often during learning, we can convert the correct response probabilities based on these similarities to error probabilities. For illustrative purposes, I have done these calculations for a point in learning at which each stimulus has been presented exactly once, and the values obtained are shown as the light bars in Fig. 2.3. For comparison, the average numbers of errors per problem during learning in the Shepard, Hovland, and Jenkins (1961) study, rescaled by a linear transform to make them visually comparable to the error probabilities derived from the model, are shown as the dark bars in Fig. 2.3.

It will be seen that the correlation between the predictions and observations is certainly appreciably above chance, and, in fact, except for the aberration for Problem II, the model does an almost perfect job of ordering these problems of varying difficulty as they are ordered in the

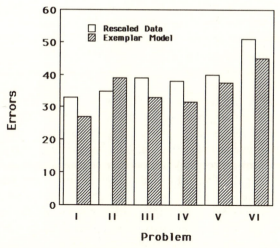

Fig. 2.3 Error data (rescaled as described in the text) for the study of Shepard, Hovland, and Jenkins (1961) compared with predictions from the core model with no free parameters.

subjects' error data. The agreement between theoretical and observed values could be substantially improved by allowing the value of s to differ for different stimulus dimensions and choosing the best values by a model-fitting program (Nosofsky 1984), but here I wish only to make the point that the simplest form of this exemplar-memory model can yield non-trivial a priori predictions about some properties of the data on the basis of assumptions that contain no reference to logical structure of the categories or strategies that might be used by the subjects.

(d) Prediction based on average prototypes or focal exemplars

Before proceeding to refinements of the exemplar model that enable it to produce quantitative accounts of learning data, I will discuss briefly the question of whether predictions for the Shepard, Hovland, and Jenkins (1961) study could equally well have been derived from models based on conceptions of abstract mental representations of categories such as prototypes.

Formal theory in the categorization area has a curious aspect in that prototype theory is by far the most visible variety in the literature (see reviews by Rosch 1978; Smith and Medin 1981; Hunt 1989; Smith 1990) although it can be credited with none of the close quantitative accounts of categorization data that have appeared during the last decade, the majority of which have been achieved by exemplar-similarity models (Medin and Schaffer 1978; Nosofsky 1984, 1986, 1987, 1988*b*, 1991*b*; Estes 1986b; Estes, Campbell, Hatsopoulis, and Hurwitz 1989; Nosofsky, Kruschke, and

McKinley 1992). The popularity of prototype theory appears to be attributable to a combination of factors, among them its intuitive appeal, its long history, and some results of experiments employing categories of objects (typically irregular polygons or dot patterns) produced by means of variations on experimenter-defined prototypes (Attneave 1957; Posner and Keele 1968, 1970).

The term *prototype* has no unique definition with respect to categorization, and may refer either to objective properties of a category or to a hypothesized mental representation of a category formed during learning. Rosch (1978) has argued strongly that only the former usage is well justified and that the notion of a prototype as a constituent of human information processing is problematic. The influential studies of Posner and Keele (1968, 1970) set the stage for the continuing practice of shifting between the two usages. Those investigators used haphazard dot patterns as stimuli and created categories by designating particular patterns as prototypes and generating category exemplars by producing small perturbations in the positions of individual dots from their positions in the prototypes. They assumed that, during learning of a categorization, subjects form mental representations of the category prototypes (by some unspecified process of abstraction) and predicted that, following a sequence of learning trials on which the prototypes never occurred, the prototypes, when presented on tests, would be categorized more efficiently than exemplars that had actually occurred during learning. Confirmation of this and related predictions was taken as strong support for a prototype model. That implication was weakened, however, when it was shown some years later that the same predictions could be derived from exemplar-similarity models (Medin and Schaffer 1978; Nosofsky 1986).

Continuing development of the prototype concept has branched into two main variants, one based on the idea of a prototype as the central tendency of a category and the other on the conception of a prototype as a highly representative exemplar of a category. Reed (1972) formalized the idea that a prototype represents the central tendency of a category. To illustrate this conception, the designs of all six of the Shepard, Horland, and Jenkins (1961) problems are presented in Table 2.13 in the standard binary coding, the entries 1 and 2 in the first, second, and third positions of each exemplar representation (i. e., the three members of each feature triad) representing the attributes dark/light, large/small, and triangle/square on the brightness, size, and form dimensions, respectively.

For these problems, it does not matter which measure of central tendency is used, and I have chosen average prototypes, shown for each problem in Table 2.13 by the entries denoted A Prototype and B Prototype for Categories A and B, respectively. In any prototype model, it is assumed that when tested on any exemplar pattern, the subject mentally compares it to the prototypes of the two categories for the given problem and assigns the

Table 2.13 Categorization problems with prototypes (Shepard, Hovland, and Jenkins 1961)

	Problem					
	I		II		III	
	A	B	A	B	A	B
	111	211	111	112	111	211
	112	212	121	211	112	122
	121	221	212	122	121	212
	122	222	222	221	221	222
Average prototype A	1.0 1.5	1.5	1.5 1.5	1.5	1.25 1.5	1.25
Average prototype B	2.0 1.5	1.5	1.5 1.5	1.5	1.75 1.5	1.75
Focal exemplars					111	212
					121	222

	Problem					
	IV		V		VI	
	A	B	A	B	A	B
	111	122	111	211	111	112
	112	212	112	122	122	121
	121	221	121	212	212	211
	211	222	222	221	221	222
Average prototype A	1.25 1.25	1.25	1.25 1.5	1.5	1.5 1.5	1.5
Average prototype B	1.75 1.75	1.75	1.75 1.5	1.5	1.5 1.5	1.5
Focal exemplars	111	222	111	211		

pattern to the category with the closer prototype. Looking across the rows of category prototypes in Table 2.13, one sees immediately that a model based on central-tendency prototypes cannot predict better than chance performance on either Problem II or Problem V, because the prototypes are the same for both categories (whereas the data reported by Shepard, Hovland, and Jenkins (1961) exhibit significant learning on both). More generally, an average prototype model cannot predict learning of any categorization in which individual features are invalid and better than chance performance depends on use of relational information, as in the XOR problem discussed above.

The notion of a prototype as a representative, or "focal" member of a category has had no formal development, but, nonetheless, seems to be the favored version (Rosch 1978; Osherson and Smith 1981; Smith and Medin 1981; Smith and Osherson 1984; Smith 1990). Within the array framework, it is natural to define the concept of a focal exemplar as the exemplar with highest summed similarity to the members of category. The focal exemplars, so defined, for each problem in the Shepard, Hovland, and Jenkins (1961) study are shown in the bottom row of Table 2.13. It turns out that only Problems IV and V have unique focal exemplars, whereas Problem III has two for each category, and Problems I, II, and VI are uninteresting cases with all members of each category having identical summed similarities.

Before considering any special role that focal exemplars might have in categorization, we should note that the definition given above needs qualification. Categorization performance would be based on focal representations in memory, which might not be the same as focal exemplars identified by looking only at the list of exemplars used in a task. In the Shepard, Hovland, and Jenkins study, all exemplars of each category occurred equally often, so we can assume that focal memory representations would be the same as the focal exemplars identified in Table 2.13. In other cases the restriction to equal frequencies might not obtain, and then it would be necessary to use frequency-weighted similarities in the computation of values of similarity-to-category and similarity ratios.

One might ask whether the exemplar model can account for the observation reported by Rosch (1973, 1978) that focal exemplars of natural categories are the fastest learned in ordinary environments. The answer has to be qualified. For the Shepard, Hovland, and Jenkins (1961) problems, the model does predict fastest learning for the focal exemplars in Problems III, IV, and V, and confirmatory results have been reported by Kruschke (1992a). However, it must be noted that in these problems, the exemplar with highest summed similarity to its own category had in each case the lowest summed similarity to the alternative category, and therefore the largest ratio between the two similarities. For the exemplar model, it is the ratio that is critical. In any problem, the exemplar with the highest ratio should be the fastest learned. It seems likely that in most experimental studies, a focal exemplar will be the one with the highest similarity ratio, but a determination needs to be made in any application before one attempts to predict relative learning rates from the model. In the case of natural categories, valid application requires that one consider the set of alternative categories that would be learned concurrently and obtain feature lists for each so that similarity ratios can be computed. These qualifications do not point to defects in the model.—The function of a model is not to provide universal, unqualified predictions of behavior, but rather to indicate what information is relevant in a given situation and how to use it in order to generate predictions.

(e) Configural prototypes

It now seems clear that even if central-tendency prototypes are formed in a learner's memory system, as some believe, they cannot provide the basis for categorization performance except under very special conditions, because these prototypes take no account of relational information. Perhaps, however, one could define a prototype concept that did not have this deficiency. A possibility that comes to mind in the context of the array framework might be termed a *configural prototype*, defined as the exemplar pattern, among all those that can be constructed from the features defined for a task, having the highest summed similarity to a category. The difference from the concept of focal exemplar is that the configural prototype, like an average prototype, need not be a pattern that actually occurs during learning of a categorization.

For an illustration, consider Problem IV in Table 2.13, and imagine a learning experiment in which pattern 111 was never allowed to occur, but the other patterns all occurred with equal frequencies. Analyzing the situation in terms of the exemplar model, we note first of all that, so long as the similarity parameter is greater than zero, a memory representation of pattern 111 will develop during learning by virtue of its similarity to exemplar patterns that do occur. In fact, if the similarity parameter is much greater than 0.5, the weight (summed similarity-to-category) of pattern 111 at the end of a learning series, of any length, so long as the stipulations about relative frequencies are met, will be the largest in its category. And in that event, we would predict that on its first test, pattern 111, the configural prototype of its category, would be correctly categorized with higher probability than any exemplars that did occur during learning. If, however, the similarity parameter were appreciably smaller than 0.5, this pattern would not qualify as a configural prototype, and on its first test it would not be correctly categorized with higher probability than the other exemplars. In an actual research situation, one would, of course, need to evaluate the similarity parameter, either from a previous experiment or from the learning data of the given experiment in order to be in a position to predict test performance at the end of learning.

I can see no obvious motivation for constructing special models incorporating the concepts of focal exemplars or configural prototypes, because within the framework of the exemplar model, representations of these are automatically formed in the memory system during category learning. There might be some interest in formulating and testing a variant of the exemplar model in which we assume that, after sufficient experience with a task, individuals shift from comparing test patterns to the full memory array to comparing them only to focal exemplars or configural prototypes of categories. I will be surprised if a model of that kind exhibits any superiority so long as attention is confined to situations in which learners acquire knowledge about categories by observing sequences of category exemplars with feedback. If, however, one were either bypassing or supplementing that kind of experience by conveying information about a categorization verbally or by demonstrations (as done in a study by Medin, Altom, and Murphy 1984), then an implication of the exemplar model is that describing or presenting configural prototypes to subjects would facilitate categorization performance, and would generally do so more effectively than presenting average prototypes.

2.2.2 On category structures and conceptual levels

Before getting into elaborations of the exemplar model, I will give one more illustration of how the model in its simplest form can be used to aid in the interpretation of a problem of general interest. This application has to do with the conception of levels of categorization.

Observations by anthropologists of the way people form taxonomies in ordinary life show that the natural categories formed for domains like plants and animals are not all of a kind, but are grouped into structures that correspond approximately to scientically based taxonomies (D'Andrade 1989). Proceeding from these observations, Rosch and Mervis (1975) and Rosch, Mervis, Gray, and Boyes-Braehm (1976) developed the idea that natural categories are typically hierarchically organized in terms of a particularly important basic level, corresponding approximately to the level of generic classes in biological taxonomies, plus superordinate and subordinate categories. An example of a basic level category is chair, with superordinate furniture and subordinates rocking chair, folding chair, etc.; another is dog with superordinate animal and subordinates spaniel, collie, etc. Many empirical studies have found that objects are most rapidly categorized at the basic level, a generalization qualified by Jolecoeur, Gluck, and Kosslyn (1984), who found that the special ease of processing at the basic level depends on exemplars at that level having higher typicalities than those at the subordinate level. Seeking a psychological basis for the ease of categorizing at the basic level, Rosch, Mervis, Gray, and Boyes-Braehm (1976) obtained evidence that more people list the same features for basic level categories than for superordinates and that exemplars at the basic level are easier to image than those at the superordinate level, perhaps because of greater commonality in shape.

In natural environments, structural properties of categories must be confounded with many other factors, so to sort out the various contributors to categorization performance, it is important to have experimental studies with necessarily simplified category structures but with control of such variables as stimulus salience and frequencies of occurrence. The first reported study of this kind (Murphy and Smith 1982) used sets of pictorial stimuli constituting artificial examples of familiar classes of objects (e. g., "pounders" and "cutters"), with class relationships intended to mirror some of the properties believed to characterize natural categories. Stimuli assigned to the basic level had relatively large numbers of features that were common to all members of a category but distinct from the features of alternative categories, whereas members of superordinate and subordinate categories had fewer of both common and differentiating features. Tests given following categorization training intended to produce asymptotic perform-ance yielded shortest correct reaction times for basic level, longer for subordinate level, and longest for superordinate level categorization responses.

To illustrate how the exemplar model can be used to analyze the learning of such a category structure, I will use the design of a more recent study that was planned with more attention to conditions of learning (Corter, Gluck, and Bower 1988, Experiment 1). The category structure, with my interpretation of the featural composition of stimuli, is shown in Table 2.14. The categories are labeled by capital letters, and exemplars are defined in terms of three qualitative features, each having four values. Thus, the exemplar belonging to subordinate category V of basic category N has value 4 on the first feature, value 4 on the second, and value 1 on the third. The structure is designed so that exemplars of a basic level category are quite similar, agreeing in two of the three features, but dissimilar to members of other categories at that level. Within a basic level category, members of different subordinate categories are again similar, agreeing in two of three features; members of different superordinate categories are more complexly related, but are uniformly differentiated by the value of feature 1. The training conditions in the study were arranged so that all category labels were applicable equally often.

Table 2.14 Category structure used by Corter, Gluck, and Bower (1988, Experiment 1)

Level				Category				
Superordinate			P				Q	
Basic		N			M		C	D
Subordinate	V	T	K	H	S	G	N	J
Exemplars								
Feature 1	4	4	3	3	2	2	1	1
Feature 2	4	3	2	1	4	3	2	1
Feature 3	1	1	2	2	2	2	1	1

Applying the simplest case of the exemplar model, with the same value of the similarity parameter used for all feature mismatches, we can compute the summed similarity of each exemplar to each of the categories it belongs to, and from these values the probability of a correct categorization after any given number of training trials. With values of the similarity parameter in the range 0.2 to 0.3, the model yields predictions of correct categorization probabilities that fall at about the level of those obtained by Corter, Gluck, and Bower (1988)* and that agree with the observed result in being highest for the basic level (e. g., 0.82, 0.96, and 0.77 for superordinate, basic, and subordinate levels, respectively when s is equal to 0.3). I have not tried an actual fit to the Corter, Gluck, and Bower data, and would not expect to obtain as good a result as they did for a suitably constructed network model. What we see again in this example is the usefulness and convenience of the simple exemplar model for analyzing stimulus similarity relationships and yielding a priori predictions, at least on an ordinal scale, about results to be expected in a novel experiment.

* Personal communication from M.A. Gluck.

3. Models for category learning

3.1 The exemplar-similarity model

3.1.1 Augmentations of the core model

The minimal exemplar-similarity model developed from first principles in the preceding sections is useful for making predictions about categorization given that we know the current state of an individual's memory, or can make plausible assumptions about it. We have seen that the basic assumptions about array storage and similarity computation alone can yield non-trivial predictions about such matters as the kinds of problems that can be learned and the relative difficulty of problems involving different category structures. However, this bare-bones model lacks the machinery needed to address the dynamics of learning. This limitation has been recognized by all investigators working in the area; consequently, several augmentations have been explored, and some of these have become standard equipment. I will briefly discuss four of these, having to do with stimulus salience, learning rate, initial state of memory, and permanence of memory storage.

(a) Stimulus salience

The first published version of an exemplar-similarity model for categorization, Medin and Schaffer (1978), was, essentially, the minimal exemplar model described in Chapter 2 plus an assumption that the stimulus attributes of a categorization problem might differ in salience, owing either to different stimulus properties (i. e., size, position, brightness) or to different validities. More salient attributes or those with higher validities would be expected to attract more attention, which in turn would yield more efficient computation of similarity. Thus, in the Medin and Schaffer model, and in later applications and extensions by Nosofsky (1984, 1986, 1987, 1988a,b), each attribute in a problem was assigned an "attentional weight" parameter, to be evaluated during the fitting of the model to data and applied as a coefficient of the similarity parameter, s (thus, in effect, allowing a different similarity parameter for each attribute). This augmentation defines what those investigators term the "context model," so named because background context and stimulus attributes combine multiplicatively in the generation of categorization probabilities. The context model has demonstrated impressive ability to describe categorization performance on tests given at the end of a learning series in experiments employing a wide variety of stimulus materials and category structures (for reviews, see Nosofsky 1988a, b, 1990;

Estes 1991*b*; Nosofsky, Kruschke, and McKinley 1992). In the remainder of this volume, because I am more concerned with predictive capability of models across a wide range of situations than with detailed accounts of particular data, I will limit attention to situations in which it is reasonable to assume equal weights across attributes and thus to get along with a single similarity parameter, *s*.

An aspect of stimulus salience that has been of special interest in the literature of discrimination theory since the 1950s pertains to situations in which one feature is completely valid and the remaining features entirely invalid (as the example of a pair of identical twins who have all perceptual features in common except a scar that marks only one, discussed in Chapter 1). It was brought out in the earlier discussion that the basic exemplar model can easily be augmented with an attentional learning function, which ensures that over a series of trials, a learner will come to attend selectively to the valid feature and thus reach the maximum level of categorization performance permitted by the dissimilarity of the valid from the invalid features. However, I regard this function as only an example of a kind of special-purpose device that can be added to the model when obviously appropriate for a particular situation; it would not be applicable, for example, to situations including features of varying degrees of partial validity. A more widely applicable way of handling attentional learning is implemented in a model that incorporates aspects of the exemplar model in an adaptive network architecture (Kruschke 1992*a*; Nosofsky, Kruschke, and McKinley 1992).

(b) Learning rate

In any but trivially easy cases, categorizations are not learned instantaneously; rather, proportions of correct responses per trial block for subjects, or even groups of subjects, typically follow an irregular course from an initial chance level to an asymptote, which often approximates optimal performance (Estes 1986*a*; Estes, Campbell, Hatsopoulis, and Hurwitz 1989). A natural way to allow for more or less gradual learning is to assume that pattern storage is probabilistic rather than deterministic. Implementation of this idea by the addition to the basic exemplar model of a parameter, *p*, representing the probability that the pattern presented on any trial is effectively stored in memory yielded quite impressive accounts of the detailed course of learning in those studies (that is, impressive at the time, for other augmentations of the model, to be discussed next, have further improved its descriptive capability).

(c) Trace decay and shift effects

A standard practice during the development of array models of memory has been to assume that, once encoded in the memory array, memory traces of stimulus patterns remain in storage and available for retrieval permanently.

It is generally recognized that this assumption may be only a convenient simplification, but it has seemed to be a viable one since typically very little retention loss is observed from one occurrence of a repeated exemplar to the next, even over many intervening trials, in category learning data (Estes 1986*b*).

However, observable retention loss is not the only way in which some deviation from the assumption of permanent storage might show up in categorization data. Another way has to do with the ability of learners to cope with shifts in the rules governing assignments of exemplar patterns to categories. Imagine, for example, that an individual is learning to classify words of a new language as adjectives (C1) or adverbs (C2). The result of the first few learning trials might be the memory array

	C1	C2
W1	2	0
W2	0	1
W3	1	3

word W1 having occurred twice with C1 indicated to be correct, and so on. Now we can predict from the exemplar model that on further tests of these words, probability of correct categorizations will be high (assuming the similarity parameter *s* to be small). But suppose it is discovered at this point that the information given the learner on these trials was incorrect, W1 actually belonging to category C2 and W2 and W3 to C1. The incorrectly stored representations cannot be erased from memory, but after only a moderate number of additional learning trials with the correct feedback rules in effect, they would be outweighed by the new experiences. The new memory array after a dozen relearning trials might be

	C1	C2
W1	2	4
W2	3	1
W3	6	3

so the learner would be well on the way toward giving correct categorizations with high probability. Suppose, however, that the discovery about incorrect feedback did not occur until much later, when the memory array was, say,

	C1	C2
W1	12	0
W2	0	6
W3	2	15

Now the same dozen relearning trials would produce

	C1	C2
W1	12	4
W2	3	6
W3	7	15

on tests at this point, the learner would still be giving categorizations that would be correct by the original but incorrect by the new rules, and many more relearning trials would be needed to produce accurate performance under the new rules. It is easy to see that, in general, relearning after a shift in categorization rules will be slower the greater the number of learning trials prior to the shift.

This prediction has been sharply disconfirmed by an appropriately designed experiment (Estes 1989*a*), which showed that speed of relearning

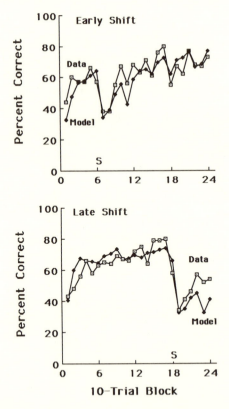

Fig. 3.1 Learning functions for early and late shift conditions of Estes (1989*a*) study fitted by exemplar model lacking a decay parameter.

proceeded at virtually identical rates after early and late shifts. It is possible to reduce the excessive inertia of the exemplar model, and improve the account of shift results, by adding the assumption that with some probability any stored pattern suffers decay (i. e., becomes less available for comparisons with newly perceived patterns) during any trial following storage. For mathematical convenience, the decay probability is denoted $1-\alpha$, where α has a value between 0 and 1; thus, α is the probability that no decay occurs on a trial. The effect of this added assumption on the exemplar model's account of the Estes (1989*a*) data is illustrated in Figs. 3.1 and 3.2, the former showing the fit of the model lacking a decay parameter and the latter the fit including one. The added "decay" process appears to be a necessary augmentation of the model, at least for applications to relatively long learning series.

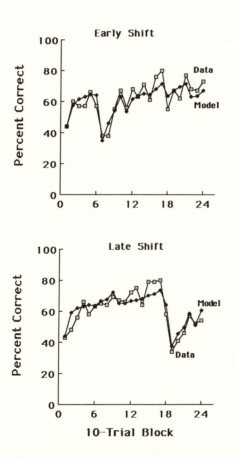

Fig. 3.2 Learning functions for early and late shift conditions of Estes (1989*a*) study fitted by exemplar model including a decay parameter.

(d) Initial memory load

In nearly all research on memory in the information-processing tradition, including the development of exemplar-similarity models from the original Medin and Schaffer (1978) study to the present, a learner is assumed to start any new experimental task with an empty memory array. Theoretical computations are thereby greatly simplified, for we need deal only with similarities of test stimuli to stored representations of others that have occurred within the experimental session. A subject engaged in an experiment simulating medical diagnosis, for example, is assumed to compare the symptoms characterizing hypothetical patients only to those for cases seen previously during the session, not also to those for patients the subject might have encountered prior to the experiment. Making this simplifying assumption seemed initially to be an innocuous way of easing the task of the theorist, but the first few applications of exemplar models to category learning (Estes 1986*b*; Estes, Campbell, Hatsopoulis, and Hurwitz 1989) showed that the simplification leads to difficulties that are far from trivial. It became clear that if a learner's memory for events of the kind encountered in a task is a blank slate at the outset of an experiment, then learning must be instantaneous in the sense that repetition of experiences would have no effect.

To see why the simplification is untenable, consider Table 3.1, which exhibits a minimal categorization task with a particular item I_1 occurring twice as often in Category A as in Category B and the reverse for item I_2.

Table 3.1 Learning of a simple categorization with an initially empty memory array

	A	B	Sim A	Sim B	Probability of A	$s = 0$	$s = 0.5$
Initial state							
I_1	0	0	0	0	Indeterminate		Indeterminate
I_2	0	0	0	0			
One cycle							
I_1	2	1	$2 + s$	$1 + 2s$	$(2 + s)/(3 + 3s)$	0.667	0.556
I_2	1	2	$1 + 2s$	$2 + s$			
Ten cycles							
I_1	20	10	$20 + 10s$	$10 + 20s$	$(20 + 10s)/(30 + 30s)$	0.667	0.556
I_2	10	20	$10 + 20s$	$20 + 10s$			

Starting with an initial state in which the memory array is empty, a learner is given a cycle of trials resulting in storage of two instances of I_1 in Category A and one in B, and the reverse for item I_2. Computation of item-category similarities in the usual way yields the expression shown for probability of categorizing item I_1 in Category A on a subsequent test, with predicted values of 0.667 and 0.556 when s equals 0 or 0.5, respectively. Proceeding to the bottom section of the table, we compute the same quantities after 20 instances of item I_1 have been stored in A and 10 in B, and the reverse for item I_2. It turns out, implausibly, that the categorization probability for item I_1 is unchanged by a tenfold increase in the number of learning trials, and of course the same would be true for the other item. This result can be shown to be quite general (Appendix 3.1), and it presents a serious problem, for we cannot live with a model that fails to accommodate the time-tested role of repetition in learning.

The solution to this problem (noted first, I believe, by Robert Nosofsky) is, happily, very simple. We need only assume that learning (at least for ordinary human adults) always begins with some relevent information already present in the memory array. The idea is not implausible theoretically, for it is probably the case that any stimuli used in a categorization task with adult learners will have some similarity to stimuli previously encountered and stored in memory in other situations. For reasons that will be discussed in a later chapter in connection with the role of context, these "old" memory traces will not be expected to have

Table 3.2 Learning of a simple categorization with an initial memory load

	A	B	Sim A	Sim B	Probability of A	$s = 0$	$s = 0.5$
Initial state							
I_1	1	1	$1 + s$	$1 + s$	$(1 + s)/2(1 + s)$	0.500	0.500
I_2	1	1	$1 + s$	$1 + s$	$(1 + s)/2(1 + s)$	0.500	0.500
One cycle							
I_1	3	2	$3 + 2s$	$2 + 3s$	$(3 + 2s)/(5 + 5s)$	0.600	0.533
I_2	2	3	$2 + 3s$	$3 + 2s$	$(2 + 3s)/(5 + 5s)$	0.400	0.467
Ten cycles							
I_1	21	11	$21 + 11s$	$11 + 21s$	$(21 + 11s)/(32 + 32s)$	0.667	0.556
I_2	11	21	$11 + 21s$	$21 + 11s$	$(11 + 21s)/(32 + 32s)$	0.333	0.444

appreciable effects on learning of a current categorization under most circumstances, except that even a small effect is enough to make gradual learning of a new categorization possible. The way this effect operates is illustrated in Table 3.2, which shows learning under conditions identical to those of Table 3.1 except that the memory array initially contains information equivalent to the storage of one instance of each item in each category. With this one change in the model, performance improves progressively over trials rather than jumping instantaneously to its asymptote after one cycle. Consequently, I and other investigators now routinely include in exemplar-similarity models a parameter, which I denote as s_0, representing the average summed similarity of any exemplar pattern to each of the alternative categories of a problem at the outset of learning (see, e. g., Hurwitz 1990; Nosofsky, Kruschke, and McKinley 1992). Of course, s_0 is a free parameter to be estimated from the learning data only when we are dealing with a situation that is entirely new to the learners. If, instead, we are dealing with a series of categorization tasks that involve the same or similar stimulus materials (as, for example, the shift experiment cited in the last section), the state of a learner's memory array at the start of the second or later task is the same as the state at the end of learning in the previous task.

3.1.2 Categorization and identification

To point up the capability of the exemplar model with this one added parameter, I will show how it enables us to address the longstanding problem of the relationship between categorization and identification. Procedurally, categorization and identification of stimulus patterns are so similar that it seems they must be closely related theoretically. Identification is perhaps the simpler, and predicting categorization from identification has often been taken as a goal for categorization models. The problem was addressed long ago by Shepard, Hovland, and Jenkins (1961) and Shepard and Chang (1963) on the supposition that a principle of stimulus generalization would mediate predictions from one paradigm to the other. Their results were mixed on this issue, suggesting that some new, "emergent" principle might be needed to handle categorization. More recently, Nosofsky (1984, 1986) addressed the same issue in the framework of exemplar-similarity models and obtained support for the idea that the same memory system may underly both identification and categorization but that in categorization a process of selective attention must be added to the exemplar model. The additional process seems to be needed because without it the value of the similarity parameter does not carry over from identification to categorization, and thus evaluation of the parameters of the model in one paradigm does not permit prediction of learning in the other. In view of Nosofsky's results, we evidently cannot expect the basic exemplar model to suffice in general for the joint treatment of categorization and identification. Nonetheless, it is possible that the model can predict qualitative relationships between the two processes, for example, relative speeds of learning, and may even yield quantitative accounts of data in situations where stimuli and training conditions are not as conducive to a major role of selective attention as those of Nosofsky's (1986) study.

I will illustrate application of the exemplar model to this problem in terms of a study reported by Reed (1978). A set of ten stimuli, schematic faces, was used in both a categorization and an identification condition. In the former, five of the stimuli were assigned randomly to each of two categories; in the latter, each of the ten stimuli was assigned a unique label. In both conditions, subjects had 15 learning trials under standard categorization or paired-associate procedures, each trial comprising a run through the set of ten

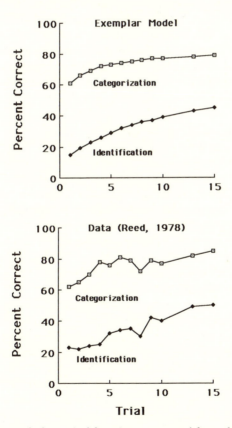

Fig. 3.3 Upper panel: theoretical functions computed from the exemplar model for categorization and identification of the same stimulus set with the same parameter values in both cases. Lower panel: comparable data from a study reported by Reed (1978).

stimuli in a random order. Thus, in effect, identification training was simply categorization training with the number of categories equal to the number of exemplars. In terms of the exemplar model, the principal difference between the tasks is that, in categorization, similarity between a test stimulus and a different stimulus stored in memory with the same category label will tend to produce a correct response; but in identification no other stimulus in the memory array has the same label as a given test stimulus, and, therefore, similarity tends to produce only errors.

Application of the exemplar model to this situation with the parameter values $s = 0.05$ and $s_0 = 0.15$ (chosen to yield roughly the same levels of correct responding as of Reed's study) yielded the theoretical learning curves presented in the upper panel of Fig. 3.3. The prediction of faster learning for categorization than identification is in agreement with Reed's (1978) study and a semi-replication by Medin, Dewey, and Murphy (1983). The learning curves from Reed's study are shown in the lower panel of Fig. 3.3, and will be seen to parallel the theoretical functions fairly well. (The fit could, of course, be improved by finding better choices for the parameter values.) In particular, the model captures the observed tendency for the categorization learning function to rise more rapidly on early trials, but with a crossover so that the identification function rises more steeply on later trials.

3.1.3 Similarity and cognitive distance

In the preceding sections, and throughout most of the rest of this volume, my applications of the product rule are limited to similarities computed on patterns composed of binary-valued attributes. For many purposes, however, it is necessary to deal with stimuli defined on continuous dimensions. To apply the product rule in such cases, we need to replace the single similarity parameter, s, with a function relating similarity between two values on a dimension to their separation, that is, to the distance between them on the given dimension. An answer to the question of what function to choose followed from the seminal insight of Nosofsky (1984) that the treatment of similarity in exemplar models of categorization can be viewed as a special case of the general conception of representing similarity in terms of distance in a multidimensional space. In a psychological, perhaps more aptly termed cognitive, space, points correspond to either representations of remembered events or representations of learned concepts, and distances between points are directly related to similarity between the events or concepts (Shepard, Romney, and Nerlove 1972; Carroll and Wish 1974; Shepard 1974). Throughout a history going back many decades, the development of this conception was isolated from the development of the perceptual and learning theories that shaded into the new (or at least rediscovered) field of cognitive psychology in the late 1950s. It began to enter into the experimental psychology of cognition when Shepard (1958) showed that a mathematical formula relating distance in a cognitive space to similarity could be derived from the concept of stimulus generalization that had arisen independently in learning theory (Hull 1943).

The notion of a psychological space in which cognitive operations can be carried out has intuitive appeal for several reasons. One is that, as evidenced both in ordinary life and in experiments (Moyer and Landauer 1967; Shepard and Cooper 1982), people can manipulate mental images, even images of abstract entities like numbers, much as they manipulate objects in the external environment. Another is that a spatial metaphor provides a convenient way of displaying and communicating relationships that are assumed to hold among hypothesized internal events or processes (Roediger 1980). For purposes of building a psychological theory of memory, however, the intuitive appeal is less important than the fact that mapping memory arrays onto cognitive spaces with different metrics has led to fruitful ways of measuring similarity (Shepard 1974; Garner 1974, 1976). A thorough review of similarity scaling in relation to cognitive models is provided by Nosofsky (1992*b*).

Only two metrics are often used in models of perception and memory, the city block and the Euclidean (Luce and Krumhansl 1988). The former is discussed below. The latter, familiar to most scientists from elementary geometry, expresses the distance between any two objects represented in a two-dimensional space as the square root of the sum of squared distances between the objects on the individual dimensions. One can obtain evidence about the appropriate metric for a given type of situation by comparing versions of a model that differ only with respect to the assumed metric. For example, in an unpublished analysis of the data of an experiment on bar-chart categorization reported in Estes (1986*b*), I compared versions of the exemplar-similarity model employed in that study with city block versus Euclidean metrics and found a clear advantage for the former. In this volume, because I am concerned more with processes than with forms of representations, it will be convenient to limit attention almost exclusively to cases in which stimuli vary on only a single dimension or in which they are multidimensional and can be represented in a city block metric.

For a typical example of a city block metric, I will use the stimuli of the Shepard, Hovland, and Jenkins (1961) study, illustrated in Fig. 2.2. By using the same similarity parameter, s, for a mismatch on any attribute in the analysis of that study, we were assuming, in effect, that the two values of brightness, form, and size were each separated by a unit distance in a psychological space. With a city block metric, the distance between any two points in a space is the sum of their distances on individual dimensions. Referring to Fig. 2.2, there is, for example, a distance of one unit between the large white and the large dark triangle or between the large white triangle and the large white square but a distance of two units between the large dark triangle and the large white square, and a distance of three units between the large dark triangle and the small white square. When objects are represented by qualitative, on/off features, the city block distance between any two objects is simply the number of mismatches between their feature lists. Throughout this volume, the metric assumed in applications will be understood to be city block unless otherwise specified.

The formal relation to be assumed between similarity and distance on any single attribute in a cognitive space is the exponential function

$$s_{ij} = e^{-cd_{ij}}, \tag{3.1}$$

where s_{ij} denotes the similarity and d_{ij} the distance between the values of items i and j on the given attribute, and c is a constant, that was introduced to the literature of cognition by Shepard (1958) and more recently argued to be the expression uniquely qualified to represent stimulus generalization gradients (Shepard 1987). Nosofsky (1984) was the first to point out that, when a city block metric is assumed, only an exponential function for similarity on individual attributes is compatible with the product rule for pattern similarity. It will be immediately apparent that similarity declines as a negatively accelerated function of distance, s_{ij}, starting at a value of unity when distance is zero and approaching zero as distance becomes large, and that the constant c, termed a sensitivity parameter by Nosofsky (1984, 1986), determines the steepness of the function.* In applications of Equation 3.1, the value of the parameter c may be assigned in advance if there is some basis for doing so. Often c is set equal to 1 merely for simplicity. When quantitative predictions of data are being attempted the value of c is generally selected so as to minimize some statistic of goodness of fit.

In the special cases when stimuli are coded by on/off features, or by attributes on which distance varies only by equal, integral steps, the exponential similarity function reduces to the form introduced in Chapter 1 in connection with the product rule and Equation 1.1. With e^{-c} set equal to s, Equation 3.1 becomes

$$s_{ij} = s^{d_{ij}}, \tag{3.2}$$

which is equivalent to Equation 1.1 when distance between two patterns is equal to the number of mismatches between them, as is true for binary-valued dimensions or on/off features.

The term d_{ij} in Equations 3.1 and 3.2 denotes distance in a psychological, or cognitive, space, but for stimuli defined on simple sensory attributes, it often suffices for practical purposes to measure d_{ij} by distance on a physical stimulus dimension. To illustrate, in a study of category learning in which the stimuli were triangles that varied by equal steps over four values of height and four values of width, the distances entered in Equation 3.1 were

---

* The parameter c was not included in the formula given by Shepard (1958, 1987) but is essential to provide the flexibility needed in fitting the model to data.

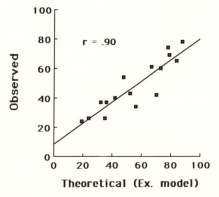

Fig. 3.4 Categorization response percentages for 16 triangle stimuli versus values computed from the exemplar (Ex.) model.

simply 1, 2, 3, and 4 units on each dimension (Estes 1992). An exemplar-memory model using this similarity function yielded a reasonable account of the observed learning curves, and a fairly high correlation between theoretical and observed total percentages of choices of one category over all 16 stimuli, as shown in Fig. 3.4. In an extension of the study not described in the published report, similarity judgments on the stimuli were subjected to a multidimensional scaling analysis, which showed that the dimensions extracted could not be equated exactly with height and width of the triangles. I have not carried the scaling analysis further, but it seems likely that an optimal choice of dimensions would reduce the scatter of observed points around the regression line seen in Fig. 3.4. Although the scaling procedure is the more elegant method, and on theoretical grounds probably better justified, I have customarily followed the practice of using distances on physical stimulus dimensions when applying Equation 3.1 in studies of memory and categorization except when there is some special reason to think that this simplification would yield appreciable distortions of model predictions.

3.1.4 Status of the exemplar-similarity model

Taking the core model together with these indicated augmentations produces what I will henceforth refer to as the exemplar-similarity model, or often for brevity just the exemplar model. The model comprises the basic array architecture with a single similarity parameter, s (or, when specified in particular applications, the parameters s and t) for comparisons between perceived and stored patterns; a parameter s_0 representing the average similarity of any exemplar pattern to any category at the outset of learning in a task; a storage probability, p; and a "decay" parameter, α. In the remainder of this volume, for simplicity, p will be assumed equal to unity, since once the decay parameter is included, allowing probabilistic storage generally has little effect on goodness of fit of the model, and also, the convention will be followed that α is equal to unity (so that there is no decay) unless otherwise specified. When appropriate, the similarity parameter, s, will be replaced by the exponential function discussed above.

My exposition of the exemplar model has been organized in a logical rather than a chronological sequence, so I will briefly recapitulate the development of the model at this point to provide some historical perspective. The basic ideas were set down by Medin and Schaffer (1978) and instigated a series of tests of the exemplar model against feature frequency models (Medin and Schwanenflugel 1981; Medin, Altom, Edelson, and Freko 1982; Estes 1986a), prototype models (Busemeyer, Dewey, and Medin 1984; Nosofsky 1984, 1986), and rule-based models (Nosofsky, Clark, and Shin 1989). These and numerous related studies yielded steadily mounting evidence for the economy, descriptive power, and generality of the exemplar model in comparison with other extant models. Concurrently, I accomplished some fine tuning of the original Medin and Schaffer model with respect to assumptions about specifics of memory storage and retrieval and generalized the structural assumptions to what I have termed the array architecture (Estes 1986a,b); and in an important series of developments, Nosofsky (1984,1986) incorporated multidimensional scaling and assumptions about the role of selective attention into the framework.

In its present form, the exemplar model is similar in many respects to a number of models that are being concurrently developed by other investigators, including Anderson (1991), Ashby and Lee (1991), Fried and Holyoak (1984), Hintzman (1986), and Kruschke (1992a). Some differences are that the models of Ashby and Lee, and Fried and Holyoak are more restricted than the exemplar model in that they assume specific statistical distributions for exemplar information, whereas Kruschke's model is more general in that it includes a network-based learning mechanism. The commonalities and differences within this family have been discussed in some detail by Estes (1986a,1991b), Nosofsky (1990, 1992a,b), and Nosofsky, Kruschke, and McKinley (1992). I think it is fair to say that, for static situations, the exemplar model is the most generally applicable of these models and has accumulated the largest number of successes in providing detailed quantitative accounts of categorization data.

3.2 Network-based learning models

3.2.1 A simple adaptive network model

Despite its many desirable properties, the exemplar model has an important limitation. Under many conditions, the model yields satisfactory accounts of category learning once its parameters have been evaluated from the data, but it generally can tell us little about the probable course of learning in advance of an experiment. One of the prime objectives I would set for a categorization model is to enable us to predict how the relative frequencies of different types of errors of categorization will change during learning. Another is to predict the asymptote of learning, that is, the level of performance that subjects can be expected to achieve after a sufficient number of training trials.

By referring again to the minimal categorization problem illustrated in Table 2.10 and discussed at the beginning of this chapter, it is easy to point up the basis of this limitation. The expression derived from the exemplar model for probability of a correct response after each training pattern had occurred once took the form $1/(1+s)$, and this same expression holds after even an indefinitely large number of trials so long as the two categories and the four exemplars occur equally often. Surely, normal human learners would reach a level of 100% correct responding after even a moderate number of trials, and this result can be predicted from the model if the similarity parameter, s, is equal to zero. However, if we assume that s is equal to zero, we run into another difficulty. It is known that in the early stages of learning of a categorization, subjects' errors of categorization are systematically related to similarities between exemplars, and the model can account for this fact only on the assumption that s is greater than zero. If we fit the model to successive blocks of trials of a lengthy learning series separately (as I have done for the data of Estes (1986b), estimates of s from the data decline over blocks. However, there is no theoretical machinery in the exemplar model to produce changes in s over a series, and introducing some arbitrary function would, of course, have no explanatory value.

I have been unable to see any way of resolving this impasse within the framework of the exemplar model, and thus have begun to look for resources that might be drawn from other approaches. The most promising, perhaps, is the family of "connectionist" network models. A convenient starting point for discussing this approach is a model adapted from the discrimination theory of Rescorla and Wagner (1972) and introduced to the categorization literature by Gluck and Bower (1988b). In the form originally presented by Gluck and Bower, the model is based on a network of nodes and connecting paths; a node is defined for each member of the set of features from which category exemplars are generated, and each is connected to the output nodes, which correspond to the categories available for choice. The path from any feature node f_i to a category node C_j has an associated *weight*, w_{ij}, whose value measures the degree to which input from the feature node tends to activate the category node. The stimulus pattern presented on any occasion activates its feature nodes, and the output from these to the category nodes determines the probability of the corresponding categorization responses.

The way the model works can be illustrated in terms of a learning trial of a simple categorization problem. We assume that the exemplar pattern presented comprises features f_1 and f_2, which activate feature nodes n_1 and n_2. The output of the network to category node C_1 is

$$o_1 = w_{11} + w_{21} \qquad (3.3)$$

and the output to C_2 is

$$o_2 = w_{12} + w_{22} \qquad (3.4)$$

The ratios of these outputs (transformed by an exponential function to avoid negative quantities, as described in the next section) determine the categorization probabilities. The probability of a Category 1 response, for example, is given by

$$P(1) = o'_1 / (o'_1 + o'_2), \qquad (3.5)$$

where o'_i signifies the transformed output. At the end of the trial, when the learner is informed of the correct category, the weights on the active paths are adjusted by a learning function with a form known in the connectionist literature as the "delta rule" (Stone 1986; Gluck and Bower 1988*b*). In this example, if Category 1 is correct, the weight on the path from feature node n_1 to category node C_1 increases according to

$$w'_{11} = w_{11} + \beta(1 - w_{11} - w_{21}) \qquad (3.6)$$

and if Category 2 is correct, decreases according to

$$w'_{11} = w_{11} + \beta(0 - w_{11} - w_{21}). \qquad (3.7)$$

The w_{ij} terms on the right sides of these equations are the values at the beginning of the given trial and the w'_{ij} terms on the left the values at the end of the trial; β is a learning parameter with a value in the range 0 to 1.

In applications to a special type of categorization task in which features are uncorrelated within categories, this model proved to be at least equal, and in a few instances superior, to the exemplar model for describing the course of category learning (Gluck and Bower 1988*b*; Estes, Campbell, Hatsopoulis, and Hurwitz 1989). However, the scope of this model is severely limited, for it cannot account for learning in the very common situations where combinations of features have higher validities than the features individually; most conspicuously, the model implies that learning of the XOR problem should be impossible. To overcome this kind of limitation, Gluck, Bower, and Hee (1989) augmented the simple model with the assumption that the network includes not only nodes representing individual features but also nodes representing pairs of features. The resulting "configural cue" model, which in general may include nodes representing feature combinations of any size, remedies the deficiencies of the simple network quite well. Still, I find this approach somewhat unsatisfying in that the number of potential configural nodes becomes very large when the category exemplars are even moderately complex, and we lack any principled way of deciding in advance of an experiment which of the potential configural nodes should be included in a network.

A different way of augmenting the simple network model is suggested by the observation that its deficiencies are precisely of the kind that were overcome by the introduction of the product rule in the case of exemplar models. Perhaps what we need is some combination of the array and network approaches that could offer the advantages of both the learning mechanism of the network and the similarity formalism of the exemplar family. A proposal that I put forward a few years ago (Estes 1988) seems to be not quite right in details, but by building on some recent work of Gluck (1991), I think it is possible to modify that proposal and assemble a combined model that can give us the best of both worlds. The approach I take is evidently "in the air," for it closely parallels the independent development of basically similar, though more complex, models by Kruschke (1990, 1992*a*) and Nosofsky, Kruschke, and McKinley (1992).

3.2.2 The similarity-network model

(a) Model for a simple discrimination

It will be convenient to introduce the basic notions of a combined model by means of an ultra-simplified experiment. We will imagine a sensory discrimination problem of a kind much studied in psychophysics and animal learning research. Suppose that a learner's task is to discriminate two shades of gray paint. Certainly we could choose two shades so close together that initially many errors of classification would occur, but different enough that perfect discrimination would be attainable with sufficient practice. The design can be represented in the standard form:

| | Category | |
	1	2
f_1	1	0
f_2	0	1

where f_1 and f_2 denote the two shades of gray, f_1 occurring with probability 1 on trials when Category 1 is correct and f_2 with probability 1 when Category 2 is correct. We will assume that test trials for which we wish to generate predictions are given following blocks of trials in which the two categories have occurred equally often. Let us first examine this situation from the standpoint of the basic exemplar model. Using the same reasoning as in the analysis of the minimal learning task discussed at the beginning of this chapter, we find the same expression for probability of correct responding,[*]

$$P(C) = 1/(1+s).\tag{3.8}$$

Again, we find that perfect performance can be predicted only if the similarity parameter, s, is equal to zero, but then we cannot predict that frequency of confusion errors during learning will be related to similarity, illustrating what has been termed the "overlap problem" in discrimination learning (Rudy and Wagner 1975).

A model that can resolve this problem is based on the same stimulus representation but combines it with the learning mechanism of the Gluck and Bower (1988*b*) model. Rather than an array of stored representations, the memory structure in this model is a network of nodes and connecting pathways. The basic representational assumption is that a node is entered in the network for each stimulus pattern (in the discrimination example, each shade of gray) perceived by the learner. Associated with each node is a featural description of the stimulus with the same properties as the representations in the exemplar model. A key assumption is that similarity between an input pattern and the featural description associated with a node is computed exactly as in the exemplar model, and the computed similarity determines the level of activation of the node (hence, the designation similarity-network model). The network also includes a node for each category defined in the given task, and a pathway connects each memory node with each category ("output") node, as illustrated in Fig. 3.5 for the discrimination task.

The most salient difference between the exemplar model and the similarity-network model pertains to the handling of repeated exemplars. When an input pattern is repeated, a new node is not formed for each repetition; rather, the tendency of that node to activate the category nodes is modified by an adaptive learning mechanism. Associated with each path between a memory node n_i and an output node C_j is a weight, w_{ij}. The weight is initially equal to 0 but is adjusted on each learning trial that involves activation of node n_i, increasing if Category j is the correct outcome and decreasing otherwise. In general, the adjustment rule is as follows.

$$w'_{ij} = w_{ij} + \beta(z_j - o_{ij})a_i ,\tag{3.9}$$

where the term w_{ij} on the right and w'_{ij} on the left sides denote the weight at the beginning and end of a trial, respectively , z_j denotes a "teaching signal," which is equal to 1 if Category j is correct and equal to 0 otherwise,

---

[*] If, for example, a test is given after 100 trials with this design, Column 1 of the memory array will contain 50 representations of f_1 and the Column 2 50 representations of f_2. Thus the summed similarity of a test stimulus f_1 to the contents of Column 1 is 50 and to Column 2 is 50s. Probability of a correct response to f_1 is, then 50/(50+50s). A test on f_2 of course yields the same result.

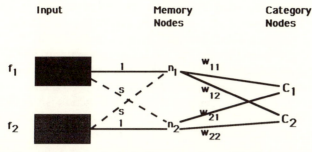

Fig. 3.5 Representation of similarity-network model for an experiment on discrimination between two shades of gray described in text.

a_i denotes the activation level of node n_i (having value 1 if n_i is active and 0 otherwise), β is a "learning rate" parameter with a value between 0 and 1, and o_{ij} is the current output of the network to category node C_j when memory node n_i is active. The output is defined by

$$o_{ij} = \Sigma a_{ik} w_{kj}, \tag{3.10}$$

where a_{ik} denotes activation level of node nk when pattern i is the input, and the summation runs over all memory nodes in the network.

Response probabilities are not computed directly from the outputs; rather, as in nearly all connectionist models, the o_{ij} values are subjected to a nonlinear transformation. In accord with previous closely related work (Gluck and Bower 1988*b*; Estes, Campbell, Hatsopoulis, and Hurwitz 1989), I use an exponential transformation, so for any two-category situation (with Categories A and B indexed by letting j in Equation 3.10 equal 1 or 2), the probability of assigning stimulus i to Category A is given by

$$P_i(A) = \frac{e^{co_{i1}}}{e^{co_{i1}} + e^{co_{i2}}}$$

$$= \frac{1}{1 + e^{-c(o_{i1}-o_{i2})}} \tag{3.11}$$

where c is a scaling parameter whose value is either chosen a priori on theoretical grounds or estimated from the data to which the model is being applied. It will be seen that response probability is an ogival function of the difference in outputs to the two category nodes, running from zero when o_{i2} is much larger than o_{i1} to unity when o_{i1} is much larger than o_{i2}.

For the discrimination problem, the adjustment rule for the weight on the path between the memory node corresponding to stimulus f_1 and the output node for Category 1 is

$$w'_{11} = w_{11} + \beta[1 - (w_{11} + sw_{21})]. \tag{3.12}$$

It will be noted that the quantity in parentheses on the right is the output to Category 1 on the given trial, as defined in Equation 3.10. Like the update function given above for the Gluck and Bower (1988*b*) model, this learning function is a special case of the "delta rule" of connectionist theory (Stone 1986) and also corresponds formally to the learning function of an influential model for classical conditioning (Rescorla and Wagner 1972).

An interesting and important property of this function is that learning is competitive in the sense that the magnitude of the adjustment to a weight on any trial depends on the weights on other concurrently active paths. Thus, in Equation 3.12, it is apparent that the increment to w_{11}, the weight on the path from stimulus f_1 to Category Node 1, is reduced as the output from stimulus f_2 to the same category node (sw_{21}) increases.

The way in which this model resolves the problem that proved to be an impasse for the exemplar model is illustrated in Fig. 3.6. The two learning functions portrayed were computed trial-by-trial from Equation 3.12 with the learning parameter, β, set equal to 0.25 and the similarity parameter, s, to 0 or 0.50. The relationship between the two functions is in line with expectations on the basis of well-known empirical results (Gynther 1957; Uhl 1964; Robbins 1970; Rudy and Wagner 1975). The difficulty of learning, indexed by the speed with which a learning curve approaches its final level, and therefore the number of errors that occur on early trials, is directly related to stimulus similarity, measured here by the magnitude of the similarity parameter, s, but both of the functions approach a final level of virtually perfect discrimination. The major advance over the exemplar model

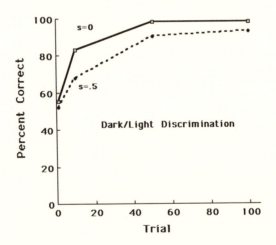

Fig. 3.6   Learning functions computed by the network of Fig. 3.5 for two values of the similarity parameter (s).

is that these predictions do not require any change in the similarity parameter over learning trials, so that if an estimate of *s* is available for a given situation from previously obtained data, the course of learning of a categorization can be predicted in advance.

(b) Categorization with multifeature stimuli

Very little modification of the network structure defined for the simple discrimination task is needed to handle more typical instances of categorization learning with multifeature stimuli. It will be convenient to illustrate the extension in terms of the categorization problem presented in Table 2.10, Chapter 2. The design of an experiment based on this problem could take the form

Exemplar	Category	
	A	B
1 1	0.5	0
1 2	0.5	0
2 1	0	0.5
2 2	0	0.5

where the entries 1 and 2 in the first column under Exemplar denote dark and light, 1 and 2 in the second column denote triangle and square, and the entry in each Category cell is the probability of occurrence of the row exemplar on trials when the given category is correct. In conventional terminology, dark and light are *relevant*, or *valid*, cues, which suffice to predict the correct category on any trial; triangle and square are *irrelevant*, or *invalid* cues, which convey no information about correct categorization. In an earlier period, it was thought that to master the categorization, the learner must somehow learn to attend only to the valid and to ignore the invalid cues, and then associate the valid cues with the appropriate category labels (see, e. g., Restle 1955; Zeaman and House 1963). However, we shall see that the similarity-network model can accomplish the task without requiring the assumption of a separate selection process.

The network representation, as illustrated in Fig. 3.7, has a memory node corresponding to each exemplar, and an output node for each category (the nodes for categories A and B being denoted C_1 and C_2, respectively). The whole structure would exist, of course, only after each exemplar pattern had occurred at least once. To reduce clutter in the figure, only the connecting paths from exemplar pattern 11 to the pattern nodes and from pattern node n_{11} to the category nodes are shown. The different thicknesses of the lines from pattern 11 to the memory nodes signify the different levels of activation that would be generated by presentation of this pattern,

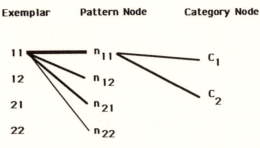

Fig. 3.7   Similarity-network representation of a categorization experiment, showing associative paths only for stimulus pattern 11.

depending on the inter-pattern similarities computed by the product rule: node n_{11} would be most strongly activated since similarity of pattern 11 to itself is 1; activation of nodes n_{12} and n_{21} would be lower since each differs from 11 with respect to one feature; and activation of node n_{22} would be lowest, since pattern 22 differs from 11 with respect to two features. Weights on the paths from the memory nodes to the output nodes are defined exactly as done for the discrimination task (Fig. 3.4), and the general function for adjustment of weights on learning trials has the same form as Equation 3.9. On a trial when the exemplar presented is pattern 11 and Category A is correct, for example, the function for adjustment of the weight on the path from pattern 11 to category node C_1 is

$$w'_{11,1} = w_{11,1} + \beta[1 - (w_{11,1} + sw_{12,1} + sw_{21,1} + s^2w_{22,1})], \quad (3.13)$$

where $w_{11,1}$ on the right and $w'_{11,1}$ on the left sides of the equation denote the old and new values, respectively. The learning functions are discussed further in Appendix 3.2.

Illustrative learning curves for the simple categorization problem were generated by setting the learning parameter, β, in Equation 3.9 equal to 0.25, the scaling parameter, c, in the output function (Equation 3.10) equal to 8, and computing changes in the weights and response probabilities trial-by-trial for the cases $s=0$, $s=0.3$, and $s=0.5$, as shown in the upper panel of Fig. 3.8. As for the simple discrimination, rate of learning and frequency of errors on early trials depend on stimulus similarity; however, for values of s smaller than about 0.3 (which would be the case with the stimulus materials used in most categorization experiments) the functions go to asymptotes close to unity.

In this task, the categorization could easily be mastered by attending only to the relevant attribute (light/dark). However, the presence of the irrelevant attribute (circle/triangle) exerts a drag on the rate of learning, as may be seen by comparing the upper panel of Fig. 3.8 with the lower panel, which

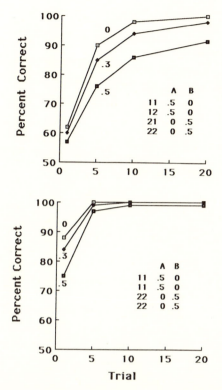

Fig. 3.8 Learning functions computed from the similarity-network model for a standard binary categorization experiment described in the text (upper panel) and a variation in which the irrelevant feature values become relevant but redundant (lower panel). The parameter is the value of the similarity parameter (s).

portrays learning by the same model for the same task except that the features of the exemplars have been rearranged so that light/dark has become a redundant, relevant attribute. Comparing the curves for $s=0$ in the upper and lower panels, we can see the effect of relevance versus irrelevance of the light/dark attribute most clearly. When similarity between light and dark or circle and triangle increases, indexed by larger values of s, the effect in the lower panel is only a modest retardation of rate of learning with virtually no change in asymptote; the effect in the upper panel is a much more prolonged retardation of learning, and, for the largest value of s an appreciable lowering of the asymptote. I do not know of any experiments designed to check on these predictions in quantitative detail, but they seem to be qualitatively in accord with a considerable literature on the role of relevant and irrelevant cues in discrimination learning (Restle 1955; Medin 1976).

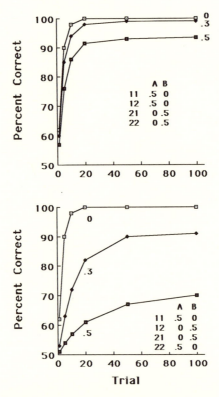

Fig. 3.9 Learning functions computed from the similarity-network model for the standard categorization experiment and a variation in which the design conforms to an XOR pattern as discussed in the text.

(c) Comparison of simple categorization and XOR problems

A still more impressive illustration of the sensitivity of the similarity-network model to the pattern of similarities among exemplars of each category is seen in Fig. 3.9, where the standard categorization problem discussed in the previous section is now compared with the "exclusive or" (XOR) problem (defined in the inset in the lower panel), with all parameters of the similarity-network model identical to those used for Fig. 3.8. In the XOR design, both attributes are irrelevant and learning of the categorization must be based entirely on the relations between exemplar patterns and categories. Although the model has no nodes in the network to represent individual features, the presence of irrelevant features greatly retards learning at the higher *s* values because of the way in which they enter into the similarity computations for pattern-node activation and for network output.*

3.2.3 Pattern to feature transfer

For an initial comparison of the exemplar and similarity-network models, I will use a task frequently set for category learning models, namely, predicting responses on tests given with individual features following a series of learning trials on categorization of exemplar patterns. Suppose, for example, that the learning task is to assign symptom charts of hypothetical patients to medical diagnostic categories, as in Gluck and Bower (1988b). During learning, subjects see some pattern of symptoms on each trial; the pattern may comprise several features (symptoms), as $f_1 f_2 f_3$ or $f_1 f_2$, or only a single feature, as f_1, presented alone. During learning, the subject is to try to assign each pattern to its correct category. On a feature test following learning, the subject is typically shown a single feature with the instruction to estimate the probability of a particular category (usually Category A in an A,B categorization problem) whenever that feature is present in an exemplar. In the study of Gluck and Bower (1988b), a simple network model appeared to be superior to a special case of the exemplar model for mediating predictions of these feature tests. However, several kinds of evidence suggest that once subjects have become used to responding to the pattern comprising a given feature alone in accord with its category probability, they simply persist in responding the same way when that feature is presented on a test trial, even though they should then respond in accord with the marginal probability of the reference category to any pattern containing the feature (Estes, Campbell, Hatsopoulis, and Hurwitz 1989; Shanks 1990).

(a) Design of a transfer study: Experiment 3.1

A hitherto unpublished study conducted in my laboratory was designed to circumvent this problem. A categorization task was arranged so that subjects would see only pairs of features during learning and would encounter single-feature displays for the first time on transfer tests given following learning. Therefore, they might be expected to respond on the tests in accord with the new instructions to estimate category probabilities given the presence of the test feature in the display.

The task described to the subjects was categorizing hypothetical people (category exemplars) according to membership in two country clubs. The

---

* Considering, for example, the learning of weight $w_{11,1}$, in the XOR design, both of the patterns with greatest similarity to pattern 11 belong to Category 2, but in the standard design only one of these belongs to Category 2, so on a pattern 11 trial at any given point in learning, output to the Category 1 node is greater in the standard than in the XOR design.

exemplars were defined by pairs of characteristics from the set "blond", "Cadillac," "Democrat," and "tennis," coded henceforth as features 1, 2, 3, and 4. The country clubs were labelled "P" and "Q," henceforth recoded as A and B. The four feature pairs presented during training and their frequencies of occurrence in the two categories were

	Category	
Exemplar	A	B
1 2	12	8
1 4	12	8
3 2	4	16
3 4	4	16

where the first entry under *Exemplar* denotes a pattern comprising features 1 and 2, and so on (see Appendix 3.3 for additional details.) Both the feature pairs (training patterns) and the individual features were only partially valid predictors of category membership. The question at issue was whether experience only with pairs would enable subjects to learn the validities of the individual features and to exhibit this knowledge when subsequently tested on single features. Instructions to the subjects at the beginning of the experiment explained the task and the procedures for the training trials but did not mention the test trials; the test instructions were given during a short break at the end of the training series.

(b) Model fits to learning data

Since there was virtually no non-zero trend in accuracy of categorization over ten-trial blocks in the learning series, the learning data are summarized in terms of percentages of Category A responses to each of the four training exemplars averaged over all blocks in Table 3.3. The table includes also the theoretical values for the similarity-network model and for the Exemplar

Table 3.3   Category A percentages to training patterns averaged over all learning trials in Experiment 3.1 (pattern-feature transfer)

Pattern	Validity	Data	Exemplar model	Similarity-network model
12	67	64	61	58
14	67	60	54	59
32	20	23	24	25
34	20	22	22	23
RMS error			11.4	13.0

Table 3.4 Category A percentages on single-feature test trials of Experiment 3.1

Feature	Validity	Data	Exemplar model	Similarity-network model
1	60	57	60	53
2	40	46	40	47
3	20	36	21	42
4	40	48	40	48
RMS error			9.1	3.5

model (with the same number of fitted parameters*). On the basis of previous work (Estes, Campbell, Hatsopoulis, and Hurwitz 1989), it was expected that the response percentages would tend to match the pattern validities,† expressed as percentages, and this expectation is quite well borne out in the data. Both models account for the data reasonably well, with the exemplar model being slightly superior.

(c) Model fits to transfer data

In many such comparisons, I have found that the exemplar and the similarity-network models yield approximately equivalent accounts of learning data when the change in response percentages over trials is not large. Thus we must look to other aspects of the data to differentiate the models—in this experiment, the results of the single-feature tests given at the end of the learning series. These are given in Table 3.4 in the form of percentages of Category A responses to each of the features, together with predictions from the exemplar and network models. It deserves emphasis that the parameters of the models were evaluated from the learning data and thus the theoretical values in Table 3.4 are genuine predictions that could have been made before the test trials were given. The exemplar model implies (contrary to the observed result) that the test percentages should closely match the feature validities,† also shown in the table. In contrast, the network model predicts quite accurately the way in which the observed values deviate from matching.

---

* The parameters of the exemplar model represented similarity (s), initial memory load (s_0) and decay, those of the similarity-network model, learning rate (β), similarity (s), and the scaling constant (c).

† Pattern validity is defined as the conditional, or Bayesian, probability of a reference category (taken here to be Category A) in the presence of the pattern. Feature validity is the same probability in the presence of the feature. Both validities are given in percentages for convenience.

Many experiments of the same design as Experiment 3.1 have been used in recent years for the purpose of comparing the fits of various versions of exemplar and network models to the learning and transfer data. Both types of models have had their striking successes, but no one has proved uniformly superior. A hypothesis that seems to merit close examination is that the superiority of particular models varies with experimental conditions in systematic ways that can be characterized by principles general enough to enable advance specification of the model that will best handle a new situation. My first efforts toward this examination are the subject of the next chapter.

Appendix 3.1 Categorization probability for the exemplar model in relation to initial memory load

We consider the categorization task of Table 2.10 and apply the exemplar model, assuming no initial memory load ($s_0=0$). After a series of n trials with the exemplars and categories occurring in the same ratios as in Table 3.1, the expected memory array will be

	A	B
I1	$n/3$	$n/6$
I2	$n/6$	$n/3$

Since categorization probability depends only on the ratios of the entries in each row, we can simplify the derivation by multiplying all of the entries by six and rewriting the array as

	A	B
I1	$2n$	n
I2	n	$2n$

then, computing the similarities-to-category and the response probabilities in the standard way, we obtain

	Sim A	*Sim B*	*Probability of A*
I1	$2n+ns$	$n+2ns$	$(2+s)/3(1+s)$
I2	$n+2ns$	$2n+ns$	$(1+s)/3(1+s)$.

Obviously, categorization probability is independent of n, and therefore the model cannot accommodate the almost ubiquitously observed facilitative effect of number of learning trials on performance.

If, instead, the learning process began with a preload, M', in each category of the memory array, then the array after n trials would have the form

	A	B
I1	$M+2n$	$M+n$
I2	$M+n$	$M+2n$

where we have set M equal to $6M'$ to simplify the expressions. Completing the derivation just as in the previous case yields

	Sim A	*Sim B*	*Probability of A*
I1	$M+2n+s(M+n)$	$M+n+s(M+2n)$	$\dfrac{M(1+s)+n(2+s)}{(2M+3n)(1+s)}$
I2	$M+n+s(M+2n)$	$M+2n+s(M+n)$	$\dfrac{M(1+s)+n(1+2s)}{(2M+3n)(1+s)}$

Now n does not cancel out of the ratios and categorization probability is an increasing function of the number of learning trials. For example, with $M=1$ and $s=0.2$, the probability of assigning exemplar I1 to Category A runs 0.50, 0.54, 0.58, 0.59 for n equal to 0, 1, 5, and 10, respectively.

Appendix 3.2 Similarity-network output and learning functions for standard four-pattern categorization

The design of the four-pattern categorization task, repeated from the text for convenience, is

Exemplar	*Category*	
	A	B
1 1	0.5	0
1 2	0.5	0
2 1	0	0.5
2 2	0	0.5

the exemplars being represented by their values on two binary attributes. With exemplar 11 used for illustrative purposes, the expression for output to Category node 1 is

$$o_{11} = w_{11} + s(w_{21} + w_{31}) + s^2 w_{41}, \tag{3.A1}$$

obtained by setting the subscript k in Equation 3.10 equal to 1, 2, 3, and 4 for the four exemplar patterns. To specialize the four activation levels, a_{1k}, in

Equation 3.10 to this example, I have substituted the similarities of each of the four patterns to pattern 1, these being 1, s, s, and s^2, since patterns 1, 2, 3, and 4 differ from pattern 1 with respect to 0, 1, 1, and 2 features, respectively. Then we need only enter this output function in Equation 3.10, and, letting a_1 equal 1 and making the appropriate changes in subscript notation, we have for the w_{11} learning function on a trial when pattern 1 is presented and Category 1 is correct,

$$w'_{11} = w_{11} + \beta(1 - o_{11}). \tag{3.A2}$$

For a trial on which pattern 1 is presented with Category B correct, the term z_j (the "teaching signal") in Equation 3.10 is set equal to 0 rather than 1, and the learning function for weight w_{11} is

$$w'_{11} = w_{11} + \beta(0 - o_{11}). \tag{3.A3}$$

The functions for the other pattern-category weights are of course obtained similarly.

Using the weight adjustment functions of the form of Equations 3.A2 and 3.A3, we could compute trial-by-trial predictions of changes in weights over a learning series, given knowledge of the exact sequence of pattern-category combinations presented. To make advance predictions for an experiment knowing only the probabilities of occurrence of categories and patterns, we have to replace the terms z_j and a_i in Equation 3.10 by their expected values. For a trial when pattern i is presented, these are:

$$E(z_j) = 0.5(p_{1j}s_{1i} + p_{2j}s_{2i} + p_{3j}s_{3i} + p_{4j}s_{4i}), \tag{3.A4}$$

for the expectation of z_j, and

$$E(a_i) = p_1 s_{1i} + p_2 s_{2i} + p_3 s_{3i} + p_4 s_{4i}), \tag{3.A5}$$

for the expected activation of pattern node i', where p_{ij} denotes probability of pattern i on a category j trial, p_i the unconditional probability of pattern i, and s_{ki} the similarity between patterns k and i. The term 0.5 in Equation 3.A4 is the probability of category j (equal to 0.5 for the experiment under discussion in the text).

Only minor adjustments are needed to convert this model for binary categorization into a model for identification of the same stimuli that were presented in the categorization task. Recalling that for a given set of N stimuli, identification is simply classification into N distinct categories, one per stimulus, we note that the conversion into a model for identification is accomplished by letting the category subscript, j, in Equations 3.A4 and 3.A5 run from 1 to 4 rather than from 1 to 2. The number of learning functions increases from 8 to 16, since there are weights from each of the four pattern nodes to each of four category nodes, but each of the functions is produced in exactly the same way as those in Equations 3.A2 and 3.A3, with the subscripts i and j in the general function, Equation 3.A4, each running from 1 to 4. Also, for the identification of four stimulus patterns, the case discussed in the text, the term 0.5 in Equation 3.A4 should be replaced by 0.25.

Appendix 3.3 Additional details of Experiment 3.1 procedure

During the 80 training trials, each exemplar pattern appeared five times, the relative frequencies in the two categories being preserved. For example, during the first 20 trials, the exemplar pattern 12 appeared three times with category A denoted correct and two times with category B denoted correct.

In the test block, given after the training series, subjects saw each of the single features once and for each estimated the probability of the reference category, given only the information that the given feature was present (i.e., that it characterized the hypothetical individual represented on the test).

4. Categorization and memory processing

The models for category learning discussed in the preceding chapters have been developed largely in conjunction with a standard experimental design in which a subject classifies category exemplars with feedback during a learning phase, often running to hundreds of trials, then is tested for transfer to new stimulus patterns of various types. There are good reasons for some standardization, but the cost is that it is not easy to relate the models to other potentially relevant bodies of memory research and theory. In this chapter, I report some efforts to modify the standard design in ways that may enable informative analyses pertaining to concepts of interference and organization in memory.

4.1 Concurrent categorizations

In ordinary life outside the laboratory, it seems to be the norm that an individual must concurrently learn a variety of categorizations. In school, for example, a student typically studies several different subjects in the course of each day; and each of these requires the learning of categorizations, one, perhaps, pertaining to parts of speech in a new language, another to plant or animal forms, another to types of governments. Learning experiences on the different categorizations are intermixed in a more or less random order, and the learner must be able to carry along a number of partly learned categorizations with minimal interference. In laboratory experiments, however, the learner normally has no previous relevant experience and receives all of the training prescribed for a task in a single session. On the relatively rare occasions when a subject is asked to learn more than one categorization task as part of a study, training is completed on one task before another is started and special precautions are taken to avoid any positive or negative carryover from one to the next. Thus, if we expect results of research on category learning to generalize beyond the laboratory, we need evidence as to whether subjects in typical experimental tasks can learn and maintain multiple categorizations simultaneously.

The experiment to be discussed in this section (Experiment 4.1) was designed to address this problem, and, as a by-product, to set the stage for some analyses bearing on modes of information processing. Salient aspects of the design are summarized in Table 4.1 and details of procedure in Appendix 4.1. Each subject had 60 training trials on each of four

Table 4.1 Design of Experiment 4.1: concurrent categorization study

	Problem			
	1	2	3	4
Features	Circulation	Temperature	Pain	Skin
	Nausea	Cramps	Nosebleed	Cough
Categories	A or B	C or D	E or F	G or H

Learning Sequence

Blocked
Trial	1–60			61–120			121–180			181–240
Problem	1			2			3			4

Random
Trial	1	2	3	4	5	6	.	.	.	.	. 240
Problem	2	4	1	3	4	1	.	.	.	.	. 240

categorization problems in a simulation of the learning of medical diagnoses. The common task was to learn to classify hypothetical patients, represented by symptom patterns, into disease categories. No symptom occurred in more than one problem, but all of the symptoms were semantically related, which might be expected to render the task rather difficult. On any one trial on a particular problem, the subject first saw on a computer screen a "chart" listing one, both, or neither of the two symptoms belonging to the problem, together with a query of the form, "Category X or Y?"; then the subject typed a letter denoting either Category X or Category Y, and finally viewed a display of the category label defined by the experimenter as correct for the trial.

The lower portion of Table 4.1 exhibits the learning conditions to which two groups of subjects were assigned. The novel one is the Random condition, in which trials representing the four problems are intermixed in a random sequence, so that, for example, the first trial might present the learner with an instance of Problem 2, the second trial an instance of Problem 4, and so on. A trial lasted about 3–4 seconds (the time required for display of the symptom chart and the subject's response, plus 2 seconds viewing time for the display of the correct category, with no additional interval between trials). Thus, the processing demands were quite severe, and rapid and efficient "mental bookkeeping" was needed to accomplish the task without interference between problems. In the more conventional blocked condition, a subject had all 60 trials on one problem before starting the next. Blocking of course greatly reduced the problem of coping with interference between problems and allowed heavier reliance on short-term memory, an aspect that will be of special interest.

Category structures were chosen to represent a variety of those commonly studied in previous research. Problems 1 and 2 had "independent cue" structures in that the features were uncorrelated within categories (as in Gluck and Bower (1988*b*) and Estes, Campbell, Hatsopoulis, and Hurwitz (1989)), whereas Problem 3 had perfectly correlated features in an "XOR" design (discussed in Chapters 2 and 3), and Problem 4 had partially correlated features.

For a preliminary theoretical analysis of the data, I will apply the exemplar and similarity-network models to each problem separately in both the blocked and random conditions.* The first task to be posed for the models at this point is predicting the relative difficulty of the problems, in terms of probability of correct categorization at the end of the learning series. To derive predictions for the exemplar model, it was assumed that all of the exemplars presented for a problem were stored in memory with their category labels, and the similarities of test patterns to categories, together with response probabilities, were computed as in previous applications of the model. Predictions for the network model were obtained by computations based on the learning functions given in Chapter 3. Details of the category structures of the four problems and the theoretical computations are given in Appendix 4.1

The predicted ordering of the problems is very similar for the two models. The value of the similarity parameter, s, has little effect on the predictions except for Problem 3, the XOR problem, in which features are entirely invalid. On the assumption that s is small, both models imply that Problem 3 should be the easiest (i.e., should yield the highest asymptotic probability correct) and Problem 4 the most difficult. Problems 1 and 2 are intermediate in predicted difficulty (but rather closer to Problem 3), with an advantage for Problem 1 over Problem 2 that is a bit larger in the similarity-network than in the exemplar model predictions.

To bring out further the capability of these models for generating genuine advance predictions about an experiment of some complexity, I have computed theoretical learning functions for all four problems from the similarity-network model with the parameters β and c having the same values, 0.1 and 2, that were used for the computation of predicted asymptotes and the similarity parameter s set equal to 0, with the result shown in Fig. 4.1.

These theoretical functions may be compared with the observed learning curves, plotted in Fig. 4.2 in terms of percentage of correct responses per

---

* The question of how the representations of the different structures are kept separate in memory and how they are accessed when examplars of one or another category are presented for categorization will be addressed in Chapter 6 in connection with the general problem of similarity relationships among categories.

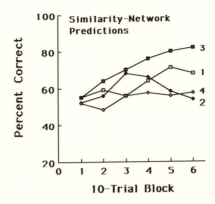

Fig. 4.1 Learning functions for problems 1–4 of Experiment 4.1 predicted a priori by the similarity-network model.

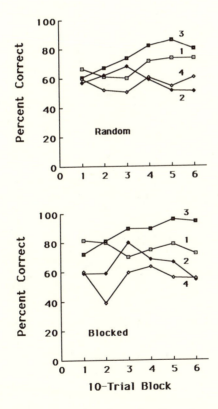

Fig. 4.2 Observed learning functions for Experiment 4.1 by condition and problem.

ten-trial block for each problem. In spite of the rather drastic difference in procedure for the blocked and random conditions, the relative difficulties of problems and the trends over blocks are quite similar for the two conditions. Learning was slightly faster in the blocked condition, at least for the two easier problems, but not as much so as might have been intuitively expected. Evidently the subjects in the random condition suffered little inter-problem interference.

In each condition, the observed functions line up quite well with the a priori predictions of the models concerning relative difficulty. Even more impressive, perhaps, is the degree to which the similarity-network learning functions predict the rather complex trends (resulting from the particular sequences of exemplar patterns presented) seen in the observed functions depicted in Fig. 4.2. The only formal basis for interpreting differences between the blocked and random conditions in either of the models lies in the decay process (represented by the decay parameter of the exemplar model and implicit in the similarity-network model). There must be more retention loss between occurrences of an item in the random condition, the

Table 4.2   Fits of the Exemplar and Similarity-Network Models in the Concurrent Categorization Study

	Problem				
	1	2	3	4	Mean
Learning					
Blocked					
Exemplar	10.9	11.4	8.6	14.6	11.3
Network	11.3	12.3	9.1	16.6	12.6
Random					
Exemplar	14.2	16.6	10.5	13.1	13.8
Network	14.7	17.1	10.4	13.2	14.0
Transfer					
Blocked					
Exemplar	18.2	2.2	8.4	16.7	13.2
Network	22.8	16.6	8.4	16.3	16.0
Random					
Exemplar	3.2	7.8	7.4	9.2	7.1
Network	7.4	6.7	8.1	0.7	5.7

Note: The measure of goodness of fit is root mean square deviation of predicted from observed correct response percentages, computed over all 60 exemplar presentations for each problem.

intervals between recurrences being longer on the average than in the blocked condition, and therefore the learning functions should rise less steeply (as observed for three of the four problems in Fig. 4.2). In addition, we might intuitively expect the learning rate parameter of the similarity-network model to have smaller values in the random condition, where rehearsal would be more difficult, but this expectation has no formal basis in the assumptions of the model.

To compare the abilities of the two models to account for the detailed course of learning given appropriate parameter values, the models were fitted to the observed learning functions with values of the three free parameters estimated by least squares for each problem. The measures of goodness of fit in terms of root mean square deviations of theoretical from observed values, shown in Table 4.2, reveal a modest advantage for the exemplar model in the blocked condition but virtual equivalence in the random condition. As anticipated, the estimated decay parameter of the exemplar model was smaller in the random than the blocked condition (values of 0.938 and 0.965, respectively),* and similarly for the rate parameter, β, of the similarity-network model (estimates of 0.235 and 0.285 for random and blocked). The predictions for test trials (a priori, since the model parameters were estimated using only the learning data) are also represented in Table 4.2. The models do not differ appreciably or systematically, and both fare much better on the random than on the blocked condition,† as is apparent also in the presentation of test data in Fig. 4.3.

Although it is clear from the results of the experiment just described that several distinct category structures can be learned concurrently with little interference, one may still ask whether any information is acquired concerning relationships between structures. Suppose, for example, that at an early stage of acquiring a new language a person is learning to classify nouns into the categories masculine versus feminine gender and verbs into the categories transitive versus intransitive under conditions similar to those of the experiment just described. In the noun task, there is a feature that belongs to all of the nouns in the practice material but to none of the verbs. To accomplish the noun classification task, the learner must, in effect, ignore this irrelevant, or "invalid," feature, which does not discriminate gender; and we saw in Chapter 2 how this problem could be handled by the exemplar model. We may ask, however, whether, after this learning is completed, the learner could be expected to be able to demonstrate knowledge that the invalid feature belongs only to nouns and not to verbs. An experiment

---

* It will be recalled that the decay parameter is defined (Chapter 3) so that a value of unity signifies no decay and a value of zero maximal decay.

† The much greater variability of the test data for the blocked condition was no doubt due to the long intervals from the end of learning to the tests (all of which were given following the 240 learning trials).

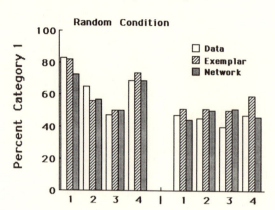

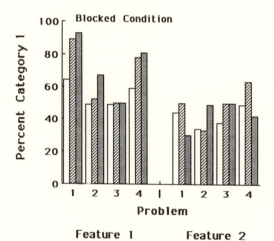

Fig. 4.3   Data for the single feature tests in Experiment 4.1 together with predictions by the exemplar and similarity-network models.

conducted in my laboratory (Experiment 4.2, described in Appendix 4.2) was designed to simulate this situation, and yielded an affirmative answer, in accord with predictions from both the exemplar and the similarity-network models. Evidently, the memory representation formed during learning, which, according to either model, constitutes simply a record of exemplar-category occurrences, contains implicit knowledge about the multiple task structure that becomes manifest in appropriate test situations. We have yet another demonstration that relational information having no explicit representation in a memory array may be generated at test when computations of global similarities are carried out via the product rule.

4.2 Categorization with constraints on memory

An idea I have been entertaining for some time is that, when performance depends mainly on short-term memory, the exemplar model may be hard to improve upon, but when retrieval of information from long-term memory is strongly implicated, a network model is superior. This hypothesis is related to a distinction between two types of learning that dates from Hebb (1949). Hebb marshalled a body of evidence in support of the idea that immature organisms are characterized by a slow, incremental form of learning that is responsible for their developing ability to recognize and classify stimulus patterns. This form of learning sometimes occurs in adults, most conspicuously during recovery from damage to the brain or sensory systems, but is normally overshadowed by a faster form of learning, basic to problem solving and other cognitive functions. The slow form might be described in terms of the formation of memory structures by the growth of associative strengths among components, the fast form in terms of reorganization of relations among the memory structures.

Learning at maturity concerns patterns and events whose parts at least are already familiar and which already have a number of other associations. . . . The characteristic adult learning . . . is learning that takes place in a few trials, or in one only. (Hebb 1949, p. 127)

Hebb was mainly concerned with shifts in the nature of learning from lower to higher phylogenetic levels and from infancy to maturity within levels. Granting those developmental trends, I think that also it is often possible to observe both slow and fast forms of learning in the same organism and in the same situation, most conspicuously in human adults. With respect to categorization learning, the thought that has emerged in my work is that, on the first few trials in a categorization task, learning is characteristically fast and describable in terms of the storage of stimulus representations in short-term memory and their retrieval after short intervals for purposes of comparison with newly perceived stimuli. As experience in a situation continues, however, gradual changes occur in strengths of associative connections between representations of exemplars and categories in a network. In contrast to the short-term representations, which are highly susceptible to displacement by new inputs, the network representation is more stable and much more resistant to interference from succeeding learning experiences. In terms of the models under discussion, learning of a new categorization is at the outset adequately interpreted in terms of the pure exemplar-similarity model, but as trials continue, the more slowly evolving process represented in the network model takes over.

Now, how might we hope to gain reasonably direct evidence concerning this dual-model conception? It has not been possible to get far by examining the existing literature because I have been unable to find any reports of categorization experiments designed so that learners would have to rely solely on short-term memory. Contriving such a design is not easy, but the following experiment, conducted in my laboratory, was a first attempt. The attempt was not entirely successful, but I will describe it briefly en route to a more satisfactory study.

4.2.1 Categorization with constrained repetition lags

Except for one constraint, which I will spell out, all aspects of the design and the procedure of this experiment (Experiment 4.3) were identical to those of Experiment 1 of the study reported by Estes, Campbell, Hatsopoulis, and Hurwitz (1989). The subjects' task was to classify hypothetical symptom charts by disease categories under an experimental routine in which Categories A and B occurred with probabilities 0.25 and 0.75, respectively, and the sampling probabilities of symptoms within categories were

	Category	
Symptom	A	B
1	0.6	0.2
2	0.4	0.3
3	0.3	0.4
4	0.2	0.6

The four symptoms were sampled randomly to generate the category exemplars (combinations of 0 to 4 symptoms) exhibited on training trials. On each trial, a subject viewed an exemplar pattern, made a categorization response, and then was shown the label for the category defined by the experimental program as correct for the trial. At the end of the 240-trial learning series, transfer tests were given on which each symptom appeared alone and the subject was to estimate the probability of Category A in the presence of the symptom.

The novel aspect of the experiment was a restriction on the lags between recurrences of exemplars to the range 0–7 intervening trials throughout the learning series. The purpose of the restriction was to ensure that when a learner encountered a repeated exemplar (i.e., had occasion to compare a perceived exemplar to a previously stored representation of the same symptom combination), the exemplar must have occurred within the last eight trials and, therefore, should be active in short-term working memory.

Our prime interest is in the relative abilities of the exemplar and similarity-network models to account for the learning and test data. The model fits summarized in Table 4.3 show that the two models are approximately equivalent with respect to the learning data, but the exemplar model predictions are distinctly superior for the test data. The latter result is in sharp contrast to the large advantage for the similarity-network model

Table 4.3 Model fits to constrained categorization data (Experiment 4.3)

Model	Learning	Tests
Exemplar	18.23	6.12
Networks		
Similarity-network	18.56	9.22
Feature/doublet	21.35	11.18

Note: Goodness of fit is indexed by root mean square differences between observed and predicted response percentages; model parameters were estimated by least squares on the learning data only.

seen in Table 3.4 for tests given after a learning series that did not have the restriction to short repetition lags. Perhaps more striking, the exemplar model is somewhat superior for learning and greatly superior for test data when compared to the configural cue model of Gluck, Bower, and Hee (1989), which has outperformed the exemplar model on several data sets from standard category learning experiments. Thus, over all, we have a suggestion that under conditions conducive to relatively heavy dependence on short-term memory, the storage and retrieval processes assumed in the exemplar model account for categorization better than do the network representations, which are generally superior when performance depends more strongly on long-term memory.

That suggestion is only tentative, however, for examination of other aspects of the data of the constrained repetition experiment raises a discordant note. Under the processing assumptions of the exemplar model, it is expected that categorization of repeated exemplars should depend on lag; that is, accuracy should be greatest for an exemplar that occurred on the immediately preceding trial and decline with an increase in the number of trials intervening between the current and the preceding occurrence. But, carrying out the indicated analysis, we find no trend over lag, mean accuracy being 67.8% for immediate repetitions and 69.2% for repetitions at a lag of seven trials (the maximum allowed in this experiment). Reflecting on this initially puzzling result, I realized that this experiment was not optimally designed for its purpose. Although the lag restriction should ensure that when a repeated exemplar is presented for categorization, its most recent previous occurrence will be in short-term memory, the computation of its categorization probability will nonetheless depend on its summed similarity to all previously stored exemplars. And, of course, as the learning series goes on, an ever smaller fraction of these will have been stored within the most recent eight trials. To enable a better test of the processing assumptions of the exemplar model, we need an experiment in which categorization probabilities depend solely on stored representations of events that have occurred within the short-term memory range.

4.2.2 Categorization based on short-term memory

In order to ensure that subjects' categorization performance would depend solely on short-term memory, we designed a new experiment (Experiment 4.4), employing the simple expedient of making the learning series extremely brief. The experimental session for any one subject included 12 distinct tasks. Each task was a miniature category learning experiment, comprising a series of eight learning trials followed by two kinds of test trials. Since individual trials took no more than about 3–4 seconds, the learning sequence could be assumed to fall comfortably within the commonly accepted span of short-term memory (specifically, *working memory* (Baddeley 1986).

In one of the tasks, subjects were asked to classify hypothetical individuals into mental disease categories on the basis of symptoms (which served as the features used to construct category exemplars). The learning sequence ran as follows:

Trial	Symptoms	Category
1	Headache and fever	E
2	Fever and nosebleed	S
3	Fever and insomnia	E
4	Fever and insomnia	E
5	Headache and nosebleed	S
6	Headache and fever	E
7	Headache and nosebleed	S
8	Fever and nosebleed	S

where E and S are labels for the disease categories. Each exemplar (symptom pair) occurred exactly twice, and was assigned to the same category on both occurrences, so a fully efficient learner could be correct on the second occurrence of each. The number of trials (lag) intervening between the two occurrences of an exemplar varied from 0 to 5, setting the stage for planned analyses bearing on the question of whether comparisons between current and previously experienced exemplars proceed via a sequential search through a chronologically ordered memory array.

Immediately following the eight learning trials, the subject received transfer tests of the same kind given in Experiment 4.3. In these tests, each symptom was presented once alone and the subject estimated the probability of a category. The symptom *insomnia* in the example had occurred in two exemplars during learning, both times with Category E correct. The symptom *fever* had occurred in six exemplars, with Category E correct four times and Category S correct twice. Thus, the most appropriate estimates of Category E probability in the presence of these symptoms would be 1 and 2/3, respectively (100 and 67 on the percentage scale actually used). Considering the brevity of the learning series, we did not expect high accuracy on these tests, but nonetheless, we wished to compare the ability of the exemplar and similarity-network models to predict the performance. If our procedure has been successful in causing the stored representations of the exemplars viewed during the learning series to be still active in short-term memory (working memory), at the time of the tests, then we may find that test performance will be better predicted by the retrieval and comparison processes of the exemplar model than by the associative strengths (network weights) of the similarity-network model, in contrast to the result found previously for conditions more conducive to dependence on long-term memory.*

Each subject completed 12 tasks, involving several different kinds of categories and features, with six tasks assigned to a high validity and six to a zero validity condition. The example given above represents one of the six high validity tasks, so called because each exemplar pattern is associated with the same category on both of its occurrences; it would be converted to a zero validity task if the correct category were changed on the second occurrence of each of the exemplars.† Additional details of the design and procedure are given in Appendix 4.3. A complete replication of the experiment was run with the only change in procedure being that, whereas the high and zero validity tasks were given in a random order in the main experiment, they were blocked in the replication—high validity first for half of the subjects and zero validity first for the other half.

4.2.3 Analyses of response frequency data

Our first concern with the results is to test the predictions of the exemplar and similarity-network models for the learning and feature-to-category test data just as was done previously for the experiments where performance was not constrained to depend on short-term memory. The fits of the models are

---

* The final phase of the task was a series of eight category-to-feature tests. In the example, one of these might be a request to estimate the relative frequency with which the sympton *headache* had occurred in Category E during learning, the appropriate answer being 50%. In the study of MacMillan (1987), with conditions conducive to categorization on the basis of long-term memory, tests of this type strongly supported network over exemplar models, so there is special interest in seeing whether the same will be the case when categorization depends primarily on short-term memory. Results of these tests will be given in Chapter 5.

† In the high validity conditions of all of the problems, all of the exemplar patterns presented and all but one of the individual features were fully valid or partially valid (i.e., occurred with different frequencies in the two categories). In the zero validity conditions, included to provide evidence about some aspects of performance on a type of test that will be discussed in Chapter 5, all exemplar patterns and all individual features were entirely invalid (i.e., occurred with equal frequencies in both categories). Only analyses of the high validity data are presented in this section, since only in that condition could category learning in the usual sense occur.

Table 4.4   Model fits to data of Experiment 4.4: categorization in short-term memory

Model	High validity		Zero validity	
	Learning	Tests	Learning	Tests
Main experiment				
Exemplar	15.17	14.14	14.53	0
Network	17.39	15.81	15.29	3.54
Replication				
Exemplar	17.43	13.69	17.71	5.48
Network	18.37	14.14	17.39	13.42

Note: Entries are root mean square differences between observed and predicted response percentages; model parameters were estimated by least squares on the learning data only.

summarized in Table 4.4, in a format paralleling that of Table 4.3, and exhibit a distinct advantage for the exemplar model, much greater for the test than for the learning data.

With respect to learning, however, we are less concerned with the overall fits than with the way categorization performance changes from the first to the second occurrence of an exemplar as a function of lag. If categorization is accomplished by comparing the current exemplar sequentially with the previously stored representations, then probability of correct categorization on the second occurrence of a repeated exemplar should decrease with lag because, with a longer lag, the representation of the first occurrence will be more likely to be unavailable for a similarity computation. The indicated analysis (performed on only the high validity conditions since only these are comparable to previous experiments) shows no change from lag 0 to lag 1 but a large change between these and longer lags. The results, together with model predictions, are summarized in Table 4.5. The drastic decline in

Table 4.5   Percentage of correct categorizations of repeated exemplars as a function of lag (Experiment 4.4)

	Lag	Data	Model	
			Exemplar	Network
Main experiment	0–1	80	84	74
	3–5	63	66	73
Replication	0–1	82	81	76
	3–5	66	67	74

performance from the shorter to the longer lags contrasts sharply with the small or absent effects that characterize experiments not similarly limited to short-term memory processing (e.g., Experiment 4.3 and the more standard experiments reported by Estes 1986*b*). It is notable also that the observed lag effect is quite accurately predicted by the exemplar model but missed entirely by the similarity-network model.

4.2.4 Analyses of reaction times

In short-term memory research, evidence concerning modes of information processing has traditionally been sought mainly in analyses of reaction times for correct recognition responses, because predictions for these seem intuitively straightforward. If, for example, comparisons of a test stimulus to memory are accomplished by a sequential search, then reaction time is expected to increase with the number of comparisons. Translated to the present situation, the hypothesis of a sequential search* implies that reaction time for categorization of an exemplar should increase as a function of the trial of occurrence, since on later trials there would be more stored representations to be compared with the to-be-categorized exemplar.

Studies of category learning under the usual conditions, nearly always using long series of trials, have yielded no support for the assumption of sequential search. A typical result is the following, taken from an unpublished experiment conducted in my laboratory. Under procedures generally the same as those used in Estes (1986*b*) and Estes, Campbell, Hatsopoulis, and Hurwitz (1989), subjects were given a 320-trial learning series with the task of classifying artificial words as adjectives or verbs. Mean reaction times (in milliseconds) for categorization responses to new and old (repeated) exemplars were

80-trial block

	1	2	3	4
New	2480	2030	1970	1750
Old	2060	2000	1710	1620

As in all similar studies I am familiar with, reaction time steadily decreases over trials. Further, a breakdown of these data by new exemplars (first occurrences) versus first repetitions shows very similar decreasing trends for both; and even an examination of the first 40 individual trials reveals no increasing trend for either first occurrences or first repetitions. We evidently have to conclude that either reaction time does not increase with increasing number of comparisons to memory required for similarity computations, or

---

* Presumably backward from the current trial, but the order is immaterial.

any increase is outweighed by some kind of practice effect that is as yet not understood. Things might be quite different when processing is restricted to short-term memory, however, so an analysis of reaction times in the short-term categorization experiment is in order.

For a first test of the sequential search hypothesis, I averaged all reaction times obtained from the high validity condition of both the main experiment and the replication (except those for trial 1, on which there would be no occasion for memory search). The trend of these means over trials yielded no obvious support for the hypothesis, the values increasing from about 1650 milliseconds (ms) on trial 2 to 2000 ms on trial 4, then steadily decreasing to 1500 ms on trial 8. However, this overall function might represent a conglomerate of different trends for subsets of the pooled data, so further analysis is needed. For a next step, I considered only reaction times on repetitions of exemplars, since only on these trials would the current exemplar be represented in the memory array. These means are plotted in Figure 4.4 as a function of the trial of the repetition, with separate curves for correct and incorrect responses. The increasing, and not far from linear, function (with a slope of 76 ms per trial) for correct reaction times is quite compatible with the hypothesis of a sequential search. The non-monotone function with a much shallower linear trend obtained for incorrect responses is not necessarily incompatible with the hypothesis, for errors may have occurred predominantly on trials when for some reason a search was not initiated or was aborted prematurely.

A long standing but still live issue in memory processing theory is whether search is exhaustive or self terminating (Townsend 1990). That is, with respect to the situation considered here, does the learner compare the currently perceived exemplar with all of those stored in the memory array before generating a response or do the comparisons stop whenever a match

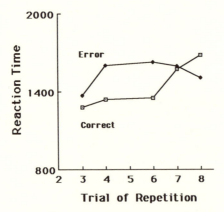

Fig. 4.4 Mean reaction times for correct and incorrect responses on second occurrences of exemplars in Experiment 4.4.

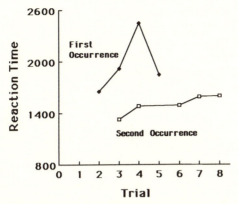

Fig. 4.5 Mean reaction times on first and second occurrences of exemplars in Experiment 4.4.

occurs? The "signature" of a self-terminating search in the short-term recognition literature is a plot of reaction time versus number of items searched in which the slope for reaction times on positive trials is half the slope for reaction times on negative trials.* In recognition research, positive and negative probes are test items that were or were not, respectively, present in the "memory set" previously presented on the trial. In the categorization situation, we can, by analogy, let reaction times on repetitions of exemplars correspond to those to positive probes in recognition and let reaction times to first occurrences of exemplars correspond to negative probes. The result of this analysis is presented in Fig. 4.5 in the form of a plot of reaction times to first occurrences and repetitions as a function of trial number (again averaged over the main experiment and replication). The slopes of linear regression lines fitted to the two functions, 113 ms per comparison for first occurrences and 49 ms per comparison for repetitions, are compatible with the hypothesis of a sequential search, and their ratio is not far from the 2:1 ratio predicted for a self-terminating search.

Another expectation about reaction times in a self-terminating search process is that there should be a greater reduction in reaction time from the first to the second occurrence of an exemplar at short than at long lags. The reduction is expected because on the second occurrence, the memory array includes a representation of the exemplar on which search may terminate with a match. The lag effect is expected because at a longer lag, the decay

---

* The basis for this prediction is the supposition that, in an exhaustive search, the test item (probe) is compared to all of those stored in the memory array, regardless of whether the probe is represented in the array. But in a self-terminating search, a match between probe and memory occurs halfway through the array on the average on trials when the probe is present in the array, and complete searches occur only on trials when the probe is absent.

Table 4.6   Reaction time difference* as a function
of repetition lag

	Main experiment	Replication
Lag		
0–1	519	925
3–5	179	346

* Difference in reaction time between first and second occurrences of repeated exemplars.

process will have acted longer and the stored representation will be at a
lower level of availability. The indicated analysis is summarized in Table 4.6,
and the results appear compatible with a self-terminating search.

Taken together with the analysis of lag functions for correct response
probabilities, these results on reaction times support the assumption that
similarities of to-be-categorized stimuli to the representations stored in
memory are computed by a sequential comparison process. The nature of
the search cannot be specified with confidence. From the present evidence,
it seems reasonable to assume that in the short-term situation, memory
search is self-terminating, but there may be some mixture of exhaustive and
self-terminating processes.

In summary, all of the kinds of evidence considered converge on the
conclusion that, uniquely under the restriction to short-term memory, the
exemplar model is never inferior and in nearly all comparisons is superior to
the similarity-network model. Further, short-term memory processing
appears to be accomplished by a sequential search over a chronologically
ordered array of item representations rather than by the kind of global
computation assumed in the similarity-network model.

4.3 A modular view of exemplar and network models

From the first appearance of an exemplar-similarity model in the work of
Medin and Schaffer (1978), it has seemed intuitively implausible that
comparisons of a currently to-be-categorized stimulus pattern to the stored
items in a large memory array could be accomplished by proceeding
sequentially through the array in a chronological order. In none of the
models developed in this tradition has the mode of processing been spelled
out in detail. However, it seems generally to have been tacitly assumed that
similarity to category is computed by a global process in which comparisons
of the currently perceived stimulus pattern to items in memory are made in
parallel, either on the items stored in the chronological array or on a
reorganized *canonical* array that preserves frequency but not order
information.

To illustrate these alternatives, suppose that an individual learning to troubleshoot a complex type of equipment knows that breakdowns fall into two main categories and studies a series of breakdowns, in each of which he observes an item of diagnostic information and then learns the cause. A record of his experiences might run

$$I_1 \quad I_2 \quad I_3 \quad I_3 \quad I_1 \quad I_2 \quad I_2 \quad I_3 \quad I_1 \quad I_2$$

$$A \quad B \quad A \quad B \quad A \quad B \quad A \quad B \quad B \quad A$$

where the I_k are the items and A and B the categories. A chronological memory array would have the same form, and a sequential search would proceed backward (right to left) from the current item. If over time the order information decays or otherwise becomes unavailable, then, in effect, the record is reorganized into a canonical array retaining only the frequency information:

Item	A	B
I_1	2	1
I_2	2	2
I_3	1	2

If, say, the next trial presented another instance of I_1, then (assuming average similarity s between any two items) its summed similarity to the stored A items would be $2+3s$ and to the B items $1+4s$; and, in the exemplar model, the probability of its being classified as an A by the observer would be 2/3. If the series were to continue, with the same item-category pairs occurring in each ten-trial block but in new random orders, then after, say, 100 trials, the stored representation of the sequence would extend much beyond the bounds of short-term memory, but the canonical array would be unchanged except for the cell frequencies:

Item	A	B
I_1	20	10
I_2	20	20
I_3	10	20

and probability of Category A computed from the exemplar model would again be 2/3. The result of computing similarity of a test stimulus to the canonical array is, of course, identical to the result of comparing it simultaneously to all of the items in a chronological array; I will refer to these formally indistinguishable modes of computation as *global processing*.

The generation of categorization probabilities on the basis of the canonical array via the computational processes of the exemplar model would account nicely for the frequently observed tendency for asymptotic categorization probabilities to reflect information about frequencies of occurrence of exemplars in categories (Experiment 4.1; Gluck and Bower 1988*b*; Shanks 1990). However, we have noted that, under some conditions, asymptotic categorization probabilities deviate from the true relative frequencies (Experiment 3.1; Estes, Campbell, Hatsopoulis, and Hurwitz 1989) in ways that are predictable from network models. Thus, a key question is whether the most promising combined model might have performance within the short-term memory range described by the exemplar model, operating on a chronologically ordered memory array via sequential search, but with a network representation of the kind assumed in the similarity-network model taking over when performance depends mainly on long-term memory. Possibly the canonical memory array is simply a fiction and the shift in the basis for categorization when the limits of short-term memory are exceeded is from the chronological array to one in which the cell entries are network weights rather than frequencies, in the example:

Item	A	B
I_1	w_{1A}	w_{1B}
I_2	w_{2A}	w_{2B}
I_3	w_{3A}	w_{3B}

where w_{ij} is the weight on the network path from item node i to category node j. A very tentative view of the categorization process is that, at the outset of a task, exemplar-storage and network formation begin more or less simultaneously and run in parallel, with the basis for categorization judgments lying initially in the exemplar array but shifting to the network over time. After additional evidence bearing on the dual-process conception has been discussed in the next chapter, it will be in order to try to specify how the two constituent models might mesh together.

Appendix 4.1 Method of Experiment 4.1

The features (symptoms) and categories (disease labels) for the four problems were

Problem	*Feature 1*	*Feature 2*	*Category*
1	circ.	nausea	A or B
2	temp.	cramps	C or D
3	pain	nosebleed	E or F
4	skin	cough	G or H

On a learning trial, the display comprised a symptom list plus a query. For Problem 1, for example, the display might be

circ.　　+　A or B?

nausea　−

or

circ.　　+　A or B?

nausea　+

a plus sign indicating that a symptom was present in the given chart and a minus sign that it was absent.

A test display for the same problem took the form

circ.　　***

nausea　+

What is the probability of disease A?

The entry *** signified that no information was available about presence or absence of the given symptom. The subject responded to the query by typing a number in the range 0–100.

Subjects were 44 Harvard undergraduates, paid for their service. Of these, 20 were assigned to the random and 24 to the blocked condition. Within conditions, half of the subjects were assigned to each of two replications that differed only in the order of problems on the test trials and the reference category (i.e., the category designated in the test display) for the test trials on each problem. All subjects in each condition received the same sequence of exemplars on learning trials, and subjects in both conditions received the same sequence of exemplars within problems. The pattern and feature validities for the four problems are shown in Table 4.A1, "validity" being defined as the conditional probability of the first category of a problem in the presence of a given pattern or feature.

The basis for predicting the relative difficulties of the problems from the exemplar model is the set of expected memory arrays shown in Table 4.A2. For each problem, the cell entries under Probabilities are the probabilities of occurrence of the exemplar patterns in each category. For example, in Problem 1, exemplar 11 occurred with probability 0.19 in both categories; exemplar 10 occurred with probability 0.56 in Category A and 0.06 in Category B; and so on. From these probabilities together with the category base rates, we can compute the average number of representations of each exemplar that would be stored in each cell of the memory array by the end of the 60 training trials. Thus, for the storage of exemplar 11 in Category A in Problem 1, we multiply the category probability, 0.75, by the probability

Table 4.A1   Pattern and feature validities in Experiment 4.1 (in terms of conditional probability of first category)

	Problem			
Pattern	1	2	3	4
f1 f2				
1 1	0.75	0.50	1	1
1 0	0.96	0.50	0	0.50
0 1	0.04	0.10	0	0
0 0	0.75	0.10	1	0.50
Feature				
f1	0.90	0.50	0.50	0.67
f2	0.50	0.25	0.50	0.50

of exemplar 11 in the category, 0.1875 (rounded to 0.19 in the table), then multiply the product by the number of trials, 60, obtaining

$$0.75 \times 0.1875 \times 60 = 0.1406 \times 60 = 8.44 \qquad (4.A1)$$

which appears as the entry for exemplar 11 under Category A in Table 4.A2.

From the expected memory arrays so obtained, we can compute categorization probabilities in the standard fashion. Continuing with Problem 1, the similarities of exemplar 11 to each of the four exemplars listed in the left-hand column are 1, s, s, and s^2; therefore the average similarities of pattern 11 to the representations stored in Categories A and B are

$$Sim_{11,A} = 8.44 + 25.31s + 2.81s + 8.44s^2, \qquad (4.A2)$$

and

$$Sim_{11,B} = 2.81 + 0.94s + 8.44s + 2.81s^2. \qquad (4.A3)$$

On the basis of previous research using the same stimuli (Estes, Campbell, Hatsopoulis, and Hurwitz 1989), we would expect the value of s to be near 0 for these problems. Substituting $s=0$, we obtain for the probability of a Category A response to exemplar 11

$$P_{11}(A) = 8.44/(8.44+2.81) = 0.75. \qquad (4.A4)$$

Computing the analogous values for the other exemplars and averaging the results (weighted by exemplar frequencies) yields the predicted probability correct, 0.85, shown as Probability Correct (ex.) for Problem 1 in Table

Table 4.A2 Category and feature probabilities and expected memory arrays for Experiment 4.1

	Problem 1				Problem 2			
	Probabilities		Expected array		Probabilities		Expected array	
	A	B	A	B	A	B	A	B
Category probability	0.75	0.25			0.25	0.75		
f1 f2								
1 1	0.19	0.19	8.44	2.80	0.38	0.12	5.62	5.62
1 0	0.56	0.06	25.31	0.94	0.38	0.12	5.62	5.62
0 1	0.06	0.56	2.81	8.44	0.12	0.38	1.88	16.88
0 0	0.19	0.19	8.44	2.81	0.12	0.38	1.88	16.88
			$s = 0.5$	$s = 0$			$s = 0.5$	$s = 0$
Probability correct (exemplar) =			0.76	0.85	0.76	0.82		
Probability correct (network) =			0.74	0.79	0.74	0.72		

	Problem 3				Problem 4			
	Probabilities		Expected array		Probabilities		Expected array	
	A	B	A	B	A	B	A	B
Category probability	0.50	0.50			0.50	0.50		
f1 f2								
1 1	0.50	0	15	0	0.33	0	10	0
1 0	0	0.50	0	15	0.33	0.33	10	10
0 1	0	0.50	0	15	0	0.33	0	10
0 0	0.50	0	15	0	0.33	0.33	10	10
			$s = 0.5$	$s = 0$			$s = 0.5$	$s = 0$
Probability correct (exemplar) =			0.56	1.00	0.56	0.66		
Probability correct (network) =			0.55	0.88	0.55	0.62		

4.A2. Substituting $s=0.5$ in the Sim_{11} expressions yields the lower value, 0.76, for probability correct, also shown in Table 4.A2. The corresponding predictions for the other problems are computed similarly.

Predictions from the similarity-network model are obtained in exactly the same way except that the similarity computations operate on the weights, w_{ij}, on the paths between pattern and category nodes. For illustrative purposes, I have computed these weights for each of the problems (using the learning and output functions given in Chapter 3 with parameter values, $\beta=0.1$ and $c=2$, characteristic of those commonly found appropriate in previous research). Substituting the obtained weights for the average frequencies in the Experimental array columns of Table 4.A2 and carrying out the same similarity computations as for the exemplar model yields the predictions for Probability Correct shown in the bottom row of the table. The differences in absolute level between the predicted values for the two models are of no significance since the level for the similarity-network model could be adjusted by changing the value of the scaling parameter, c.

Appendix 4.2   Learning about invalid cues in concurrent categorizations: Experiment 4.2

Method

An overview of the design is given in Table 4.A3. A subject concurrently learned two categorizations ("problems") with trials on the two intermixed as in the random condition of Experiment 4.1. The task was to classify descriptions of houses, presented as feature lists, according to the type of family that would be a potential buyer from the standpoint of a real-estate agent. The features used for the two problems were distinct but semantically related. The first feature listed for each exemplar was completely valid; the second and third were invalid, differing in that the value of the second attribute varied from trial to trial whereas the value of the third was constant. A series of 32 learning trials, given under the same procedures as those of Experiment 4.1 with all categories and exemplars occurring equally

Table 4.A3   Illustrative problem structures in Experiment 4.2, invalid feature learning

Problem 1		Problem 2	
House	Category	House	Category
Stone, large, garage	A	Urban, victorian, patio	C
Stone, small, garage	A	Urban, modern, patio	C
Brick, large, garage	B	Rural, victorian, patio	D
Brick, small, garage	B	Rural, modern, patio	D

Tests		
Feature type	Example	
Valid	Stone	A or C ?
Varying invalid	Large	B or D ?
Constant invalid	Garage	A or C ?

Table 4.A4 Design of Experiment 4.2 learning series

Problem 1			Problem 2		
Exemplar	Category		Exemplar	Category	
	A	B		C	D
Problem set 1					
a1b1c1	4	0	d1e1f1	4	0
a2b1c1	0	4	d2e1f1	0	4
a1b2c1	4	0	d1e2f1	4	0
a2b2c1	0	4	d2e2f1	0	4
Problem set 2					
a1b1c1	4	0	d1e1f1	4	0
a2b1c1	0	4	d2e1f1	0	4
a1b2c2	4	0	d1e2f2	4	0
a2b2c2	0	4	d2e2f2	0	4

often, was followed by test trials of the types shown at the bottom of the table. Details of the design of the learning series are summarized in Table 4A.2.

Two different task orientations were used, each with a different set of stimuli and categories. In one, the subject was to take on the role of a real-estate agent showing houses to families and assigned the task of classifying descriptions of houses according to the type of family (category) that would be a prospective buyer. Descriptions of houses were presented in the form of triads of features comprising one value each of a, b, and c or one value each of d, e, and f in the following list:

a stone-brick   d urban-rural
b large-small   e Victorian-modern
c garage-carport   f patio-deck

In the other task, the subject was to imagine that she or he was planning some fishing trips and needed to learn what water and weather conditions are appropriate for different types of bait (categories). Descriptions were formed as above from the following list:

a day–night   d rapid–calm
b fresh–salt   e clear–weeds
c April–October   f warm–cool

Following the learning series on a problem set, test trials were given on which the subject saw a display of the form:

> garage
> A or C?
> 1–100

and was to estimate, by typing a number in the range 1–100, the probability that the right-hand category would be correct for an exemplar (house in this example) having the displayed feature. The test might present a valid feature, like a1 in Table 4.A4, a constant invalid feature, like c1 in Problem set1, or a varying invalid feature, like c1 in Problem set 2.* In each case, the test paired one of the categories that occurred during learning on the problem to which the feature belonged with one of the categories that occurred during learning on the other problem of the problem set. The display shown above represents a test trial for the constant, invalid feature of problem 1 in Problem set 1.

Subjects were 24 Harvard undergraduates, paid for their service; 12 were assigned to each of two replications involving different relative positions of features a, b, and c, or d, e, and f on the display screen; assignments of the actual features (e.g., stone or large) to valid and invalid roles; orders of learning and test trials; and definition of the reference category (C in the example above) for test trials. Data reported are pooled over the replications.

Results

Our primary interest is in the results of the tests on invalid features, summarized in Table 4.A5 Consider first the feature *large*, which occurred on half of the Problem 1 learning trials, equally often when Categories A and B were correct (hence the label "varying invalid"). If presented with this feature and the query "A or B?", we should expect a subject to choose responses A and B each about 50% of the time, but what should be predicted about a test on which the feature occurred with the query "A or C?"? Even though *large* is invalid with respect to A vs. B, might the learners exhibit knowledge that it belongs to Problem 1 rather than Problem 2 by choosing A over C? The exemplar model, with the processing assumptions described above, implies that A should be the predominant choice, as does the similarity-network model with similar processing assumptions, and the common prediction is supported by the observed result shown in the row for *large* in Table 4.A5. A comparable strong tendency to choose C over A

---

* There were also tests on some feature pairs, like a1c1, which will not be discussed in this report.

Table 4.A5 Tests on invalid features in Experiment 4.2

Feature	Alternatives	Percent choice of A		
		Data	Exemplar	Network
Constant invalid				
Garage	A or C	61	80	62
Patio	A or C	37	22	38
Varying invalid				
Large	A or C	72	80	62
Victorian	A or C	34	12	38

Note: Alternative categories for each feature during learning were:

Feature	Alternatives
Garage	A or B
Patio	C or D
Large	A or B
Victorian	C or D

in the test on *Victorian*, which belongs to Problem 2, is predicted and observed (bottom row of Table 4.A5). Much the same reasoning applies to the "constant invalid" features *garage* and *patio*, although, for reasons not taken into account by either model, we might expect them to receive less attention than the varying features during the learning trials. The test results for these show preferences for the appropriate alternative only slightly less marked than those observed for the varying invalid features.

A similar interpretation holds for the tests on valid features, results of which are given in Table 4.A6. When a test pairs the correct category for a

Table 4.A6 Tests on valid features in Experiment 4.2

Feature	Alternatives	% choice of A or B		
		Data	Exemplar	Network
Stone	A or C	82	88	74
Urban	A or C	22	22	26
Stone	B or D	44	52	42
Urban	B or D	49	48	58

Note: Feature-category assignments during learning were:

Feature	Alternatives	Correct category
Stone	A or B	A
Urban	C or D	C

valid feature with a category from the other problem (e.g., stone A or C?), the preference for the appropriate category should be accentuated over the comparable invalid case because the memory array will contain a larger number of representations of the type stone A. In contrast when a valid feature test pairs its incorrect category with a category from the other problem (stone B or D?), the preference should be eliminated because the memory array will contain no representations of the type stone B. Both of these expectations are confirmed in the data, in qualitative agreement with both of the models.

Regarding the relative merits of the two models, the similarity-network yields considerably more accurate predictions for the invalid feature tests (Table 4.A4) but is not quite as accurate as the exemplar model for the valid feature tests (Table 4.A5). What can be said with assurance is that the family of models within which the exemplar model and similarity-network are close relatives receives new support from this study.

Appendix 4.3 Method of Experiment 4.4: categorization in short-term memory

The main experiment and replication were each conducted with 24 subjects, Harvard undergraduates who were paid for their service, and differed only with respect to the order of conditions, as described in the text. For each subject, the experiment consisted of 12 categorization tasks, each having eight categorization learning trials, run under the standard procedure (as in Experiments 4.1 and 4.2), followed by 12 test trials. On the first eight test trials, the subject was asked to estimate the probability of a particular feature in a given category; on the last four test trials, the subject was asked to estimate the probability that a category (Category A) was correct given that a particular feature was present.

There were six basic tasks, each instantiated once under the high and once under the zero validity conditions with distinct sets of features and pairs of category labels. The category exemplars in the six tasks were descriptions formed from pairs of features of the following types:

1. CVCs (consonant–vowel–consonant syllables)
2. Disease symptoms
3. Attributes of buildings
4. Characteristics of people
5. CVCs-2
6. Disease symptoms-2.

Each set of features was coupled with a unique pair of letters or digits that served as the category label with semantic interpretations such as word-types for the CVCs, and diseases for the symptoms). The features used are listed in Table 4.A7.

Table 4.A7 Feature sets used in Experiment 4.4

	CVC		CVC-2	
1	fop	gac	hiz	sak
2	qav	kel	wos	pom
3	rex	tij	naf	jig
4	mub	duy	veh	zun
	Diseases		Diseases-2	
1	Anxious	Headache	Cramps	Depressed
2	Dizzy	Fever	Rash	Irritable
3	Drowsy	Insomnia	Nausea	Disoriented
4	Moody	Nosebleed	Hives	Distracted
	Buildings		People	
1	Garage	Brick	Industrious	Charismatic
2	Patio	Small	Practical	Generous
3	Mailbox	Victorian	Intelligent	Determined
4	Driveway	Fireplace	Warm	Competent

Table 4.A8 Pattern and feature validities in Experiment 4.4

High validity			Zero validity		
Pattern	Category		Pattern	Category	
	A	B		A	B
12	2	0	34	1	1
24	0	2	14	1	1
23	2	0	12	1	1
14	0	2	13	1	1
Feature	Category		Feature	Category	
	A	B		A	B
1	2	2	1	3	3
2	4	2	2	1	1
3	2	0	3	2	2
4	0	4	4	2	2

117

The frequencies of occurrence of exemplars in categories in the high and zero validity conditions are given in the upper portion of Table 4.A8 in a standard format—the exemplars being represented by pairs of feature numbers, the categories by the labels A and B; the cell entries are the frequencies of occurrence in an eight-trial learning series. The lower portion of Table 4.A8 shows the feature validities in the same format. It will be apparent that in the zero validity condition there was nothing to be learned except the relative frequencies of occurrence of the features within categories. However, the task was presented to the subjects as a categorization problem in the zero just as in the high validity condition; thus any learning that occurred with respect to feature frequencies would be of the kind termed "implicit" in the current and "incidental" in the earlier cognitive literature.

5. On the storage and retrieval of categorical information

Our main concern in the preceding chapters has been to develop a simple but powerful account of category learning and transfer under the most commonly used experimental conditions. Now we shall take a closer look at necessary and sufficient aspects of the usual training methods and raise new questions about the retrieval of information from once acquired category structures. In the development of models for category learning to date, it has almost universally been tacitly assumed that differences among training procedures need not be addressed explicitly—all that matters is that necessary information is communicated somehow to learners. But among current models, some are and some are not based on an assumption that learning is driven by an error-correcting process that depends on informative feedback following learners' categorization responses. Thus, it is time to take a closer look at correspondences between assumptions of the models and learning procedures. Again, nearly all categorization research has been concerned largely with learners' abilities to classify exemplars of categories, as in making diagnoses. However, the realization is emerging that other aspects of categorization may be of at least as much practical importance (Corter and Gluck 1992; Heit 1992), and examining some of these aspects will be the second main task of this chapter.

5.1 Standard versus observational training procedures

The vast majority of studies of category learning have been conducted with what may well be termed a standard training procedure. On each training trial, the learner views a stimulus pattern and either assigns it to a category or rates the likelihood of its belonging to alternative categories, then is informed of the correct category for the trial. This procedure maps in a very intuitive way onto either the exemplar or the network model. In terms of the former, the information supplied on a trial suffices to direct the storage in memory of a representation of the stimulus pattern together with its category label. In terms of the latter, the learner's disposition to make a given categorization response corresponds to a weight on the associative path from the stimulus to the category representation in the memory network; the effect of the feedback on a trial is to cause the associative weight to change in a direction that will reduce error on subsequent trials.

In an alternative training procedure, used in a number of earlier studies of paired-associate and probability learning (Izawa 1967; Reber and Millward 1968; Estes 1976), the learner observes presentations of stimuli together with information about correct responses on learning trials, but makes no responses to the stimuli. Applied to category learning, the observational procedure constitutes simply a presentation of a stimulus pattern together with a category label on each trial. The observational and standard procedures appear equally appropriate to the assumptions of the exemplar model. The same does not seem to be true for the network model, however, because the observation trial includes no opportunity to compare a response with a feedback event corresponding to the *teaching signal* of the model. A direct comparison of category learning under the two procedures seems clearly desirable, and is afforded by two experiments conducted in my laboratory.*

5.1.1 Method for comparison of training procedures

In both of the experiments, henceforth identified as Experiments 5.1 and 5.2, the subjects' primary task was to learn to assign stimulus patterns to categories, and separate groups were trained under standard and observational procedures. For half of the subjects in each group, the patterns were bar charts, representing symptoms of hypothetical patients and the categories were diseases. For the other half, the patterns were schematic faces and the categories were personality types. The eight training patterns (category exemplars) were formed from all combinations of three binary features (high or low bars in the charts, large or small distances between parts of the faces). In Experiment 5.1, the assignments of the patterns to two categories, A and B, were the same as those of Problem type V of the study of Shepard, Hovland, and Jenkins (1961), shown in Table 2.13 of Chapter 2. The design produced correlations among features within categories, as will be apparent in Table 5.1, which presents the frequencies of occurrence of exemplar patterns in categories during each block of learning trials.† In Experiment 5.2, the stimuli were the same, but individual features were assigned different probabilities in the two categories (value 1 of features 1, 2, and 3, respectively, having probabilities of 0.67, 0.17, and 0.67 in Category A and 0.33, 0.83, and 0.33 in Category B), and examplar patterns were generated by independent sampling from the feature set. I will refer to the distinction between the experiments as one of *correlated* versus *independent* features. The distinction is crucial with respect to predictions of the models pertaining to identification of prototypes.

---

* W. Todd Maddox assisted in all aspects of these experiments.

† On Category A trials in the full condition, for example, a value of 1 for the first feature of an exemplar is accompanied by a value of 1 for the second feature with probability 2/3, whereas if the features were independent, this probability would be 1/2.

Table 5.1 Design of Experiment 5.1 in terms of frequencies of exemplars in categories A and B during learning for each problem type

Exemplar pattern	Problem type			
	Full		Partial	
	A	B	A	B
111	2	0	0	0
112	2	0	2	0
121	2	0	2	0
222	2	0	2	0
122	0	2	0	2
212	0	2	0	2
221	0	2	0	2
211	0	2	0	2

On each training trial in the standard procedure, the subject saw a stimulus pattern, made a categorization response, and was informed of the correct category for the trial. Following each block of training trials,* there was a block of categorization test trials that differed from training trials only in that the informative feedback was omitted. On each training trial in the observational procedure, the subject saw a category label (making no overt response to it), then a stimulus pattern that was an exemplar of the category.† After each block of training trials, these subjects had a block of test trials on which they categorized the patterns presented, without feedback, exactly as done by subjects in the standard condition.

In Experiment 5.1 only, the procedural groups were divided into subgroups assigned to "full" or "partial" conditions. As may be seen in Table 5.1, in the partial condition one of the eight exemplar patterns never occurred on training trials; however, it was presented on test trials (so we could monitor changes in performance due to generalization from the other patterns). Further details of design and procedure for both experiments are given in Appendices 5.1 and 5.2.

---

* In Experiment 5.1, each of the four training blocks included two instances of each exemplar pattern, a total of 16 trials. In Experiment 5.2, training was extended to six blocks of 27 trials because, with the probabilistically defined categories, learning was expected to be more difficult.

† This inverse order of presenting the category label and the exemplar was used in order to prevent subjects from defeating the intended comparison by making implicit categorization responses to the patterns shown on the training trials before seeing the correct category label.

5.1.2 Results for comparisons of training procedures

To enable controlled comparisons of the effects of the different types of training, learning was measured for both procedural conditions in terms of the responses on the test blocks only. Learning proved to be somewhat more rapid with the observational than with the standard procedure: for example, in the first test block, percentages of correct responses for the observational and standard groups, respectively, were 76 and 69 for Experiment 5.1 (full condition) and 77 and 70 for Experiment 5.2. The superiority of the observational procedure may seem surprising to some, but it is in agreement with similar comparisons previously reported for both probability learning and paired-associate learning (Estes 1976; Izawa 1985). The term "superiority" should be qualified, however, for in Experiment 5.2, with the much longer training series, performance of the observational group actually declined from 77% in block 1 to 73% in blocks 5–6 while the standard group was increasing from 70% to 79%.

These differences in performance between early and late training blocks for standard versus observational procedures may be related to an interesting pattern of interactions that emerges when the exemplar and similarity-network models are applied to the learning data. The fits of the models are summarized in Table 5.2 in terms of root mean square deviations between predicted and observed categorization percentages. In the upper panel of the table, both experiments show better fits of the exemplar model for the initial block but better fits of the network model for the final blocks. In the lower panel of the table, both experiments show better fits of the exemplar model in the observational groups but better fits of the network model in the

Table 5.2 Interactions of model fits* with training block and training procedure in Experiments 5.1 and 5.2

Model	Experiment 5.1 Block		Experiment 5.2 Block	
	1	4	1	5–6
Exemplar	5.83	8.84	6.33	7.45
Network	6.83	7.85	9.61	6.33
	Procedure		Procedure	
	Standard	Observational	Standard	Observational
Exemplar	7.20	7.47	7.66	6.12
Network	6.83	7.85	6.44	9.50

* Entries are root mean square disparities between observed and predicted values.

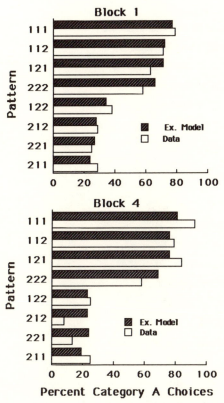

Fig. 5.1 Performance in first and last training blocks of Experiment 5.1 (standard procedure, full condition) together with predictions from the exemplar model (Ex. Model).

standard groups. To give an idea of the adequacy of prediction of the data signified by the goodness-of-fit measures, predictions by the exemplar model are compared with data values for early and late blocks in Figs. 5.1 and 5.2 for Experiments 5.1 and 5.2, respectively.

The better account of learning under the standard procedure by the network model, seems intuitively quite reasonable in view of the fact that the procedure of responding with feedback on each trial corresponds closely to the process of error correction assumed in the model. Overall, the results of the model comparisons fit very well the suggestion that emerged from quite different analyses discussed in Chapter 4 to the effect that, in the early stages of category learning, where operations on short-term memory may be implicated to a significant degree, processing is better represented by the exemplar model, but in the later stages, where dependence on long-term

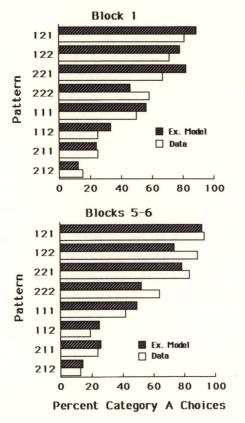

Fig. 5.2 Performance in first and last training blocks of Experiment 5.2 (Standard procedure) together with predictions from the exemplar model (Ex. Model).

memory is stronger, processing is better represented by the network model.

5.2 Learning on the basis of average or configural prototypes[*]

Although numerous comparisons of prototype and exemplar models have been published (reviewed by Nosofsky 1992*a*), Experiments 5.1 and 5.2 are particularly apt for this purpose. The principal difference between these experiments was that the sets of category exemplars comprised features that were correlated within categories in Experiment 5.1 but independent (uncorrelated within categories) in Experiment 5.2. The relevance of this difference arises from theoretical analyses showing that, in the independent

---

[*] Both types of prototypes were defined in Chapter 2, pp. 51–55.

case, predictions about categorization performance derived from average prototype versus exemplar models are virtually indistinguishable, and in some important cases identical, although in the case of correlated features they may differ widely (Estes 1986a).

We should note before continuing that all of the prototype models that have appeared in the literature are performance models, not learning models. The common assumption of prototype models is that, given knowledge of the category prototypes, learners arrive at categorization judgments by comparing the similarity of a test pattern to the average or configural prototypes of the alternative categories (or distances between the test pattern and the prototypes in a similarity space). However, no models have been reported that provide detailed accounts of how mental representations of prototypes might evolve trial-by-trial during the course of learning. It seems that there would be motivation to try to develop such models only if the prediction of asymptotic learning data and of the results of transfer tests following learning proved to be at least comparable to those of the exemplar and network models, so I turn next to that type of comparison.

For estimates of asymptotic categorization performance, I have taken the percentages of Category A responses to each exemplar pattern on the tests given at the end of the final block of training trials, in each case averaged over standard and observational procedures.* These data are presented in Table 5.3, along with predictions from average and configural prototypes and from the exemplar model. Estimates of the similarity parameter, s, required for all of the predictions, were obtained by fitting the exemplar model in the usual way to the learning data and using these estimates to compute predictions for for each model.†

The category structure of Experiment 5.1 is well suited to bring out a special problem for prototype models, although it was not designed especially for the purpose (having been taken from the study of Shepard, Hovland, and Jenkins (1961)). The set of exemplar patterns assigned to each category during training includes two that are maximally dissimilar, 111 and 222 in Category A and 211 and 122 in Category B. As can be seen in the upper panel of Table 5.3, subjects performed quite well (averaging over 85% correct) on patterns 111 and 211, which were the configural prototypes of

---

* The pattern of comparisons was very similar for the two procedures. In the case of Experiment 5.1, only data for the full condition were used because there was no unique configural prototype for Category A in the partial condition.

† As in previous related studies (Estes 1986a; Nosofsky 1992a), predctions for each type of prototype were obtained by computing the similarity of a test pattern to the prototypes of Categories A and B and taking the ratio of the similarity to A to the sum of similarities to A and B as the estimate of probability of a Category A response. The computations differed from those for the exemplar model only in the replacement of similarities to stored category exemplars with similarities to prototypes. The observed pattern of deviations of prototype predictions from the data is independent of the value of the similarity parameter.

Table 5.3   Predictions of final learning performance from exemplar model and from prototypes in terms of percentage of Category A responses to each pattern

Pattern	Category	Data	Average Prototype	Configural prototype	Exemplar model
Experiment 5.1: Correlated features					
111*	A	92	76	91	85
112	A	90	76	91	80
121	A	88	76	91	80
222	A	68	24	9	74
122	B	25	76	91	26
212	B	6	24	9	20
221	B	17	24	9	20
211*	B	21	24	9	26
Experiment 5.2: Independent features					
121*	A	94	96	100	90
122	A	81	80	90	74
221	A	82	80	90	76
222	A	52	49	10	51
111	B	48	51	90	48
112	B	20	20	10	24
211	B	26	20	10	26
212*	B	8	4	0	13

* Configural prototype.

the categories, and appreciably less well (averaging 72% correct), though still much above chance, on 222 and 122, the result predicted by the exemplar model. In contrast, the prediction from either average or configural prototypes is much lower than chance performance on patterns 222 and 122, widely disparate from the data. In the lower panel of Table 5.3, we see that the data obtained with the independent feature structure of Experiment 5.2 are well predicted from average prototypes (as expected, since, asymptotically, the average prototype mimics the exemplar model in this case), but responding on the basis of the configural prototypes would again produce performance deviating widely from the data on some patterns.

Beyond the question of how well performance can be predicted from prototype conceptions, it is interesting to inquire how the efficiency of categorization on the basis of prototypes compares to the efficiency developed by human learners through experience with category exemplars. For the conditions of Experiments 5.1 and 5.2, it can readily be calculated from the information in Table 5.3 that in the case of correlated features, categorization on the basis of either average or configural prototypes (averaging 63% and 70% correct, respectively) would be far short of the level of 84% attained by the subjects. In the case of independent features, the average prototype matches the 76% attained by the human subjects, but the configural prototype is somewhat inferior at 72%.

Curiously, in spite of the long-standing popularity of prototype concepts, there has been very little experimental research on categorization performance by learners who are tested after having been given information about prototypes but no actual experience with category exemplars. Tests of this type were imbedded in experiments reported by Medin, Altom, and Murphy (1984), with results qualitatively in line with expectations from the analysis above. The category structures studied were closer to that of Experiment 5.2 than that of Experiment 5.1 (all features having high validity as predictors of categories), and the effect of describing the prototypes of the categories to one group of subjects prior to a learning series was a modest facilitation of performance during learning in comparison to that of a group not given the prior information.

In the framework of the exemplar model, the consequence of informing a learner about the prototype of a category is the storage of a representation of the prototypic pattern (possibly more than one, if the prototype is rehearsed) in the same memory array that will contain representations of exemplars presented during learning. To illustrate the derivation of predictions from the exemplar model, I will consider a simplified counterpart of the design used by Medin, Altom, and Murphy (1984), taking the form

Category A	*Category B*
121	221
211	212
112	122

where the entries in the column under a category label are the values of the exemplars of the category on three binary features. Suppose that learners were given one trial on each pattern under standard conditions and then a test on any one pattern, say 121. We could predict the result from the exemplar model by computing the similarities to the patterns stored in Categories A and B in the usual way, and for $s=0.5$, for example, we would obtain a probability correct of 0.57. If, instead, the learners were informed of the configural prototypes of the categories, 111 for Category A and 222 for Category B, and then tested immediately, the memory array would contain only 111 in Category A and 222 in Category B. Then the similarity of pattern 121 to Category A would be s and to Category B, s^2, and the predicted probability of assigning the pattern to Category A would be

$$P(A) = s/(s+s^2) = 1/(1+s). \qquad (5.1)$$

With s equal to 0.5, the probability of a correct response would be 0.67. But suppose that the learners were informed of the average, rather than the configural prototypes. These are 1.33, 1.33, 1.33 for Category A and 1.67, 1.67, 1.67 for Category B. With only these representations stored in the memory array, the probability of a correct response on the test, with s again equal to 0.5, would be 0.56. Thus, in this example, information about configural prototypes produces better performance and information about average prototypes produces poorer performance than a learning sequence on the category exemplars.

Precise predictions for any design of course require actual similarity computations. The model can, however, provide the basis for qualitative expectations that should hold quite generally. In particular, direct information about configural prototypes of categories will always be facilitatory and, in many circumstances, will yield better performance than learning experience with a set of category exemplars that does not include the configural prototype. Direct information about average or other central-tendency prototypes will be beneficial under some circumstances, useless in some, and a hindrance under others, and analysis in terms of the model is needed to distinguish these cases.

5.3 Inducing prototypes

In view of the fact that either a central-tendency or a configural prototype encapsulates summary information about a category in a form that can be readily communicated, and that can under some circumstances facilitate categorization performance, it is of interest to know whether learners can induce prototypes from experience with category exemplars. It can, in fact, be predicted from the exemplar model that a by-product of category learning should be some capability for identifying prototypes, the extent depending on specific conditions.

The process of "learning prototypes" has been studied by Busemeyer and Myung (1988), but not with materials suitable for analysis in terms of the models under consideration here. However, Experiments 5.1 and 5.2 were designed with a view to providing appropriate data. In both experiments, the instructions given to the subjects prior to category learning specified that, in addition to assigning exemplars to categories, they were to try to induce the prototype of each category in preparation for a later test. The concept of a prototype was explained as a base pattern from which exemplars of a category could be generated by means of small alterations of values on individual attributes or features. Following the category learning series in both experiments, subjects were tested by presentation of each of the patterns from the learning task (which necessarily included the configural prototypes) intermixed with patterns representing the average prototype of each category and (to avoid making the prototypes conspicuous because of

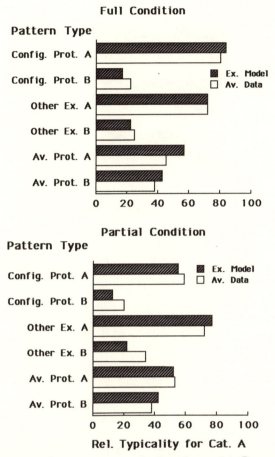

Fig. 5.3 Results of prototype tests in Experiment 5.1. Data are average relative typicalities (defined in the text) for Category A, and theoretical values are probabilities of Category A computed from the exemplar model. See text for definitions of pattern types.

their novelty) a few other new patterns. Subjects were asked to rate each of these stimuli on a scale of 0 to 100 with respect to its goodness as a prototype of an indicated category (each pattern being tested once for Category A and once for Category B).

The rating scores, averaged over the standard and observational training conditions, which did not differ greatly, are the basis for the portrayal of prototype judgments to various kinds of test patterns in Figs. 5.3 and 5.4. To put these mean ratings on the same scale as the model predictions,* each

---

* This transformation was needed because the subjects' ratings of a given pattern as a Category A and as a Category B prototype did not necessarily sum to 100.

Type of Pattern

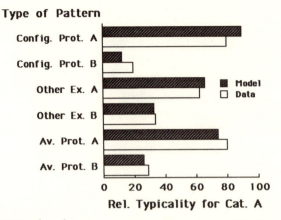

Rel. Typicality for Cat. A

Fig. 5.4 Results of prototype tests in Experiment 5.2. Data are average relative typicalities for Category A, and theoretical values are probabilities of Category A computed from the exemplar model. The labels "Other Ex. A" and "Other Ex. B" denote patterns, other than the configural prototypes, that occurred more often in Category A or in Category B, respectively, during training.

mean score was converted to a relative typicality for Category A, defined as the rating of the given pattern for Category A divided by the sum of its ratings for Categories A and B; the corresponding theoretical measures are probabilities of Category A at the end of training, computed from models in the usual way. (For convenience, both the empirical and the theoretical measures are converted to percentages.)

With the correlated-feature structure of Experiment 5.1, the configural prototypes are expected to be highly rated. This prediction is easily derivable from the exemplar model on the premise that these ratings, like categorization probabilities, result from similarity comparisons between perceived patterns and stored representations of previously experienced patterns; and it is clearly borne out in Fig. 5.3. For the full condition (upper panel), the configural prototypes of Categories A and B received the highest and lowest relative typicality scores for Category A, followed by the other exemplars of each category, and finally the average prototypes, which yielded very little discrimination between the categories. In the partial condition, where the configural prototype of Category A had never occurred on training trials, this pattern was nonetheless rated higher than the average prototype, though not as high as the other exemplars of Category A that had occurred during training and were therefore represented in the Category A and B memory arrays. As in the full condition, the configural prototype of Category B had the lowest relative typicality rating for Category A and the average prototypes yielded little discrimination between the categories.

Results for Experiment 5.2 are exhibited similarly (except that there was no partial condition) in Fig. 5.4. Again, the configural prototypes of the two categories are the best rated; but with the independent feature structure, the average prototypes also differentiate the categories quite well. Perhaps the most striking aspect of these analyses is the degree to which the exemplar model was able to predict the entire pattern of prototype ratings.

Loosely speaking, our subjects prove quite able to learn simultaneously to assign exemplars to categories and to induce prototypes. More rigorously speaking, the experiences entailed in either standard or observational categorization training build up memory arrays on which appropriate computations provide the basis for either categorization judgments or identification of prototypes. However, these two kinds of responses only begin to tap the variety of information that can be retrieved from the memory array in response to appropriate interrogation. We turn now to another type that is of both theoretical and practical significance.

5.4 Predicting features from categories

In this section, we reverse the emphasis of the preceding chapters by shifting attention from the learning of category assignments to the prediction of feature frequencies within categories. One of the main values of learning a categorization is that, once it has been accomplished, discovering to which category an object or event belongs immediately yields information about properties of the object or event that might not be directly perceptible (Corter and Gluck 1992; Heit 1992; Estes, in press). This function of categorization may be important even at a relatively primitive level. Animals or young children, for example, might use visual properties, among others, when learning to categorize some varieties of plants into those that do or do not have bitter tastes and then be able to respond adaptively to new instances when only visual features are available. Category-to-feature inference must be ubiquitous in human adults, who have learned many categorizations and who thus can be given information verbally about the category memberships of objects or events whose non-perceptual properties are not immediately available. Suppose, for example, that I call an auto rental agency and am told that it has a "compact" car available. This category label gives me quite a bit of useful information—the probable cost of the rental, the approximate size of the car, what gasoline mileage can be expected, and so on. Similarly, if I am going to a dinner meeting and am told that a "right-wing senator" will speak, I know what to expect regarding the speaker's postion on the National Rifle Association, big spending in Washington, and logging the National Forests.

In the experiments on category learning discussed in preceding sections (as in nearly all published studies), the behavioral indicator of learning is categorization performance, that is, the assignment of exemplars to categories. This orientation is reflected in all of the models that have been developed. We should expect, however, that in these experiments, just as in ordinary life, appropriate interrogation of the learners might show that they are capable of reversing the usual task and producing estimates of the likelihoods that particular features will occur in exemplars of a category.

5.4.1 Feature-frequency estimates based on long-term memory

To my knowledge, the first experiments to include category-to-feature tests were reported in an unpublished manuscript by Gluck (1984), summarized in Appendix 5.3. With the same sets of objects and categories, subjects were given training on either the standard task (assigning objects to categories) or on the novel task of predicting what features would appear in exemplars of indicated categories, then were given both feature-to-category and category-to-feature tests. The rather surprising result was that subjects produced appropriate test responses only on the type of test that corresponded to their training condition. In particular, following standard training, subjects' estimates of the relative frequencies of features in categories not only failed to mirror the true frequencies but were negatively correlated with them. It appeared that, in this case, even after learning a categorization to a rather strict criterion, subjects could access no information in memory that would enable prediction of the features to be expected in new category members.*

However, it is always hazardous to draw conclusions about memory representations on the basis of a single response measure, and in this instance, a quite different picture emerged from a subsequent study by MacMillan (1987) that differed from Gluck's most critically in employing a different response measure, numerical estimates of feature frequencies, on category-to-feature tests.

Up to a point, MacMillan's experiment resembles others on category learning discussed in preceding sections. Stimulus materials were lists of symptoms characterizing hypothetical individuals (cases), and the task for the experimental subjects was to learn to assign cases to the categories Disease or No disease. The design of MacMillan's Experiment 1 is shown in Table 5.4 in terms of percentage occurrences of exemplars in categories during categorization training, with the labels actually used for categories and symptom values in MacMillan's study replaced by our standard notation. Different groups of subjects learned under the high validity and zero validity conditions.† The term *validity* refers to features and was defined in terms of the conditional probability of a category in the presence of a feature value. For the two values of each feature, the probability of Category A was different in the high validity condition, but the same in the

---

* An analogous result has been reported from a more recent study using similar procedures (Cobos, Rando, and Lopez Gutierrez 1992).

† The study included also a partial validity condition, not included in this analysis.

Table 5.4 Design of study on estimation of feature frequencies (MacMillan 1987, Experiment 1)

Exemplar		Condition			
		High validity Category		Zero validity Category	
f_1	f_2	A	B	A	B
1	1	55	10	55	55
1	2	15	30	15	15
2	1	15	30	15	15
2	2	15	30	15	15

Note: Categories A and B were labeled disease and non-disease; features f_1 and f_2 were labeled CSF count and PKU level, with the feature values 1 and 2 denoting high and low counts or levels. Category base rates (relative frequencies) were 33 and 67 for Categories A and B, respectively.

zero validity condition. In Table 5.4, it may be seen that, in the high validity condition, the exemplar having value 1 on each feature occurs predominantly on Category A and the other three exemplars predominantly on Category B trials, so it is possible for a learner to reach a reasonable level of proficiency (78 % correct categorizations on the average). In the zero validity condition, however, all exemplars occur equally often in both categories, so nothing can be learned about feature validities that will contribute to correct performance; the maximum level of proficiency is 67%, attainable by learning the category base rates (i.e., the relative frequencies of Categories A and B, which during learning were 33:67) and always choosing Category B.

The empirical question of prime interest in this study was whether, under either or both validity conditions, subjects would acquire information about the category structure that would enable them to produce veridical judgments about the relative frequencies of different symptoms within categories. To address this question, subjects in both groups were tested at the end of a 200-trial training series with questions asking them to estimate the relative frequency of occurrence of each symptom value in the presence of the disease (i.e., in Category A). I will give an overview of the results bearing on this question, then, after deriving predictions from the exemplar and similarity-network models, examine the data in more detail.

It is apparent from Table 5.4, which presents the design of this experiment, that value 1 of each feature occurred on 70% and value 2 on 30% of Category A trials during learning. The subjects' mean estimates of these percentages are compared to the true values in Table 5.5. In the high validity condition, the subjects' estimates are quite close to the true relative

Table 5.5 Results on estimation of feature frequencies in disease category (Category A) (MacMillan 1987, Experiment 1)

Symptom level	Condition							
	High validity				Zero validity			
	True frequencies	Subjects' estimates	Exemplar model	Network model	True frequencies	Subjects' estimates	Exemplar model	Network model
High	70	65	65	70	70	42	65	52
Low	30	30	35	30	30	54	35	48

Note: High and low symptom levels correspond to feature values 1 and 2 in Table 5.4. Cell entries are relative frequencies expressed as percentages. For the true frequencies and the model predictions, the percentages in each column must sum to 100; however, the experimental subjects estimated the frequencies of high and low symptom levels separately, so their estimates do not necessarily sum to 100.

frequencies. Taking this result together with those of other experiments of similar design that will be described below, we may evidently conclude that under the conditions of standard training with positive feature validities, subjects acquire veridical information about feature frequencies. It is not entirely clear why this information becomes manifest on tests when subjects estimate feature frequencies but not when they choose from a pair of features or feature values the feature or value that occurred more often in an indicated category (as in Gluck 1984, and Cobos, Rando, and Lopez Gutierrez 1992). However, it has been found in related studies that subjects have difficulty in shifting their task orientation between training and test trials when the same response mechanism (choice between alternatives) is employed on both (Estes, Campbell, Hatsopoulis, and Hurwitz 1989).

The data shown in Table 5.5 for the novel zero validity condition differ sharply from those for the high validity condition, the mean estimates differing little from the chance level of 0.50 and failing to reflect the true values even qualitatively. It might seem that the zero validity subjects learned nothing about the feature frequencies. However, this implication should be held in abeyance until we have considered the analysis of the experiment in terms of the models.

The main theoretical question at issue is whether either the exemplar or the similarity-network model can yield accurate predictions of performance on the feature-frequency tests. A description of the derivations is necessarily somewhat intricate, so I present it in Appendix 5.4 and only discuss the predictions here.

Referring first to Table 5.5, the prediction of the large observed difference between the high and zero validity conditions on the feature-frequency estimates presents a striking confirmation of the similarity-network model. So far as I know, no extant version of exemplar, feature-frequency, or prototype models (reviewed in Reed 1972; Estes 1986a; Nosofsky 1986 1992a) can predict this result. On the other hand, within the network family, the prediction is not unique to the similarity-network model. It can, for example, be derived from the model of Gluck and Bower (1988b), which differs from similarity-network in being based on a network whose nodes represent feature values.

It is important to be clear as to just what is predicted by the network model for the zero validity condition. It would not be correct to conclude that, according to the model, the subjects remain at chance throughout training with respect to estimating frequencies of features in categories. This fact is pointed up in Fig. 5.5, which exhibits the learning curve predicted by the similarity-network model for learner's estimates of the relative frequency of high symptom values in Category A in the zero validity condition. The prediction is that the estimates should start near chance, rise to a maximum, then decline toward chance as trials continue. The reason for this perhaps surprising prediction can be understood by reference to the

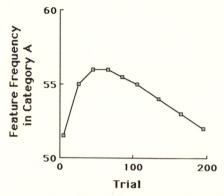

Fig. 5.5 Function predicted by similarity-network model for changes in estimates of feature frequency over trials in the zero validity condition of MacMillan (1987) Experiment 1.

design table for this experiment (Table 5.4). Exemplar pattern 11 occurs much more frequently than the other patterns; consequently, although the asymptotic weights will be the same for all patterns in each category,* the weights for pattern 11 will rise toward the common asymptote much faster than the others. These weights occur in the numerators of the theoretical expressions for the relative frequency estimates for feature 1 (Appendix 5.4), and therefore these estimates will rise above chance till they reach a maximum, then decline toward chance as all of the exemplar weights for each category approach their common asymptote.

No empirical check on the non-monotone function of Fig. 5.5 is available for this experiment because feature frequency estimates were obtained from the subjects only at the end of the learning scries. In another part of MacMillan's study (1987, Experiment 3), however, different groups were asked for feature frequency estimates after different numbers of learning trials. The procedures were generally similar to those of MacMillan's Experiment 1 except that only 80 learning trials were given and different groups of subjects made feature frequency estimates after 10, 20, 40, or 80 learning trials. The design matrices were similar in essentials to those of Experiment 1, although the particular feature frequencies differed and exemplar pattern 22 was omitted. The observed functions for feature frequency estimates and theoretical predictions from the similarity-network model are shown in Fig. 5.6. The non-monotone trend implied by the model is not only clearly evident, but closely represents the observed trend. It will be noted that a non-monotone function is predicted also for the high validity

---

* Because, in the zero validity condition, all exemplars occur equally frequently in both categories.

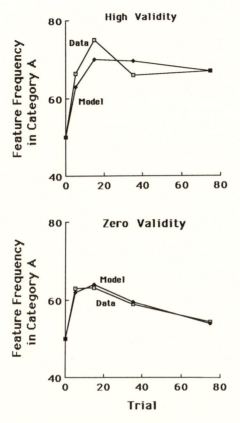

Fig. 5.6   Observed and theoretical (similarity-network model) learning functions for feature-frequency estimation in MacMillan (1987) Experiment 3.

condition, for the same reasons as in the zero validity case, and is clearly evident in the data.

The non-monotone learning function cannot be predicted by the exemplar model (even the augmented version). Thus, these results provide the clearest evidence available to date that, at least when categorization depends on relatively long-term memory, the nature of the category learning process is captured better by an adaptive network model than by models that represent learning simply in terms of trial-by-trial storage of exemplar or feature representations.

5.4.2 Feature-frequency estimation based on shorter-term memory

In view of the evidence brought out in Chapter 4, there is reason to believe that the network models may not show the same superiority when categorization depends on short-term memory. The category-to-feature tests given at the end of the experiment on categorization in short-term memory described in Chapter 4 (Experiment 4.3) are relevant to this suggestion. The model fits for that experiment, in terms of root mean square deviations of predicted from observed values, on a percentage scale, were virtually identical for the exemplar and similarity-network models (20.1 and 20.2, respectively, in the high validity and 13.1 and 13.1 in the low validity conditions, averaged over the main experiment and replication).

The large values of these deviation measures reflect a pattern that may be seen in Figs. 5.7 and 5.8, which compare mean feature-frequency estimates with predictions from the exemplar and similarity-network models in the high validity and zero validity conditions, respectively. The errors of

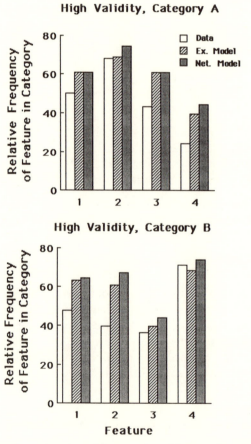

Fig. 5.7 Data for estimation of frequencies of features in categories in Experiment 4.3, high validity conditions, together with predictions from the exemplar (Ex.) and similarity-network (Net.) models.

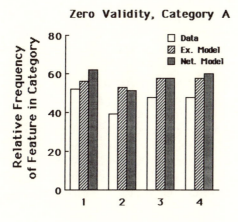

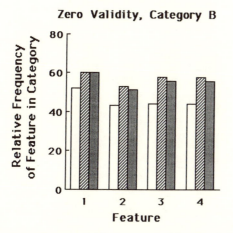

Fig. 5.8 Data for estimation of frequencies of features in categories in Experiment 4.3, zero validity conditions, together with predictions from the exemplar (Ex.) and similarity-network (Net.) models.

prediction are large on an absolute scale, but the correlations of predicted with observed values are quite high. It appears that in giving their numerical estimates of feature frequencies, the subjects had a constant tendency to avoid high ratings, a tendency that has been reported previously for numerical estimates of category probabilities (Estes, Campbell, Hatsopoulis, and Hurwitz 1989). However, in each panel of both Figs, the pattern of predicted values for both models mirrors quite closely the pattern of observed values. Taking correlations of predicted with observed ratings as our criterion of fit, it is clear that, in contrast with the results of MacMillan's (1987) study, the exemplar and network models account for the feature-frequency data about equally well even in the zero validity condition. Presumably the critical difference between the studies is that in Experiment 4.3 the learning series was not long enough to allow the appearance of the non-monotone learning function for feature-frequency predicted by the network model.

The category-to-feature tests that were included in Experiment 5.1 have the additional virtue of providing comparisons of the two learning procedures and the full and partial category structures. In this experiment, test performance could not be expected to be based primarily on short-term memory, but in view of the relatively short training series, the dependence on long-term memory may be less than in MacMillan's (1987) study. The analyses to be presented are based on subjects' ratings, on a percentage scale, of the relative frequency with which value 2 of each feature had occurred in

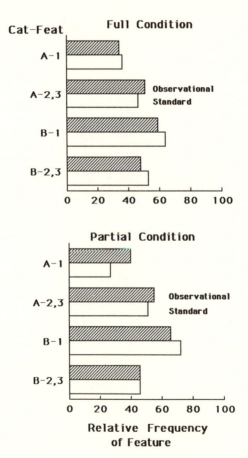

Fig. 5.9 Data for estimation of frequencies of features in categories (Cat-Feat) in Experiment 5.1, by training procedure and condition.

an indicated category during learning. The true frequencies over the entire training series in the full condition were 25, 50, and 50 for features 1, 2, and 3 in Category A and 75, 50, and 50 in Category B. In the partial condition, the corresponding values were 33, 67, and 67 for A and 75, 50, and 50 for B. In contrast to MacMillan's study, which had a much longer training series, performance was not expected to approach these values closely, but the pattern of ratings obtained does reflect the pattern of true values reasonably well, as may be seen in Fig. 5.9. Values for features 2 and 3 vary around the true value of 50 in both categories, with those for feature 1 being lower in Category A and higher in Category B. These relationships hold similarly for standard versus observational training and for the full versus partial conditions.

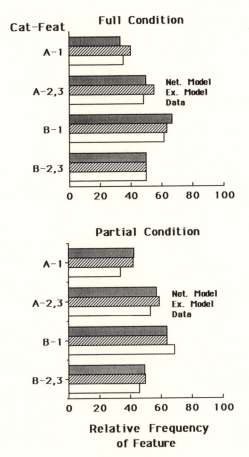

Fig. 5.10 Data for estimation of frequencies of features in categories (Cat-Feat) in Experiment 5.1, averaged over training procedures, together with predictions from the exemplar (Ex.) and similarity-network (Net.) models.

The fits of the exemplar and similarity-network models, presented in Fig. 5.10 (with observed and predicted values averaged over the standard and observational procedures), are almost indistinguishable in the partial condition, but the network model fares better in the full condition. In view of the fact that the network has one more free parameter to be estimated from the learning data, however, the appropriate conclusion appears to be that, with tests following a relatively small amount of training, the models are approximately on a par.

The studies we have reviewed all support a concept of feature-frequency learning as a robust phenomenon, demonstrable under conditions calling for retrieval of information from either short- or long-term memory. It occurs during category learning under either standard or observational procedures; it occurs whether or not the features are valid predictors of categories; and it does not depend on learners' knowing at the time of category learning that memory for this kind of information will be tested. In traditional psychological terms, it seems that this learning can appropriately be described as *unconscious*. We would not be justified at this point in terming it *automatic*, however, for a strategy of attending to category-to-feature relationships during category learning may be a *control process* (in the terminology of Schneider and Shiffrin 1977) acquired during experiences in ordinary life when category-to-feature inferences have been important (Corter and Gluck 1992).

5.5 Pattern completion

Answers to queries about assignment of patterns to categories, prototype recognition, and category-to-feature inference by no means exhaust the kinds of information that are accessible from the memory arrays formed during category learning. Another kind that is both theoretically and practically important pertains to the phenomenon of pattern completion, of central concern in current connectionist modelling but well known under the label *redintegration* in the earlier memory literature, dating from Hamilton (1859) and Hollingworth (1928). To illustrate, suppose that, on the first three trials of a categorization experiment, the exemplar-category presentations were 111A, 121B, 122A, and at that point the learner was presented with the partial pattern 11– and asked to estimate the probability that the pattern should be completed with value 1 for the third feature. To predict the learner's response from the exemplar model, we would compute the similarity of the partial pattern completed with either value 1 or value 2 to the current memory array, obtaining a global similarity to the full array of $1+s+s^2$ for 111 and $2s+s^2$ for 112. Entering these quantities in the standard expression for response probability, we obtain

$$P(1) = (1+s+s^2)/(1+3s+2s^2) \tag{5.2}$$

Table 5.6 Results* of pattern-completion tests in Experiment 5.2

Partial pattern	True value	Learning condition	
		Standard	Observational
11–	44	45	38
12–	63	57	55
21–	36	44	42
22–	58	54	60
1–1	31	47	49
1–2	50	54	51
2–1	50	51	52
2–2	71	62	69
–11	44	46	44
–12	36	43	49
–21	63	52	55
–22	58	56	64

* Mean estimates of relative frequency of completion by feature value 1, on a percentage scale

for the probability that the learner would complete the partial pattern to yield 111 (i.e., for the learner's estimate of the probability that 111 would be the correct completion). For a small value of the similarity parameter, s, this probability obviously approaches unity, which seems intuitively appropriate for this example.

To allow assessment of the degree to which this pattern-completion capability actually develops as a by-product of category learning under either standard or observational procedures, tests were given at the end of Experiment 5.2 on which each of the two-feature partial patterns that can be formed from the eight exemplar patterns was presented with a request that the subject estimate the relative frequency with which the partial pattern had been completed with an indicated feature value during learning.

The basic data from the pattern-completion tests following both training procedures are presented in Table 5.6 in terms of mean estimates of the relative frequency with which each partial pattern was completed by value 1 for the missing feature during the training series, together with the true values. It is immediately apparent that, even though these tests followed those on prototype recognition, the subjects demonstrated impressive ability at pattern completion, somewhat more so in the standard than in the observational learning group (correlations of mean judgments with true values being 0.90 and 0.78, respectively).

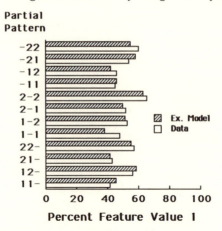

Fig. 5.11 Data for pattern-completion tests, in terms of estimated percentage of completion by value 1 of the missing feature, together with predictions from the exemplar (Ex.) model (Experiment 5.2).

Predictions from both models were generated for the pattern completion data, using the parameter estimates based on learning data. For reasons that I cannot yet explain, the similarity-network yielded an extremely poor fit, all predicted values clustering close to 0.50. Predictions from the exemplar model, however, mirror the pattern of the data very well, as may be seen in Fig. 5.11.

It is interesting to note that the subjects had, in effect, learned a set of implicit categorizations as a by-product of learning the categorization called for by the training task. When, for example, the primary task was categorizing schematic faces according to personality types, the subjects developed also the capability of assigning the partial patterns based on the noses and mouths of the faces to categories defined by closely or widely spaced eyes. I will return to some other implications of this finding in the next chapter.

Appendix 5.1 Induction of prototypes in a correlated-feature category structure: Experiment 5.1

From both empirical evidence and theoretical analyses reviewed in previous chapters, we conclude that categorization performance is generally accomplished by computations on an information-rich memory array rather than by comparing stimulus patterns to abstract representations of category prototypes. Nonetheless, the concept of a prototype continues to be of interest in its own right. A prototype is a partial summary description of a category and thus can be used to give an individual information that can facilitate categorization performance (Medin, Altom, and Murphy 1984).

Also, in experimental studies of categorization, category exemplars are sometimes generated by producing variations on a priori defined prototypes (as in Posner and Keele 1968, 1970), and categories encountered in ordinary life often have the same character (as when different models of an automobile are produced by variations on a single basic design).

Thus, it is of interest to ask how well people can induce the prototypes of categories from experience with instances and how well their learning can be accounted for by array models. The process of learning to induce prototypes has been examined by other investigators (Hull 1920; Breen and Schvane-veldt 1986; Busemeyer and Myung 1988), but not with procedures yielding data amenable to application of array models and not with attention to the important distinction between correlated and independent features. In this experiment, the question is examined for a category task in which features of exemplars are correlated within categories; in Experiment 5.2, the same is done for a task in which exemplars are generated by random sampling of independent (uncorrelated) features.

The abstract structure of the categories studied in this experiment was drawn from the study by Shepard, Hovland, and Jenkins (1961) but realized with different stimulus materials—schematic faces in one replication and bar charts in another. The gist of the experiment was to give subjects experience with a set of category exemplars under instructions both to categorize the stimulus patterns and, concurrently, to try to induce the prototypes of the categories, then to give tests for the subjects' ability to recognize two types of prototypes (average or configural, as discussed in Chapter 2) and tests of their ability to estimate relative frequencies of features within categories. In view of the fact that under the standard learning procedure, the necessity for subjects to attend to the informative feedback of each trial might interfere with the task of inducing category prototypes, we included a comparison of the standard procedure with one in which the subjects simply observed the sequence of training exemplars, with progress being monitored by occasion-ally interpolated blocks of no-feedback test trials. Finally, because of its relevance to the process of learning about prototypes, we included a condition in which the configural prototype of one category never appeared on training trials.

Method

Subjects and stimuli

The subjects were Harvard undergraduates, 24 assigned to the standard and 24 to the observational learning condition. In the interest of generality, two types of stimuli were used, the complete design of the experiment being replicated with each type for each subject. One type comprised bar charts, each display presenting three vertical bars that varied in height, low and high corresponding to 1 and 2 in the coded representations of the patterns; the subjects were instructed to think of these as symptom charts for hypothetical patients who were to be assigned to disease categories A or B. The other stimulus type comprised schematic faces differing in eye separation, nose length, and height of mouth, the two values of each corresponding to 1 and 2 in the coded representations.

Design of training series

Within the experimental session, each subject took part in two complete replications of the experiment, one with each stimulus type. For each stimulus type, there were two kinds of pattern sets, denoted full and partial. A full pattern set included all eight of the combinations of value 1 or 2 for each of the three features; a partial pattern set omitted pattern 111. The resulting sets of patterns and their frequencies of presentation by category during categorization training are shown in Table 5.1 in the text. An important property of the design that will be apparent in Table 5.1 is that relative frequencies of feature values varied within categories. In the full condition, for example, value 1 of feature 1 occurred six times but value 1 of the other features only four times in Category A . For each type of pattern set, full and partial, there were two random orders of presentation of the patterns during training, each order used with both charts and faces. Within a training condition, standard or observational, three subjects were assigned to each combination of stimulus order by stimulus type/pattern set (three to order 1 with faces and the full set, three to order 1 with faces and the partial set, and so on).

Training Procedure

Each problem began with four blocks of training trials. In the full condition, there were 16 training trials per block, two on each of the eight patterns, and in the partial condition 14 training trials, two on each pattern except 111. Each training block was followed by eight test trials, one on each pattern (including pattern 111 in the partial condition). Instructions to the subjects read, in part, as follows.

For the Standard procedure:

In one experiment you will be shown schematic faces and will be asked to categorize them into one of two personality types, which will be labelled X and Y. In the other experiment you will be shown symptom charts for hypothetical patients and will be asked to categorize them into one of two disease categories, which will be labelled A and B. On most of the trials, your response will be followed by a display of the correct category. However, from time to time there will be a short section of "test" trials on which this information is omitted.

For the Observational procedure:

In one experiment you will be shown schematic faces of people from two personality types, which will be labelled X and Y. In the other experiment you will be shown symptom charts for hypothetical patients who suffer from one of two disease categories, which will be labelled A and B. During the observational learning trials you will be shown the personality type (or disease) for an individual along with their face (or symptom chart). From time to time there will be a short section of "test" trials on which you will be shown a face (or symptom chart) and will be asked to provide the correct category label.

Stimuli were presented on the screen of a Macintosh microcomputer and responses were typed on the keyboard. Under the standard training procedure, each trial began with the display of a stimulus pattern, and, below it, the category labels, A or B for bar charts and X or Y for faces (all coded as A or B in the design and analysis tables in this report). The display remained in view until the subject chose a category by pressing one of two appropriately labelled keys, following which the chosen category together with the label of the correct category for the trial appeared on the screen for 1.5 seconds; then after a 0.5 second blank interval, the next trial started. Under the observational learning condition, a trial began with a 1.5 second display of a category label; then a stimulus pattern was added, both remaining in view for an additional 3 seconds (approximately equal to the average stimulus duration in the standard condition). After a 0.5 second blank interval, the next trial started. The procedure on the test blocks interspersed with the training blocks was exactly like that of the training trials in the standard condition except that the correct category label was not displayed following the response.

Prototype and feature-frequency tests

1. Prototype tests. Along with the training instructions, subjects were prepared for these tests, to be given immediately following the training series, by instructions that read, in part, as follows.

In the first set of special "test" trials, you will be shown a face or symptom chart along with a category label. You will be asked to rate how strongly you feel this face or chart is the "prototype" of the category...on a scale from 0 to 100 ... For faces, a prototype may be thought of as the most typical face in a category. Imagine that in preparing the particular faces, the experimenter started with the prototype and then made small changes to the prototype (e.g., lengthening or shortening the nose) to produce individual faces. In this test you are to judge how close the test faces are to the prototype. The prototype of the symptom charts can be thought of in the same way.

On the prototype tests, each of the eight patterns for a given condition was shown once with each category label. In addition, the average prototype for each category was shown once with each category label as were each of three other patterns that differed by small (but easily discriminable) amounts from the prototypes on each featural dimension. The entire set of test stimuli was presented in a random order.

2. Feature-frequency tests. Instructions for the second set of tests indicated that on each trial a single feature (e.g., the eyes from a schematic face or a single bar from a bar chart) would be shown together with a category label, and the subject would indicate on a scale from 0 (never) to 100 (always) how often the feature occurred in the category during the training series.

On the feature-frequency tests, a single feature (specifically, the value 2 of the feature in the coded format) from a stimulus pattern, e.g., the eyes or the nose from a face, was presented together with a category label. Three of these tests were given for each category.

Results
Learning

For comparability between the standard and observational training procedures, learning is assessed in terms of categorization responses in the four blocks of no-feedback test trials interspersed with the four blocks of training trials. The level of performance reached by the end of training, over 80% correct responses, was satisfactory in terms of the objective of setting the stage for the prototype and feature-frequency tests.

Prototype tests

The raw data for the prototype tests were the subjects' ratings, on a 0–100 scale, of the degree to which they judged each presented pattern represented the prototype of the indicated category. These ratings cannot be interpreted as probability estimates because all of the exemplars of each category received mean ratings greater than 50 on the prototype tests for that category. The subjects appear to have interpreted the instructions to mean that the rating for a given pattern, X, relative to Category A should correspond to the probability that X was the prototype of Category A rather than Category B. Therefore, for purposes of analysis in relation to predictions from the models, the mean ratings have been converted to values that may be termed relative typicalities for Category A. (Relative typicality of a pattern for Category B is 100 minus its relative typicality for A.) For example, the group assigned to the full condition and standard training procedure produced a mean rating of 70 for pattern 111 as the Category A prototype and 14 as the Category B prototype. These ratings yield for the relative typicality of this pattern

$$70/(70+14) = 0.83.$$

Relative typicalities so computed, and multiplied by 100 to put them on a percentage scale, are presented in Tables 5.3 and 5.4 of the text.

Appendix 5.2 Induction of prototypes in an independent-feature category structure: Experiment 5.2

The purpose of this experiment was again to examine induction of prototypes under both standard and observational training procedures with the same tasks and stimuli as in Experiment 5.1 but with category exemplars generated by independent sampling of features from different distributions defined for the two categories. Thus, whereas perfect learning of the categorizations was possible in Experiment 5.1, because all exemplar patterns (although not all individual features) were fully valid predictors of the categories, the same was not true of the fuzzy (probabilistically defined) categories of Experiment 5.2. A secondary purpose of this study was to test following categorization training for a kind of information retrieval that might be termed pattern completion.

Method
Subjects and stimuli

The subjects were again Harvard undergraduates, 27 assigned to the standard and 24 to the observational learning condition. The stimuli and the task and instructions were the same as those of Experiment 5.1, except for the substitution of pattern-completion for category-to-feature tests.

Design of the training series

With features of the stimuli, bar charts or faces, defined as in Experiment 5.1, the probabilities of occurrence of feature values in categories during training were as follows.

		Category	
Feature	*Value*	A	B
1	1	0.67	0.33
1	2	0.33	0.67
2	1	0.17	0.83
2	2	0.83	0.17
3	1	0.67	0.33
3	2	0.33	0.67

To generate the exemplar pattern for a training trial, the category for the trial was selected (each category having probability 0.5), and then the values of the three features for that trial were obtained by referring to a random number table with the appropriate probabilities listed under that category. For purposes of defining the points for insertion of test blocks (and for later data analysis), the training series was regarded as comprising six blocks of 27 trials. The constraints were imposed that each category be represented on 81

Table 5.A1   Design of Experiment 5.2 in terms of frequencies of exemplars in categories during learning

Pattern	"Correct" response	Category	
		A	B
121	A	30	1
122	A	15	3
221	A	15	3
222	A	7	6
111	B	6	8
112	B	3	15
211	B	3	15
212	B	2	30

training trials and that each block include 13 patterns from one category and 14 from the other. The resulting frequencies of occurrence of the eight stimulus patterns (the partial condition being omitted from this experiment) are summarized in Table 5.A1. In contrast to Experiment 5.1, the patterns were only partially valid predictors of the categories (the maximum average accuracy of categorization attainable being 83%).

The average prototypes of the categories were 1.33, 1.83, and 1.33, respectively, for Category A and 1.67, 1.17, and 1.67 for Category B. It will be apparent from Table 5.A1 that the focal exemplars of the categories were 121 for A and 212 for B. Because the average prototypes are very similar in form to the focal exemplars in this experiment, we can anticipate much better performance on tests for recognition of the average prototypes than in Experiment 5.1.

Prototype and pattern-completion tests

The prototype tests given at the end of the training series were conducted exactly as in Experiment 5.1. For the pattern completion tests, subjects were presented once with each two-feature partial pattern (11–, 12–, 1–1, –22, etc.) that could be formed from the eight training exemplars and asked to rate on a 0–100 scale the relative frequency with which the pattern had been completed on training trials by the indicated value for the missing feature.

Appendix 5.3 Method and results of Gluck (1984) study

In Gluck's study, 18 exemplars of each of two categories were composed from a set of six typographic symbols, with a structure such that individual features (symbols) occurred in category exemplars with frequencies ranging from 1 to 8 in each block of 36 learning trials. In Experiment 1, training to a relatively strict criterion of accurate performance was given in the usual way, with a subject viewing an exemplar pattern, making a categorization response, and being informed of the correct category on each trial. Then two types of tests were given—a set on which the subjects' task was to choose the correct category when shown a feature, and a set on which the task was to choose the more frequent of two features when shown a category label. The results of the feature-to-category tests were proportions of categorization responses that approximated the true probabilities of the categories in the presence of the test features. The category-to-feature tests, however, yielded choice proportions that were far from (and, in fact, negatively correlated with) the true probabilities.

In Gluck's Experiment 2, the materials and procedures were the same except that during training, the subject was shown a category label on each trial and asked to predict whether or not an exemplar of the category would or would not have a designated feature, then received appropriate informative feedback. On category-to-feature tests, the response proportions again approximated the true probabilities. But on the feature-to-category tests, results were essentially the reverse of those of Experiment 1, the response proportions being negatively correlated with the true values. Thus, it appeared that the information a subject had available at the time of a test depended strongly on the learning procedure.

Appendix 5.4 Derivations of predictions from exemplar and similarity-network models for MacMillan (1987) study

We will examine the way in which predictions can be generated from each model. Starting with the exemplar model, we need first of all to characterize the memory array at the point of the tests. To this end, we can calculate from the relative frequencies in Table 5.4 of the text that, over the 200-trial learning series, the average frequencies of occurrence of exemplars in categories should be as shown in Table 5.A2 (and, rounded to integral values, these were the actual frequencies). To apply the simple form of the exemplar model, assuming no decay process, we assume that the presentation frequencies are also the frequencies of stored representations of exemplars in the memory array. In the high validity condition, for example, 37 instances of pattern 11 would be stored in the Category A column and 13 in the Category B column of the array. We do not know the value of the similarity parameter, s, of the model, but the level of performance reached by the high validity group during learning (see upper panel of Fig. 5.5) indicates that s is small, so I will assume $s=0$ in making predictions. With this assumption, the predicted asymptotic probability of a learner's assigning pattern 11 to Category A on a test would be $37/(37+13)$, and the probabilities for each of the other patterns would be $10/(10+40)$; from these probabilities we can compute an asymptotic percentage correct of approximately 78.

Table 5.A2   Frequencies of occurrence of exemplars in Categories A and B during learning (MacMillan 1987, Experiment 1)

Exemplar		High validity		Zero validity	
f_1	f_2	A	B	A	B
1	1	37	13	37	73
1	2	10	40	10	20
2	1	10	40	10	20
2	2	10	40	10	20

However, our primary interest here is in what we can predict about performance when subjects are asked to estimate the relative frequency with which, say, value 1 of feature 1 occurs on Category A trials. We assume that the desired estimate is the expected relative frequency with which patterns 11 and 12, which contain the given feature value, occur in Category A. The prediction for the exemplar model, is given by a calculation exactly analogous to that used to predict categorization performance except that ratios of summed similarities are computed within columns of the memory array rather than across rows. Thus, referring again to the expected memory array for this group, the predicted relative frequency would be $(37+10)/(37+10+10+10)$, or approximately 0.70. More generally, with the value of s not constrained to be 0, the result would be $(47+20s)/(67+67s)$, so we could predict in advance of the experiment that the observed mean estimate for this feature value in Category A, expressed as a percentage, should fall between 50 and 70.

Now let us turn to the novel condition of this experiment, that of the zero validity group. For these subjects, the expected memory array at the end of 200 learning trials would be as shown in the right-hand portion of Table 5.A2, and obviously the prediction for an estimate of relative frequency of feature value 1 in Category A is the same as for the high validity condition.* Thus, prior to the experiment, we could have predicted that, for the zero validity, as for the high validity group, frequency estimates for the high symptom values should fall between 50 and 70. Again assuming on the basis of the level of performance reached during learning that the value of s for these subjects is near 0, we obtain the predicted estimates shown under

---

* With the particular design used, this predicted estimate holds also for feature 2, value 1 in Category A (and also for both feature values in Category B). In view of this equivalence, the observed symptom frequency estimates for this experiment shown in Table 5.4 are averages for the high and low values of the two symptoms.

Exemplar model in Table 5.5 of the text. It will be observed that the prediction agrees quite well with the data for the high validity group but is far off for the zero validity group.

For our treatment of this experiment in terms of the similarity-network model, we will start with the same network illustrated in Fig. 3.3 of Chapter 3 for the categorization problem represented in Table 3.1. A portrayal of the expected memory array at the end of the learning series has the same form as that of the exemplar model, but the cell entries are not frequencies, but rather the weights on the paths between exemplar memory nodes and category nodes:

Exemplar	*Node*	A	B
11	1	w_{11}	w_{12}
12	2	w_{21}	w_{22}
21	3	w_{31}	w_{32}
22	4	w_{41}	w_{42}

The network nodes correspond to exemplar patterns numbered from 1 to 4 from top to bottom, and the w_{ij} denote the weights for the connections of exemplar i to category j.

Preparatory to examining the success of the network model at predicting the results of the feature-frequency tests, we estimated its parameters by application to the obtained learning functions, plotted in terms of percentage of correct categorization responses per 20-trial block in Fig. 5.A1. The high validity function, shown in the upper panel, is accompanied by a theoretical curve computed from the similarity-network model that provides a reasonable graduation of the empirical values. A function computed with the same parameter values ($\beta = 0.05$, $c = 2$, $s = 0.1$), shown for the zero validity group in the lower panel, runs slightly above the highly irregular empirical function. These subjects seem to have found learning in the absence of relevant feature information inordinately difficult, and no orderly function could describe their learning function very well.

To generate predictions about feature frequency estimates, the values of the w_{ij} were obtained by running the model through 200 learning trials (applying the learning functions given in Chapter 3 on each trial) and computing the weights at the point of the feature frequency test; the same parameter values used to compute the theoretical learning functions shown in Fig. 5.A1 yield the terminal weights

---

* Correct responding is defined for the high validity group as choosing Category A for pattern 11 and Category B for the other three patterns; for the zero validity group, correct responding was defined as choosing the more frequent category (Category B) for all patterns.

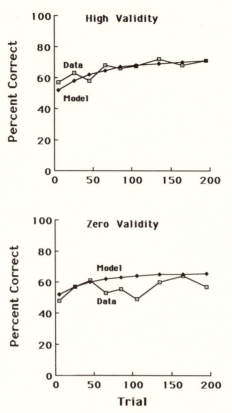

Fig. 5.A1 Observed and theoretical (similarity-network model) category learning functions for MacMillan (1987) Experiment 1.

Exemplar	Node	A	B
11	1	0.578	0.227
12	2	0.168	0.638
21	3	0.168	0.638
22	4	0.160	0.646

The assumption linking the weights to feature frequency estimates is similar to the one illustrated above for the exemplar model. For example, taking s equal to 0, the basis for predicting learners' mean estimate of the relative frequency of feature 1, value 1 in Category A is

$$\frac{(w_{11}+w_{21})}{(w_{11}+w_{21}) + (w_{31}+w_{41})} \tag{5.A1}$$

For technical reasons, just as in the derivation of functions for categorization probabilities, the summed weights within parentheses are subjected to an exponential transformation, so the function we use to predict the feature frequency estimate is

$$\frac{e^{c(w_{11}+w_{21})}}{e^{c(w_{11}+w_{21})} + e^{c(w_{31}+w_{41})}} \tag{5.A2}$$

Substituting the w_{ij} values listed above and letting c equal 2 yields

$$\frac{4.45}{4.45 + 1.93} = 0.70,$$

which is entered in Table 5.A2 as the similarity-network prediction for the high validity condition.

Noting that the exemplar frequencies in Category A are the same for the zero validity as for the high validity condition (Table 5.4 of the text), one might suppose that the similarity-network model prediction for feature frequency estimates in Category A would be the same for both conditions, as it is for the exemplar model. That supposition would, however, be quite wrong. When we compute the trial-by-trial weight changes for the zero validity condition, even though we use the same parameter values as for the high validity computation, we obtain a quite different set of weights (w_{ij} values) at the end of the 200-trial learning series), viz.

	A	B
11	0.282	0.566
12	0.253	0.507
21	0.253	0.507
22	0.244	0.489

And, employing these values in the same way as we did for the high validity case, we arrive at a prediction of 52% for the estimate of relative frequency of high symptom levels in Category A, which is entered in Table 5.5 of the text for the zero validity condition.

6. Extensions and new applications of the exemplar-similarity model

This chapter addresses two tasks. The first is to review the processing assumptions of the array-similarity model for categorization and revise the formulation discussed in Chapters 2–5 by allowing for varying degrees of similarity between categories (an extension suggested by the results on pattern completion discussed in Chapter 5). The second is to apply the exemplar model, so revised, to a number of problems not previously addressed by categorization models, including the learning of confusable categories, transfer between categorizations, changes in discriminability of features with experience, the interpretation of causal judgments, and cued recall.

The notion of category similarity can be explicated by means of the following example. Suppose that a consultant to a large corporation has the task of learning to classify cities as desirable (Category D) or undesirable (Category U) places for employees to live. The necessary learning experience, modeled on a standard categorization experiment, constitutes a series of episodes in each of which the learner is shown a description of a city in terms of a number of attributes together with its desirability rating. In the first few episodes, the learner might encounter the city-category combinations

Large, inland, industrial	U
Large, coastal, commercial	U
Small, coastal, commercial	D

If tested after a delay with the description "large, inland, commercial," or even just "large, inland," the learner would probably give U as the category. However, from the results on pattern completion discussed in Chapter 5, we know that if, instead, we presented the partial description "large, inland" and asked the learner to classify its business activity as industrial or commercial, he would probably respond "industrial." While engaged in the primary task, he would have learned secondarily to categorize cities described in terms of size and location in terms of predominant business activity. Thus, "industrial" and "commercial," which served as features of the exemplars in the primary task can be regarded as the categories (which might be denoted I and C) of the implicit secondary task. In terms of the exemplar-similarity model, the similarity of the features I and C in the primary task would have been assumed to have some value s, and we would expect small values of s to lead to rapid learning. There is no reason to think that the similarity of these features should change when the experimenter shifts attention to the implicit, secondary task, and we would expect small values of s, now interpreted as category similarity, to lead to rapid learning of the secondary classification.

6.1 Processing assumptions

In this revision, the principal departure from the formulation of exemplar models in the previous chapters of this volume and in the earlier literature (Medin and Schaffer 1978; Nosofsky 1984; Estes 1986*a*) is that category labels are assumed to have the same properties as the features or attributes of the stimulus patterns that serve as category exemplars. If, in a category structure, the category exemplars are defined in terms of N attributes (an attribute being either a dimension or an on/off feature), then a memory representation of the occurrence of an exemplar plus a category label is defined on $N+1$ attributes, one of which may be termed a categorical attribute. This idea is not novel (Hintzman 1988; Mordkowitz 1990; Heit 1992), but the implications of similarity relations among category labels have not been explored. In summary, the revised assumptions, expressed in terms of a binary categorization, are as follows.

1. On each learning trial, a featural description of the stimulus pattern and correct category label is stored in the memory array.

2. The similarity between any two different category labels (i.e., values on the categorical attribute) is represented by a parameter σ having the same properties as the parameter s, which represents similarity between two different stimulus features.*

3. When a stimulus pattern Π is presented to an individual for categorization with C_j and C_k as the alternative categories, the individual mentally combines the features of Π with those of each category label to form two vectors (feature lists), which may be denoted Π, C_j and Π, C_k. The summed similarity of each of these to the current contents of the full memory array, denoted $Sim(\Pi, C_j)$ and $Sim(\Pi, C_k)$, respectively, is then computed, using the product rule in the standard fashion. The ratio of these summed similarities determines the categorization probability according to the usual formula,

$$P(C_j) = Sim(\Pi, C_j)/(Sim(\Pi, C_j) + Sim(\Pi, C_k)). \qquad (6.1)$$

---

* For the applications to be discussed in this chapter, there will be no occasion to refer to the constituent features of category labels, and for any set of categories, A, B, C, . . ., the labels will be treated as unitary features, or values on a "categorical" attribute. More generally, the parameter σ would denote the pairwise similarity of features of category lebels, and similarities between labels would be computed by application of the product rule.

To illustrate the computation of categorization probability in terms of Assumptions 1–3, let us assume that a categorization task requires classification of a set of items into categories A and B. The items might, for example, be the light or dark triangles or squares used in earlier illustrations. Suppose that the first few trials run

$$\text{LT A   LS A   DS B   LS A   DT B}$$

The attribute values, light and dark in the first feature position, are coded as L or D, and triangle or square in the second position are coded as T or S. We assume that a corresponding array is stored in memory, the entry LT,A, for example, comprising the features of the light triangle plus the feature corresponding to the Category A label. Suppose that following these trials, a test is given on the light triangle. The computational procedure is to combine the stimulus pattern with each of the alternative category labels and compute the similarity of the resulting "feature vectors," LT,A and LT,B, to the current memory array. Applying the product rule in the standard way, we obtain for similarity of LT,A to the array

$$\text{Sim(LT,A)} = 1+s+s^2\sigma+s+s\sigma, \qquad (6.2)$$

since similarity of LT,A to itself is 1, to LS,A is s (there being a mismatch only in the second stimulus position), to DS,B is $s^2\sigma$ (there being mismatches on both stimulus features and on the category feature), and so on. Analogously, we obtain for similarity of LT,B to the array

$$\text{Sim(LT,B)} = s+s\sigma+s^2+s\sigma+s. \qquad (6.3)$$

For the probability of assigning item LT to category A, we obtain, upon entering these similarities into Equation 6.1,

$$P(A) = (1+2s+s\sigma+s^2\sigma)/(1+4s+s^2+3s\sigma+s^2\sigma). \qquad (6.4)$$

In the special case when σ is equal to 0, this expression reduces to

$$P(A) = (1+2s)/(1+4s+s^2), \qquad (6.5)$$

exactly the result that would have been produced by the computational scheme used for the exemplar model in Chapters 1–3. The effect of increasing the value of the category similarity parameter, σ, for a binary categorization is to move the categorization probabilities toward 0.5. With, say, s equal to 0.5, if σ is equal to 0, we have

$$P(A) = (1+1)/(1+2+0.25) = 2/3.25 = 0.615; \qquad (6.6)$$

but if σ is increased to 0.2, this probability becomes

$$P(A) = (1+1+0.1+0.05)/(1+2+0.25+0.3+0.05) = 2.15/3.6 = 0.597. \qquad (6.7)$$

6.2 Extensions and applications

In general, when we take account of possible variations in category confusability, the extended processing assumptions can yield results not obtainable with the original computational scheme. For convenience while discussing a variety of applications, I will refer to the extended model simply as the *exemplar model* when application is to a form of categorization but as the *array model* when application is to a cognitive activity not ordinarily labelled categorization.

6.2.1 Confusable categories

Let us imagine that the items in the example above were, not geometric figures, but, rather, brief descriptions of patients in the emergency ward of a hospital, who were classified, for purposes of reports to relatives, as "critical" or "fair," these labels corresponding to Categories A and B. A question that might be raised is how the categorization probabilities would be affected if we changed the labels to the more similar designations "critical" or "serious." To prepare for derivation of an answer, we assume that the similarity between Categories A and B has some value, σ, greater than zero, and consider a trial sequence

$$I_1 \ A \quad I_2 \ A \quad I_3 \ B \quad I_4 \ A \quad I_5 \ B$$

where I_i denotes an item of information (case description). To predict categorization on a test of item I_1 at the end of this sequence, we combine I_1 with A and with B and compute the similarity of each combination to the memory array, obtaining

$$\text{Sim}(I_1,A) \ = \ 1+2s+2s\sigma \tag{6.8}$$

and

$$\text{Sim}(I_1,B) \ = \ 2s+\sigma+2s\sigma, \tag{6.9}$$

and for the probability of assigning the item to Category A, we have

$$P(A) \ = \ (1+2s+2s\sigma)/(1+4s+\sigma+4s\sigma). \tag{6.10}$$

If, for example, we let $s=0.5$ and $\sigma=0$, then $P(A)=0.67$ and $P(B)=0.33$. If $\sigma=0.2$, then $P(A)=0.61$ and $P(B) \ = \ 0.39$. It is easily verified that $P(A)$ and $P(B)$ both move toward 1/2 as σ increases from 0 to 1.

By means of a variation on this example, we can bring out another aspect of category confusability. For a categorization task involving more than two categories, an increase in the mutual confusability of a subset of categories will increase the probability that a test exemplar will be assigned to that subset rather than to a category outside the subset. To illustrate, we will expand the example above to a three-category situation in which Categories A and B have similarity σ to each other but each has similarity zero to

Category C. In terms of the accident ward scenario, Categories A and B might be "critical" and "serious" and Category C "stable." A trial sequence (and memory array at the end) might then be

$$I_1 \ A \quad I_2 \ B \quad I_3 \ C \quad I_4 \ A \quad I_5 \ C$$

for which a test on I_1 would yield the category similarities

$$\text{Sim}(I_1,A) = 1+s\sigma+0+s+0, \tag{6.11}$$

$$\text{Sim}(I_1,B) = \sigma+s+0+s\sigma+0, \tag{6.12}$$

$$\text{Sim}(I_1,C) = 0+0+s+0+s, \tag{6.13}$$

where the terms are entered in the order of the trial sequence. Then we have for the categorization probabilities on a test with I_1

$$P(A) = (1+s+s\sigma)/(1+4s+\sigma+2s\sigma), \tag{6.14}$$

$$P(B) = (s+\sigma+s\sigma)/(1+4s+\sigma+2s\sigma), \tag{6.15}$$

and

$$P(C) = 2s/(1+4s+\sigma+2s\sigma). \tag{6.16}$$

Again letting $s = 0.5$ and $\sigma = 0$, these probabilities are $P(A) = 0.50$, $P(B) = 0.17$, and $P(C) = 0.33$; but if σ increases to 0.2, the probabilities are $P(A) = 0.47$, $P(B) = 0.24$, and $P(C) = 0.29$; and we see that the probability of A and B combined has increased at the expense of C.

A comment is in order about the sense in which the term category confusability, or category similarity, is being used. When, in this computation, the experience of perceiving item I_1 together with category label A is represented as I_1, A in the memory array of the exemplar model, the element A is being interpreted as a value on a "categorical" attribute, which in the example has B and C as the other possible values. When I speak of the confusability, or similarity, between category labels (or, for brevity, just "categories") A and B, for example, I am referring, not to similarity between the printed labels "A" and "B" but rather to similarity between their mental representations. When the labels are arbitrary symbols, which is sometimes the case in experimental studies, their mental representations may comprise simply the visual or auditory features of the symbols. But when the labels are meaningful (as in the case of critical, serious, stable), the representations include semantic features or attributes.

The general idea is that categories may be conceived to be represented as points in a similarity space, with similarity between particular categories inversely related to their separation in the space, just as has been assumed for objects (category exemplars) and features of objects in the discussions of similarity in Chapters 1–5. For purposes of operating with the model, all we need to know, or assume, about the detailed properties of a categorical attribute is wrapped up in the similarity parameter, σ, whose numerical value in a given situation is estimable in the same way as any other similarity

Table 6.1 Design of illustrative experiment on transfer of a categorization

	Condition			
	Transfer		Control	
	C_1	C_2		
a	n_0	0		
b	0	n_0		
	C_3	C_4	C_3	C_4
a	n	0	n	0
b	0	n	0	n
$P_a(C_3) =$	$\dfrac{n+\sigma n_0+s_0}{(1+s)(n+\sigma n_0)+2s_0}$		$\dfrac{n+s_0}{n(1+s)+2s_0}$	

parameter.* Thus, people can be given the task of making similarity judgments between the categories mammal and marsupial or fish and reptile just as they make such judgments between particular mammals or particular fish. And the results from the similarity judgments can be used to estimate the similarity parameter σ just as judgments of featural similarity can be used to estimate the parameter s in the exemplar model.

6.2.2 Transfer between categorizations

The positive transfer that would be expected between related categorizations can be interpreted in terms of the augmented array model, which takes account of similarity between categories. To illustrate the kind of transfer I refer to, imagine a person from some third country who has visited both the US and Britain and has occasion while in Britain to learn to discriminate between the Labour and Tory parties on the basis of certain attributes of members. We might expect that learning this categorization would be easier if the person had previously learned to categorize Democrats versus Republicans in the US on the basis of the same or similar attributes. In Table 6.1, this illustration is translated into a design for an experiment that could

---

* In experimental research, and probably for the most part in ordinary life, labels for categories are chosen so as to be dissimilar enough to make confusability of labels negligible. In an application of the exemplar model to any situation in which confusability of labels did occur, labels would be treated as features and similarity on this feature would be computed in the same way as similarity on other features. For an instructive discussion of the distinction between forming a category representation and attaching a label, or name, to the category, see Schyns (1991).

test for such transfer. Starting from the initial memory state, I_0, for each category, a learner in the Transfer condition first has n_0 trials on feature a with category C_1 correct intermixed with n_0 trials on feature b with C_2 correct and subsequently n trials on feature a with C_3 correct and n trials on feature b with C_4 correct. In the control condition, the first phase is omitted, so we can compare rate of learning of the C_3/C_4 categorization with or without the prior experience on the C_1/C_2 categorization.

We assume that similarities between C_1 and C_3 and between C_2 and C_4 each have some positive value (i.e., $\sigma > 0$) and that all other between-category similarities are equal to zero. The similarity-to-category values for a test on either feature following the C_3/C_4 training, computed in the usual way, are entered in the standard formula to obtain the probability of assigning the

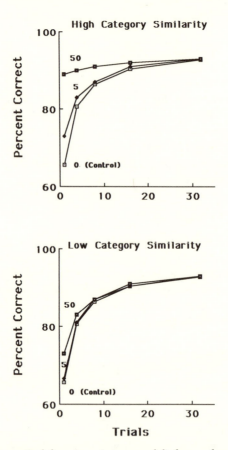

Fig. 6.1 Theoretical functions (array model) for performance on a new category learning task after previous learning of a related categorization. Category similarity is 0.20 in the upper and 0.02 in the lower panel, and the parameter of the curve family within each panel is number of trials on the previous categorization.

feature to a category. The resulting expressions for the probability of response C_3 to feature a (the probability of C_4 to feature b would be the same) are shown for the transfer and control conditions at the bottom of Table 6.1. Obviously, the probability will be higher for the transfer condition whenever n_0 is greater than 0, meaning that there will generally be a positive transfer effect with a magnitude directly related to the value of σ.

To illustrate the predictions, learning curves for the second (C_3/C_4) categorization following 0, 5, or 50 trials on the first categorization were computed for two levels of category similarity and are exhibited in Fig. 6.1. The parameter values were $s = 0.05$, $s_0 = 1$, and $\sigma = 0.20$ for the upper and $s = .02$ for the lower panel.

The prior training on C_1/C_2 yields an advantage over the control condition on the first C_3/C_4 trial. The advantage is much greater for the larger value of category similarity, but it quickly dissipates as learning on C_3/C_4 continues.

I do not know of formal experiments designed to test for this kind of transfer, but it may often be involved in second language learning, in view of the familiar observation that learning the phonetic and grammatical categories of a second language is easier the more closely the new categories resemble those of the learner's first language.

6.2.3 The burden of the past: interference in learning successive categorizations or discriminations

The residue of earlier experiences in memory can hinder as well as facilitate the learning of later categorizations. For example, it may be difficult to learn an actually significant relation between intake of a particular substance and a disease if in one's earlier experience the substance has been observed to be unrelated to health conditions. In a familiar experimental paradigm for the analysis of this kind of interference, a group of subjects first has experience with a categorization task in which a particular set of cues is irrelevant (i.e., an invalid predictor of category membership), then is given continued training with the task unaltered except that the formerly irrelevant set of cues becomes relevant (i.e., is now a valid predictor). Learning in the second phase regularly proves to be retarded in comparison with that of control subjects for whom the first phase was omitted (LaBerge 1959; Levine 1971; Nelson 1976).

The applicability of the array model to this problem can be illustrated with reference to the schematic summary of this paradigm presented in Table 6.2. First, let us consider only the left-hand portion of the table, labelled Same because the same categories are involved in both Phase 1 and Phase 2. In Phase 1, the cues a and b (which may denote either single features or combinations of features) are invalid predictors of categories C_1 and C_2, each

Table 6.2 Retardation of category learning in a current task (phase 2) when cues basic to the current categorization were irrelevant in a previous task (Phase 1)

		Categorical relationship				
		Same			Different	
	Cue	C_1'	C_2	Cue	C_3	C_4
Phase 1	a	n_0	n_0	c	n_0	n_0
	b	n_0	n_0	d	n_0	n_0
		C_1	C_2		C_1	C_2
Phase 2	a	n	0	c	n	0
	b	0	n	d	0	n
$P_r(1) =$		$\dfrac{n+n_0(1+s)}{(n+2n_0)(1+s)}$			$\dfrac{n+\sigma n_0(1+s)}{(n+2\sigma n_0)(1+s)}$	

Note: s denotes similarity between cues; σ denotes similarity between categories C_1 and C_3 and between C_2 and C_4; similarities between C_1 and C_2 and between C_3 and C_4 are equal to zero.

occurring in each category on n_0 trials. In Phase 2, these cues become valid predictors, a occurring n times in Category 1 and b occurring n times in category 2. Analogously to previous applications of the model to category learning, we assume that the memory arrays at the end of Phase 2 have the same form as the design matrices shown in Table 6.2 (so the number of stored instances of cue a in category C_1 is n_0+n, and so on).

For a test on cue a (or b) at the end of Phase 2, application of the product rule to the memory arrays in the usual way yields the probabilities of correct categorization shown at the bottom of the table. With the value of s, the parameter for similarity between a and b, set equal to zero, the left-hand equation at the bottom of Table 6.2 yields the functions shown in the upper panel of Fig. 6.2 for the development of the categorization over n Phase 2 trials preceded by 100, 500, or 5000 earlier, non-differentiating, trials. The functions all begin with probability of correct categorization at chance, of course, then diverge as the categorization is learned, with rate of learning inversely related to number of Phase 1 trials.

The model predicts that similar interference should be observed if the categories involved in Phase 1 and Phase 2 are not identical but only related by similarity. For an everyday life example, learning that taking aspirin is related to the risk of heart disease might be retarded by earlier experience in which taking aspirin was observed to be unrelated to risk of catching the common cold. I do not know of any relevant formal experiments, but one

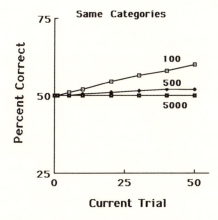

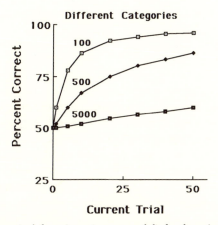

Fig. 6.2 Theoretical functions (array model) for learning of a new categorization based on certain cues after previous experience (100, 500, or 5000 trials) with a task in which the same cues were randomly related to the categories.

could easily be devised, and an appropriate design would have the form illustrated in the right-hand part of Table 6.2. Cues c and d are irrelevant during learning of the C_3 versus C_4 categorization in Phase 1 but become relevant during learning of the C_1 versus C_2 categorization in Phase 2. In terms of the example, c and d correspond to presence and absence of aspirin intake, C_3 and C_4 to presence and absence of a cold and C_1 and C_2 to presence and absence of heart disease. We assume that the category similarity parameter, σ, is greater than zero for comparison of C_1 with C_3 and C_2 with C_4. Computation of categorization probability at the end of Phase 2 is shown at the bottom of Table 6.2 and the predicted relation between rate of learning in Phase 2 and number of trials in Phase 1 is shown in the lower panel of Fig. 6.2.

A phenomenon that might be interpreted in terms of these predicted relationships is a striking and well-documented phenomenon in linguistics— the great difficulty often exhibited by adult speakers of a language in discriminating speech sounds that belong to the same phonetic category in the language but that are known to be discriminable by infants in the same culture (Kuhl, Williams, Lacerda, Stevens, and Lindblom 1992). A familiar example is the difficulty many adult Japanese have in distinguishing spoken English words that differ only with respect to the sounds r and l (technically, written /r/ and /l/), which in Japanese belong to the same phonetic category and therefore do not differentiate spoken words. A possible explanation of this phenomenon follows directly from the assumptions of the array-similarity model, the crux being that earlier experience during which the two sounds fall in the same category builds up a residue in memory that weighs against later ability to discriminate the sounds or to learn a new categorization based on them.

6.2.4 Learning multiple categorizations

A bonus for adopting the revised processing assumptions is that they permit an effective answer to a question that arises concerning situations in which several categorizations are learned concurrently (as in the study discussed in Chapter 4, pp. 90–96). Namely, how does the learner segregate the portions of the current memory array that represent individual categorizations so that a particular test pattern can be compared only to representations in the appropriate subarray? The answer is that no such segregation is needed. The pattern is compared to the entire memory array for the situation, and the product rule, applied to both item and category similarities, ensures that only the appropriate part of the array will contribute to the global similarity computation. This point can be conveniently illustrated in terms of an example representing a simplified version of the concurrent-categorization study discussed in Chapter 4 (Experiment 4.1).

Suppose that a task calls for the concurrent learning of three probabilistic categorizations ("problems"). Problem I involves categories 1 and 2 and a stimulus pattern, a, that occurs more often in category 1 than category 2; Problem II involves categories 3 and 4 and a pattern, b, that occurs more often in category 4 than category 3; and Problem III involves categories 5 and 6 and a pattern, c, that occurs predominantly in category 6. On each trial of a learning series, a problem is randomly selected and the learner is shown the appropriate stimulus pattern and choice of categories, (for example, if Problem II is chosen, the display is "b: Category 3 or Category 4?"). A series of trials would generate a memory array like the one portrayed in Table 6.3. To predict the result of a test on Problem I at this point (the query

Table 6.3 Memory array formed during learning of concurrent categorizations

Exemplar	Category					
	1	2	3	4	5	6
a	2	1	0	0	0	0
b	0	0	1	3	0	0
c	0	0	0	0	1	2

The array is the result of 10 trials, three each on Problems I and III, and four on Problem II. Cell entries are frequencies of occurrence of exemplars in categories.

to the learner being "a: Category 1 or Category 2?"), we first compute total similarities. In this example, we will assume that the pairwise similarities of the exemplar patterns all have the same value, s, that the similarity between the two category labels within any problem is 0, and that the similarities between category labels of different problems all have the same value, σ, which in general is greater than 0. With those assumptions, we obtain for similarity of the combination of exemplar a and Category 1 to the array

$$Sim(a,1) = 2+\sigma s(1+3+1+2) = 2+7\sigma s, \qquad (6.17)$$

and for the combination of exemplar a and category 2

$$Sim(a,2) = 1+\sigma s(1+3+1+2) = 1+7\sigma s. \qquad (6.18)$$

These similarities yield for the probability of choosing category 1

$$P(1) = (2+7\sigma s)/(3+14\sigma s). \qquad (6.19)$$

We see that if either similarity parameter is equal to 0, $P(1)$ is equal to 2/3, the proportion of trials with Problem I on which exemplar a occurred with category 1 designated correct; but if both similarity parameters are not zero, $P(1)$ will have a lower value.

With the category similarity parameter, σ, added to the model, expressions for response probabilities in Experiment 4.1 would have the same general form as the one derived for this example. In terms of the model, the subjects in that experiment were able to learn four concurrent problems with very little inter-problem interference only because the value of σ was near zero for the category labels used in the study.

6.2.5 Category learning in relation to number of categories

In studies of expertise, it has been suggested that expert problem solvers tend to segment their domains into finer and more specific categories than do novices (Schyns 1991; Tanaka and Taylor 1991). Doubtless many factors are at work, but with the model at hand, we can address a basic question of some interest: how does category learning depend on the number of categories defined for a task? We cannot hope for a completely general answer because all other relevant factors cannot be held constant while number of categories varies. If, for example, the number of exemplars per category is held constant, then the total number of exemplars entering into learning necessarily increases with the number of categories. If, instead, the total number of exemplars is held constant, then the number of exemplars per category must vary. I will apply the model to the latter case, which seems the more interesting in connection with the research on expertise.

I will start with a simple example and then generalize the results. The task will involve a total of six exemplar patterns, indexed by $k=1,2,\ldots,6$, with pairwise similarities all equal to the same parameter s, and all exemplars being perfectly valid predictors of their categories. For a 2-category task, the memory array after a learning experience in which each exemplar occurs once* will be

Exemplar	Category	
	A	B
1	1	0
2	1	0
3	1	0
4	0	1
5	0	1
6	0	1

and we will proceed to derive the probability of correct categorization of exemplar 1 on a test. Denoting the category-similarity parameter by σ, as before, we obtain for the similarities of exemplar 1 to Categories A and B

$$\text{Sim}(1,A) = 1+2s+3s\sigma \tag{6.20}$$

and

$$\text{Sim}(1,B) = 3s+\sigma+2s\sigma, \tag{6.21}$$

yielding,

$$P(A) = (1+2s+3s\sigma)/(1+5s+\sigma+5s\sigma). \tag{6.22}$$

For $s=0.5$ and $\sigma=0.2$, these quantities take on the values

$$\text{Sim}(1,A) = 1+1+0.3 = 2.3$$

$$\text{Sim}(1,B) = 1.5+0.2+0.2 = 1.9$$

and

$$P(A) = 2.3/4.2 = 0.548.$$

---

* All results derived in this section will hold for any number n of occurrences for each exemplar. In terms of the exemplar-similarity model of Chapter 3, I am, for simplicity, letting the preload parameter, s_0, equal 0 and assuming no decay.

If we now keep all other specifications constant but expand the number of categories to three, the memory array becomes

Exemplar	A	B	C
1	1	0	0
2	1	0	0
3	0	1	0
4	0	1	0
5	0	0	1
6	0	0	1

and we obtain

$$\mathrm{Sim}(1,\mathrm{A}) = 1+s+4s\sigma \tag{6.23}$$

$$\mathrm{Sim}(1,\mathrm{B}) = \mathrm{Sim}(1,\mathrm{C}) = 2s+\sigma(1+s)+2s\sigma, \tag{6.24}$$

and

$$P(\mathrm{A}) = (1+s+4s\sigma)/(1+5s+2\sigma+10s\sigma). \tag{6.25}$$

For $s=0.5$ and $\sigma=0.2$, these quantities take on the values

$$\mathrm{Sim}(1,\mathrm{A}) = 1+0.5+0.4 = 1.9$$

$$\mathrm{Sim}(1,\mathrm{B}) = 1+0.2+0.1+0.2 = 1.5$$

and

$$P(\mathrm{A}) = 1.9/4.9 = 0.388,$$

so increasing the number of categories from 2 to 3 has lowered the probability of a correct categorization.

In general, for this structure, with K categories and m exemplars per category, the similarities are

$$\mathrm{Sim}(1,\mathrm{A}) = 1+(m-1)s+(K-1)ms\sigma, \tag{6.27}$$

and

$$\mathrm{Sim}(1,\mathrm{X}) = ms+\sigma(1+(m-1)s)+(K-2)ms\sigma, \tag{6.27}$$

where X denotes any of the $K-1$ categories other than A. For the categorization probability on a test of exemplar 1, we then have

$$P(\mathrm{A}) = \mathrm{Sim}(1,\mathrm{A})/(\mathrm{Sim}(1,\mathrm{A})+(K-1)\mathrm{Sim}(1,\mathrm{X})). \tag{6.28}$$

This function is illustrated in Fig. 6.3 for several combinations of feature and category similarity in cases with the total number of exemplars equal to 24 or 72. Probability of a correct categorization decreases as a function of the number of categories in all instances, with the decrease being steeper for larger similarities and for the larger total number of exemplars.

The specific trends over number of categories seen in Fig. 6.3 depend, of course, on the simplifying assumptions in the derivation, especially the

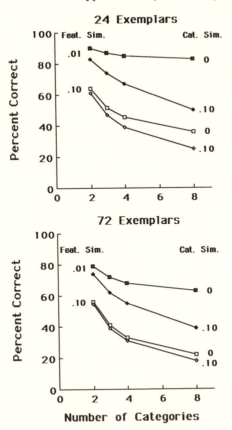

Fig. 6.3 Predictions of the array model for categorization as a function of number of categories at two category sizes with feature similarity (Feat. Sim.), and category similarity (Cat. Sim.) as parameters.

assumptions of equal pairwise similarities between exemplars and of equal frequencies of occurrence of all exemplars. The trends may be quite robust over moderate departures from these constraints, as illustrated by the following example in which the assumption of equal presentation frequencies is relaxed. Consider the 2- and 3- exemplar designs

Exemplar	Category	
	A	B
1–3	2	0
4–6	1	0
7–9	0	2
10–12	0	1

and

	A	B	C
1,2	2	0	0
4,5	1	0	0
3,7	0	2	0
6,10	0	1	0
8,9	0	0	2
11,12	0	0	1

Deriving the similarities and categorization probabilities as before, and again letting $s=0.5$ and $\sigma=0.2$, we obtain 0.533 and 0.382 for probability of a correct categorization on a test of an exemplar that occurred twice during learning in the 2- and 3-category cases, respectively, and 0.518 and 0.353 on a test of an exemplar that occurred once—the effect of number of categories thus being not very different from that computed above under the assumption of equal presentation frequencies.

The import of these results for the question of how performance on cognitive tasks may be affected by the fineness of classification imposed on a set of patterns is not simple. When the category structure to be learned is prescribed by an experimenter or by a task environment, we must evidently expect the level of learning to be reduced as the number of categories increases. There are compensating factors, however. We noted in Chapter 5 that one of the most important purposes of categorization is to enable the learner to predict or recall frequencies of occurrence of patterns or features within categories; and, as a fixed set of patterns is mapped onto an increasing number of categories, the sizes of the categories must decrease, generally resulting in an increase in the probability of predicting or recalling the most frequent exemplar or the most frequent feature within any category. Further, the analysis underlying Fig. 6.3 depends on the assumption that pairwise similarities of exemplar patterns are constant, at least on the average, within and between categories. However, in situations where an individual is free to form a category structure (that is, to choose the number of categories and the mode of assignment of patterns to categories), this assumption may be systematically violated in a way that could cause the level of learning attainable to increase with increasing numbers of categories. The value of the model in more complex and less constrained cases is to indicate the kind of information that must be obtained and how it must enter into computations in order to enable appropriate predictions.

6.2.6 Effects of category size

Several studies yield the overall impression that the level of performance reached in category learning increases with category size (Homa and Vosburgh 1976; Homa, Sterling, and Trepel 1981; Knapp and Anderson 1984; Breen and Schvaneveldt 1986; Shin and Nosofsky 1991), but, as with number of categories, there are many potentially confounding factors. In order to examine effects of size independently of number of categories, I will limit consideration to cases in which the number of categories is fixed. Within this class, it might seem straightforward to compare the learning of groups of subjects with each group having a different number of exemplars per category; however, category size would be confounded with total number of items presented during learning, which in itself is a strong determiner of test performance. More interesting is a commonly used design in which the total number of items is fixed but different numbers of exemplars are assigned to different categories and all exemplars occur with equal frequency during learning (Breen and Schvaneveldt 1986; Shin and Nosofsky 1991, Experiment 2). Predictions for this case can readily be derived from the exemplar model.

For a convenient illustrative design, I will fix the total number of exemplars at 72 and the number of categories at 3 and consider three particular arrangements, two unequal-frequency cases, one with 12, 24, and 36 and one with 6, 24, and 42 exemplars assigned to Categories A, B, and C, respectively, and an equal-frequency case with 24 exemplars assigned to each category. As in the analysis of number of categories, I assume that all exemplar patterns have the same pairwise similarity, s. The pattern of predictions will be independent of the number of learning trials, as long as the number is the same for all exemplars, so I have carried out computations for the simplest case of a test of an exemplar from each category following a learning series in which each exemplar occurs once. The computation of global similarities of test items to categories and, based on these, categorization probabilities on the tests, proceeds exactly as in the analysis given above for number of categories, so I will give only illustrative results obtained for a sample of parameter combinations—s=0.10 or 0.01 and σ=0.05 or 0.

For a picture of the effect of category size, I have combined the results for the three category structures to obtain the functions relating percentage of correct categorizations to category size shown in Fig. 6.4. Over the range of category sizes considered, the functions prove to be virtually linear, with the slopes determined mainly by item similarity for the parameter values used in the computations. I have no data at hand suitable for quantitative testing of the model, but the predictions appear to be qualitatively in line with published results.

Another question that can be raised concerning this design is how the distribution of exemplars over the three categories affects the average level of test performance for a task. From the same computations that generated Fig. 6.4, the predicted levels for each of the three category structures can readily be calculated, and these are summarized in Table 6.4. Average percentages of correct categorizations of test items increase uniformly across the rows, as both item similarity and category similarity decrease; and, more inter-

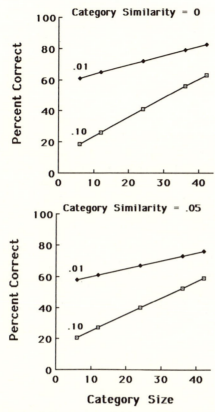

Fig. 6.4 Predictions of the array model for categorization as a function of category size at two levels of category similarity with feature similarity (0.01 or 0.10) as a parameter.

Table 6.4 Predicted performance levels (percentage correct) in tasks with different numbers of exemplars per category

Numbers of exemplars			Item Similarity			
			0.10		0.01	
Category			Category Similarity		Category Similarity	
A	B	C	0.05	0	0.05	0
24	24	24	40	41	67	72
12	24	36	44	46	69	74
6	24	42	49	52	71	77

estingly, these percentages also increase uniformly from the uniform (24,24,24) to the most diverse (6,24,42) distribution of exemplars to categories.

6.2.7 Causal relations

For another illustration of the convenience of operating with processing assumptions 1–3, let us consider the situation that might arise if one were learning a causal relationship purely from a series of observations. Similarity is a key factor, as in previous treatments of category-based induction (Rips 1975; Osherson, Smith, Wilkie, Lopez, and Shafir 1990; Smith, Lopez, and Osherson 1992). For an everyday illustration, consider a situation comprising a panel with a switch that, when moved to the "on" position, may start a motor. Denoting the background context in which the relevant events occur by x, a causal variable (turning the switch on) by v, an effect of v (starting of the motor) by E, and absence of E by E_0, we can represent an initial situation in which the context alone is present and E does not occur by xE_0 and a subsequent occasion on which v is present and E does occur by xvE. To apply the exemplar model, I will assume that features corresponding to x, v, E, and E_0 are stored in memory, yielding the memory array

$$xE_0$$

$$xvE$$

If we now test the learner by presenting xv and asking whether E will occur, similarities of the test pattern xv to the memory array are computed just as in the example above:

$$\text{Sim}(xv,E) = 1+s\sigma \tag{6.29}$$

$$\text{Sim}(xv,E_0) = s+\sigma, \tag{6.30}$$

where s and σ are again the similarity parameters for features and category labels, respectively; and for the expectation of the effect (that is, the probability of classifying the test situation as one in which E will occur), we obtain

$$P(E) = (1+s\sigma)/(1+s)(1+\sigma). \tag{6.31}$$

If σ is equal to 0, probably the most typical case, this expression reduces to

$$P(E) = 1/(1+s), \tag{6.32}$$

and $P(E)$ depends only on the perceived similarity between presence and absence of the causal variable v.

To look at the effect of repetition, suppose that, in the same situation, operation of the switch were observed (that is, the combination xvE occurred) K times. Then Equations 6.29 and 6.30 become

$$\text{Sim}(xv,E) = K+s\sigma \qquad (6.33)$$

and

$$\text{Sim}(xv,E_0) = s+K\sigma, \qquad (6.34)$$

respectively, and for expectation of the effect, we have

$$P(E) = (K+s\sigma)/(K+s)(1+\sigma). \qquad (6.35)$$

If E and E_0 are distinct, that is, σ is equal to 0, Equation 6.35 reduces to

$$P(E) = K/(K+s) \qquad (6.36)$$

and obviously $P(E)$ approaches unity as K becomes large, regardless of the value of s. Increasing the value of σ (making presence and absence of E more

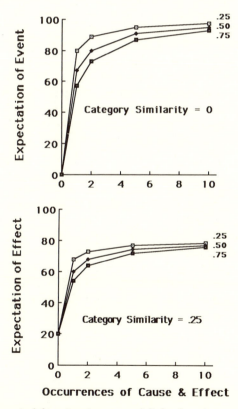

Fig. 6.5 Theoretical function (array model) for learning to expect an event E (an effect) in the presence of a causal variable v. The parameters of the families of curves are values of the inter-item similarity parameter, s.

similar) reduces $P(E)$, the expectation of the effect, at every value of K, as illustrated in Fig. 6.5. When K is equal to 0 in Equations 6.35 and 6.36, $P(E)$ is, of course, the expectation that the effect will occur in the presence of v when neither v nor E has yet occurred (i.e., only x, E_0 has been observed).

To give the model a more strenuous exercise, let us examine an experiment on the evaluation of evidence in causal inference reported by Schustack and Sternberg (1981). Their subjects were asked to judge the strength of a causal relationship between a set of events (hypothesized causes) and an outcome (effect). A problem consisted of a hypothesis and a description of several situations, each including a number of possibly causal events. The three problems used in each of three experiments are presented in abstract format in Table 6.5. In Problem 2 of Experiment 1, for example, the outcome of interest is labelled G and its absence –G; the causal events are denoted a, b, c, d, and e. In the first of five situations presented, events a, b, and c occurred and were followed by outcome G. In the second situation, event d occurred and events a and c were specified to be absent, and outcome G did not follow. The hypothesis to be evaluated, denoted a > G, was that event a causes outcome G.*

On the basis of Schustack and Sternberg's analyses of the ways in which various kinds of causal evidence might be used by the subjects, the problems in the three columns of Table 6.5, from left to right, were expected to yield high, moderate, and low likelihood judgments, respectively; the results were in qualitative accord with these expectations and were quite well described by a linear regression model. A question of prime interest with respect to the array model is whether it is able to generate a priori predictions of the order of the observed likelihood judgments for the three problems in all three experiments.

To analyze this study in terms of the model, I assume that on each study trial the subject stores in memory a representation of the events and the outcome just as in a categorization task, generating a memory array for each problem of the same form as the problem representation in Table 6.5 (with the addition of a preload item, described in Appendix 6.1). To evaluate the likelihood that the outcome specified in the hypothesis will be produced by the cause, the subject computes the probability that a situation comprising only the event specified in the hypothesis belongs to the the class of situations that have included the outcome rather than the class that have not,

---

* The problems of Experiment 3 were presented to additional groups of subjects in the form of fictional scenarios. One scenario, for example, had to do with epidemics, and a hypothesis to be evaluated was that introduction of a new hair dye in a city would lead to an epidemic of a certain disease, causal events in the situations presented including introduction of the hair dye, break in a water main, and stopping inspection of food service workers. The subject's response to a situation was an estimate of the likelihood that the event specified in the hypothesis would produce the outcome. Results for these groups did not differ greatly from those for the group receiving the abstract format.

Table 6.5 Abstract designs of causal reasoning problems (after Schustack and Sternberg 1981)

			Strength of Evidence			
High		Moderate		Low		
Event	Outcome	Event	Outcome	Event	Outcome
Experiment 1					
z	–M	abc	G	h	B
sy	M	d	–G	r	–B
y	M	bde	G	fh	B
		abd	G	a	–B
		e	–G		
Hypothesis: y>M		a>G		d>B	
Experiment 2					
qw	U	skvp	J	uwbq	–J
w	U	svp	J	yfkm	J
rw	U			ywkm	–J
				ywbm	–J
				ykm	–J
Hypothesis: w>U		s>J		w>J	
Experiment 3					
lwv	N	swnt	R	d	G
w	N	snz	–R	bd	–G
zwv	N	swtz	R	v	G
w	N	t	–R	bj	–G
Hypothesis: w>N		s>R		b>G	

just as in a categorization task (the details of the computation being illustrated in Appendix 6.1). The expressions derived for probabilities associated with the hypotheses of the problems are summarized in Table 6.6. A little algebra shows that for any combination of parameter values (except both equal to 0) these probabilities predict the observed order of difficulty of the three problems in all three experiments. With the similarity parameter, s, set equal to 0.2 and the background similarity parameter equal to 1, we obtain the probabilities (predicted likelihood judgments) shown in Table 6.7. These values do not, of course, predict the data as well as the regression model (with many more parameters) fitted to the data by Schustack and Sternberg (1981), but they do illustrate that it is possible to account for the main trends quite well on the basis only of assumptions about similarity

Table 6.6　Expressions for predicted likelihood judgments in Schustack and Sternberg (1981) study

Experiment	Observed level of judgments		
	High	Moderate	Low
1	$2/(2+s+s_0)$	$(2+s)/(2+3s+s_0)$	$2s/(4s+s_0)$
2	$3/(3+s_0)$	$2/(2+s_0)$	$s/(3+2s+s_0)$
3	$4/(4+s_0)$	$2/(3+s+s_0)$	$2s/(2s+2+s_0)$

Table 6.7　Illustrative predictions of cause-effect likelihood judgments computed from formulas in Table 6.6

Experiment	Observed level of judgments		
	High	Moderate	Low
1	0.65	0.46	0.19
2	0.75	0.40	0.13
3	0.74	0.35	0.10
	Predicted level of judgments		
1	0.63	0.61	0.22
2	0.75	0.67	0.05
3	0.80	0.49	0.12

Note: Predictions base on parameter values $s=0.15$, $s_c=0.95$

relationships. Without denying that other factors undoubtedly enter into the subjects' evaluations of causal evidence, we find support for the idea that one important basis for causal evaluations is to be found in the similarity relations between the events described in a hypothesis and those previously experienced in relevant situations.

6.2.8 The "dilution effect"

An aspect of causal judgments that is of interest in social psychology has to do with people's expectations about the behavior of others given information about possibly relevant causal factors. In a study reported by Nisbett, Zukier, and Lemley (1981), for example, experimental subjects (college students) were presented with vignettes describing a hypothetical situation in which other students who were participating in a study of the properties of a certain pain-suppressant drug were asked to accept as strong an electric shock, delivered to the fingertips, as they could stand. On an experimental trial, a subject was given information about a hypothetical student and predicted whether she or he would accept a particular shock intensity. As illustrated in Table 6.8, two types of information were provided. (1) Information that may be termed "diagnostic," comprising attributes that students believe to be relevant to the likelihood of taking shock; for example, A might be an engineering major and B a music major. (2) Information that may be termed "non-diagnostic," comprising attributes that students believe to be irrelevant; for example, one of the entries e, f, g, or h might be year in school. The principal finding was that when subjects were given only diagnostic information about two hypothetical students, say that S1 was an engineering major and S2 a music major, they predicted a large difference (on the order of 35 percentage points) in the students' likelihoods of taking a shock, but when given the same diagnostic information accompanied by some non-diagnostic information, the subjects predicted a much smaller difference (on the order of 12 percentage points). The investigators termed this phenomenon the "dilution effect"—a

Table 6.8 Memory array for an illustration of the dilution effect

Attribute		Outcome	
		Shock	No shock
A		5	1
B		1	5
e		3	3
f		3	3
g		3	3
h		3	3

Test attributes	$P(S)$*	Value of s		
		0	0.05	0.10
A	$\dfrac{5+13s}{6+30s}$	0.83	0.75	0.70
Aef	$\dfrac{11+7s}{18(1+s)}$	0.61	0.60	0.59
Aefgh	$\dfrac{17+s}{30+6s}$	0.57	0.56	0.56

* $P(S)$ denotes probability of accepting shock.

tendency for the effect of diagnostic information on causal predictions to be diluted by the addition of non-diagnostic information.

Looking at the dilution effect in terms of the array model, we assume that the key factor must be the effect of non-diagnostic information on the set of similarity comparisons that underlies the subjects' judgments. When asked to predict whether a hypothetical student will or will not take a shock (the events labeled Shock and No shock in Table 6.8), a subject is assumed to compare the information given about the student with the contents of the relevant memory array and assign the student to the category of people who do take the given shock intensity or the category of those who do not. With the actual experimental design of Nisbett, Zukier, and Lemley (1981) simplified a bit for convenience, prediction probabilities were computed in the standard manner and these results are shown in Table 6.8. The numerical entries under Shock and No shock signify the subjects' expectation that a student with attribute A would take shock five times out of six, a student with attribute B, one time out of six, a student with attribute e, 3 times out of 6, and so on. To predict test probabilities, the set of features presented on the test is compared to the columns of the memory array for Shock and No shock and the similarities computed just as in a categorization task. The result is that (except for the uninteresting case of $s=1$) the dilution effect is predicted—as the number of non-diagnostic features presented on the test increases, the subject's expectation that the student will take the shock decreases.

6.3 From categorization to recall

6.3.1 Simple cued recall of paired associates

Within the framework of the array model family, it is a short step from categorization to phenomena of memory that do not obviously involve classification and that customarily go under other labels. An important case is recall. Although some varieties of recall require analyses that would take us too far afield at this point, cued recall from a limited set of response alternatives can be treated in exactly the same way as forced-choice pattern completion (discussed in Chapter 5).

Extension of the core array-similarity model from binary categorization to cued recall of a typical paired-associate list can be conveniently illustrated in terms of a study reported by Medin, Dewey, and Murphy (1983). The two conditions of their study that are relevant to this discussion are illustrated in Table 6.9. The stimuli, numbered 1–8 in the table, were photographs of women's faces. In the categorization condition, subjects were told that the women belonged to two families. On each trial, a photo was shown; the subject tried to assign it to the proper category (family) by selecting one of two surnames, Asch or Boyd; following the response, the correct surname

Table 6.9 Extension of the array-similarity model from categorization to paired-associate learning

Photo	Category		Name							
	Asch	Boyd	Anne	Sara	Cora	Emma	Mary	Joan	Lucy	Ruth
1	n	0	n	0	0	0	0	0	0	0
2	n	0	0	n	0	0	0	0	0	0
3	n	0	0	0	n	0	0	0	0	0
4	n	0	0	0	0	n	0	0	0	0
5	0	n	0	0	0	0	n	0	0	0
6	0	n	0	0	0	0	0	n	0	0
7	0	n	0	0	0	0	0	0	n	0
8	0	n	0	0	0	0	0	0	0	n

was displayed. In the paired-associate condition, the subjects' task was to learn the first names of the women. On each trial, a photo was shown; the subject chose one of the eight alternative names* (the list of names having been made available in advance); following the response, the correct name was shown.

The two columns under Category in Table 6.9 can be taken to represent the memory array at the end of n training trials for a subject in the categorization condition, n representations of faces 1–4 being stored with Asch as the category label and n representations of faces 5–8 being stored with Boyd as the category label. The remaining columns represent the memory array for a subject under the paired-associate learning condition, n representations of each face being stored with one of the names as the correct response label.

Computation of categorization probabilities is done exactly as in the applications of the revised processing assumptions presented in the previous sections of this chapter and yields for the probability of assigning any face to the correct category

$$P(C) = (1+3s)/(1+7s), \tag{6.37}$$

where s is the stimulus similarity parameter (and the category similarity parameter has been assumed equal to 0).

To deal with the paired-associate condition, it will be convenient to replace the "name" column headings in Table 6.9 by response numbers 1–8 and to start with the assumption that the category similarity (interpreted in this case as response similarity) parameter is equal to 0. On a test with a

---

* The Medin, Dewey, and Murphy (1983) study actually had five stimuli in the Asch and four in the Boyd category. I have dropped one member of the Asch category to simplify the illustrative calculations.

particular stimulus, say Face 1, we first combine it with Response 1 and note that similarity of this combination to the memory array is equal to n since all cells in the Response 1 column except the first have 0 entries. Next, we combine stimulus 1 with any one of the remaining responses and obtain ns for similarity of the combination to the memory array. Thus, we obtain for probability of a correct response (Response 1) to Face 1

$$P(C) = n/(n+7ns) = 1/(1+7s). \qquad (6.38)$$

Probability of a correct response to any of the other faces takes the same form. Comparing Equations 6.37 and 6.38, it is apparent that correct response probability in the categorization condition will always be equal to or greater than in the paired-associate condition. For example, if s equals 0.1, the probabilities are 0.76 and 0.59, respectively; if s equals 0.05, they are 0.85 and 0.74; if s equals 0.01, they are 0.96 and 0.93. Obviously, the two expressions converge as s tends to 0. I have no way of estimating s for the Medin, Dewey and Murphy (1983) study (because training was carried to a criterion for each subject), but the inequality between conditions predicted by the model is qualitatively in line with their result.

The prediction that, in both the categorization and the paired-associate conditions, learning is retarded by stimulus similarity is of course in agreement with an enormous literature. Response similarity has had much less attention, but it has occasionally been examined in the paired-associate paradigm. The principal finding is that, if the response sets are thoroughly familiar to the learners, paired-associate acquisition is retarded by response similarity (Underwood, Runquist, and Schulz 1959). This relationship is readily interpreted in terms of the array model by allowing for non-zero values of the category-similarity parameter, σ, which in this case measures response similarity. To illustrate, let us assume that the value of σ is relatively high, say 0.5, for Responses 2 and 3 (i.e, the names Sara and Cora) in Table 6.9 but is equal to 0 for all other response pairs. Recomputing the similarity functions in the same way as was done in the analysis of category similarity in Chapter 5, we obtain for a test on any face except 2 or 3

$$P(C) = n/(n+7ns+2ns\sigma) = 1/(1+7s+2s\sigma), \qquad (6.39)$$

and for a test on Face 2 or 3,

$$P(C) = (n+ns\sigma)/(n+7ns+2ns\sigma) = (1+s\sigma)/(1+7s+2s\sigma). \qquad (6.40)$$

In line with the empirical result, correct response probability is reduced for both types of faces, and therefore learning is retarded for the whole list when σ is greater than 0. Perhaps counterintuitively, the decrement is greater for the stimuli with non-confusable responses than for those with confusable responses. Inserting the same values of s used above in the application of Equations 6.37 and 6.38, 0.1, 0.05, and 0.01, together with $\sigma=0.5$, we obtain $P(C)$ values of 0.58, 0.73, and 0.93 for the confusable responses (Equation

6.40) and 0.56, 0.71, and 0.93 for non-confusable responses (Equation 6.39). These values may be compared with the values 0.59, 0.74, and 0.93 obtained above for the same stimulus list with all non-confusable responses (Equation 6.38). The reason for the asymmetry between the values generated by Equations 6.39 and 6.40 is that confusions between similar responses may generate "false positives." For example, referring to the paired-associate condition of Table 6.9, some of the correct responses to Face 2 in the $\sigma=0.5$ case may be said to have come from trials on which Face 2 was misidentified as Face 3 but Response 2 occurred because of a response confusion.

6.3.2 Ordered recall

Another form of recall that has been studied extensively is ordered recall of a sequence or list of items, as in the familiar memory span test or in the short-term recall paradigm initiated by Conrad (1964, 1967). The latter will be the more convenient case for examination in terms of the array model because the procedure is better controlled and yields richer quantitative data for analysis. On each trial in an experiment of this type, the subject views a new random sequence of items, typically letters or words, on a display screen, presented at a rate that just permits vocal "shadowing" (naming) of the items as they appear. Either at the end of the sequence or after a delay during which the subject shadows a series of random digits (to prevent rehearsal), a recall test is given on which the task is to enter the items in their correct order in a row of response boxes on an answer form. The data from a series of trials are summarized in a table taking the form of a matrix with rows corresponding to list items in order of presentation and columns to the positions in which the items were recalled.

The memory array at the end of a trial on which four items, denoted a, b, c, and d, were presented is shown in Table 6.10. Referring to the matrix at the left in the table, positions 1–4 take on the same role in the model as the stimuli in categorization or paired-associate learning and the items a–d take

Table 6.10 Memory array and similarity matrix for ordered recall with immediate test

Recall Position	Memory array Item				Similarities Item			
	a	b	c	d	a	b	c	d
1	1	0	0	0	1	s	s^2	s^3
2	0	1	0	0	s	1	s	s^2
3	0	0	1	0	s^2	s	1	s
4	0	0	0	1	s^3	s^2	s	1

on the role of categories or responses. The similarity parameter s measures similarity between any two adjacent response positions (the measure for two positions separated by one step, e.g., 1 and 3, being s^2 and for two positions separated by two steps s^3). The parameter σ measures the similarity between any two non-identical items (responses); however, in this first analysis, we will assume $\sigma=0$. The cell entries indicate that one representation of each position-item combination in the presented list has been stored.

Applying the exemplar-model processing assumptions to this situation, we assume that at the start of recall, the learner pairs response a with position 1 and computes the similarity of this combination to the array, then pairs b, c, and d successively with position 1 and performs the same computation, the result being the similarities 1, s, s^2, and s^3, entered in the first row of the righthand matrix in Table 6.10. Computing response probability in the usual way, we have for the probability of response a in position 1,

$$P_1(a) = 1/(1+s+s^2+s^3),\qquad(6.41)$$

for the probability of response b in position 1

$$P_1(b) = s/(1+s+s^2+s^3),\qquad(6.42)$$

and so on. The entries for the remaining columns of the matrix are obtained similarly by probing memory with each recall position combined with each of the four responses. Entering a particular value for s, e.g., 0.5, in each cell of the matrix and computing response probabilities, we can generate the set of predicted curves for probability of recall as a function of input and output position shown in the upper panel of Fig. 6.6. For each output (recall) position, the prediction is that the item presented in that position will be recalled there with highest probability and items presented in other positions will be recalled there with probabilities that decrease with increasing separation of input and output position, a pattern seen in numerous studies of recall in the Conrad paradigm (e.g., Healy 1974; Lee and Estes 1977). The peaks of the four curves in the figure, representing percentages of responses correct in position, exhibit the familar form of the serial position curve for this situation.

The predictions shown in the upper panel of Fig. 6.6 are for recall on a test given immediately after list presentation. Usually, however, in studies done in this paradigm, tests are given after different retention intervals, and the uniform finding is that probability of correct recall decreases and distance functions flatten progressively as the retention interval lengthens (Bjork and Healy 1974; Healy 1974; Lee 1992). These phenomena have been addressed in terms of a "perturbation model," in which it is assumed that, during each short interval (of the duration of an item presentation) following list presentation, there is some probability that the positional code in memory for any list item is randomly perturbed by a unit value (Estes 1972; Lee and

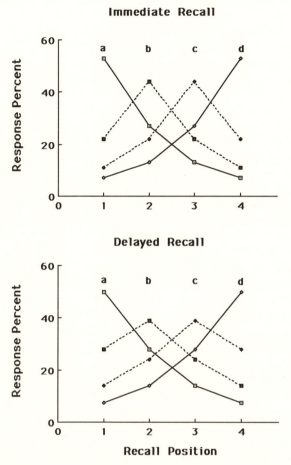

Fig. 6.6 Theoretical distance functions (array model) for ordered recall. Items a, b, c, and d were presented in that order, and on an immediate (upper panel) or delayed (lower panel) test, predicted relative frequencies of recall in positions 1–4 are as shown for each item.

Estes 1981). The situation assumed in terms of the model is shown in Table 6.11, which has the same format as Table 6.10 except that a cell entry may be interpreted as the probability with which the item presented in the column position is encoded in memory as being at the row position. Consider, for example, the column headed b after one unit interval. Item b, which started at position 2, remains at that position in the memory representation with probability $1-\theta$, where θ denotes the "perturbation probability," and moves to positions 1 and 3 each with probability $\theta/2$. To predict recall probabilities,

Table 6.11 Theoretical memory array for ordered recall after a unit retention interval

List Position	Item			
	a	b	c	d
1	$1-\theta/2$	$\theta/2$	0	0
2	$\theta/2$	$1-\theta$	$\theta/2$	0
3	0	$\theta/2$	$1-\theta$	$\theta/2$
4	0	0	$\theta/2$	$1-\theta/2$

we simply carry out similarity computations on the memory array of Table 6.11 exactly as was done above on the array of Table 6.10; the result is shown in the lower panel of Fig. 6.6. It will be seen that the model predicts the observed flattening of the distance functions.

A variable of considerable interest in this type of short-term recall is auditory similarity, or confusability, between items. The standard finding is that confusion errors increase with auditory similarity (Bjork and Healy 1974). To address this phenomenon in terms of the array model, let us suppose that in the experiment giving rise to Fig. 6.6, item c were replaced with another item, c′, that was auditorily similar to item d, all of the other inter-item similarities being low. We can implement this substitution in the model by letting the response similarity parameter, σ, have a value greater than 0, say 0.2, for the pair c′,d. Recomputing the similarities with this change, we find that the probability of incorrectly recalling item d in position 3 increases from 0.22 to 0.28 and the probability of recalling item c′ in position 4 increases from the value 0.27 that obtained for item c in the original calculation to 0.32.

So far, in considering the short-term recall situation, we have taken account only of positional errors, that is, errors scored when an item presented in a given position is recalled in a different position (e.g., the sequence presented was abcd but the recall protocol is acbd). However, under nearly all conditions, one observes also intrusion errors, that is, instances when an item presented on a trial is supplanted in recall by some non-presented item (e.g., abcd was presented but agcd recalled). Examination of a large body of data obtained with the Conrad procedure has shown that nearly all intrusion errors arise when an item presented on trial $n-1$ of a series "migrates" into the recall protocol of trial n (Lee and Estes 1981; Estes 1991*b*). Further, the intruding item is most likely to appear on trial n in the same ordinal position in which it was presented on trial $n-1$. This phenomenon is predictable by the array model on the premise that the memory representation of the list presented on a trial is not completely "cleared" at the end of the trial, so that the memory array on which

Table 6.12 Theoretical memory array for predicting intertrial intrusion errors in short-term recall

	Trial $n-1$				Trial n			
	e	f	g	h	a	b	c	d
List position								
1	1	0	0	0	1	0	0	0
2	0	1	0	0	0	1	0	0
3	0	0	1	0	0	0	1	0
4	0	0	0	1	0	0	0	1
Test position								
1	t	st	s^2t	s^3t	1	s	s^2	s^3
2	st	t	st	s^2t	s	1	s	s^2

similarity computations are performed on trial n contains not only the items of trial n but also those of at least one preceding trial. This idea is formalized by the assumption that each list item stored in memory on a trial includes a context feature, which is the same for all items of the list but differs from the context features of the lists presented on preceding trials, the difference increasing with separation (Estes 1991b).

The way in which the model operates with this augmentation can be illustrated with the aid of Table 6.12. For simplicity, I have assumed that the change of context with time is rapid enough so that we need take account of the memory array only for the trial on which recall is tested, labelled n, and the immediately preceding trial, $n-1$. To predict recall probabilities, we proceed exactly as in the example associated with Table 6.10. Starting with recall position 1, we compute the similarities of the combinations 1e, 1f, and so on to the memory array, obtaining the similarities shown in the row for Test position 1 at the bottom of the table. The entries for the trial n items are the same as those of the right-hand portion (similarity matrix) of Table 6.10, and each of them is multiplied by a parameter t, representing the similarity between the trial n and trial $n-1$ contexts, to obtain the value for the corresponding $n-1$ item. The similarities in the row are then summed to yield the denominator of the expressions for the probabilities that each item will occur in the recall protocol at position 1. Row 2 is dealt with similarly, and the rows for test positions 3 and 4 can be filled in by symmetry. With values of 0.5 for s and 0.25 (characteristic of actual applications, as in Lee and Estes 1977, 1981) for θ, these expressions yield the distance functions shown in Fig. 6.7. The functions in the upper panel are very similar to those in the upper panel of Fig. 6.6, but slightly flattened because of the allowance for intrusion errors. The gradients for the intrusion errors are shown in the lower panel and exhibit the empirically observed pattern (Estes 1991*b*), an

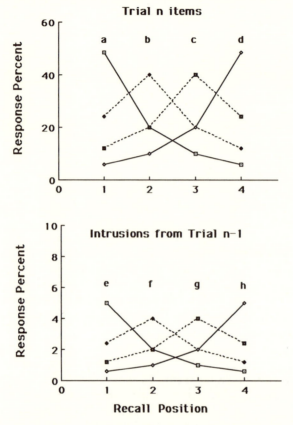

Fig. 6.7   The upper panel shows distance functions similar to those in the upper panel of Fig. 6.6 except that the levels of correct recall on a given trial, n, have been lowered somewhat because of intrusion errors from the list (e,f,g,h) presented on the preceding trial, $n-1$. The lower panel shows predicted relative frequencies of occurrence of the intruding items in positions 1–4 of the recall protocol on trial n.

item occurring in a given ordinal position on trial $n-1$ being most likely to appear in the same ordinal position as an intrusion error on trial n and increasingly less likely to appear at progressively more remote positions.

In this example all of the items presented on trial n are different from those presented on trial $n-1$. It is easy to see, however, that if an item is common to the two sets and occurs in the same position in both (e.g., item a in afgh, abcd), the intrusion from trial $n-1$ will cause an increase in probability of correct recall at that position on trial n. And, if a common item occurs in different positions on the two trials (e.g., eagh, abcd), the predicted effect will be complex: an increase in probability that the common item will be recalled on trial n but a decrease in probability that it will be recalled in the correct position. All of these predictions are in line with empirical results (Estes 1991*b*).

6.3.3 The crossover effect in sentence memory

The adaptation of the exemplar model to paired-associate learning can be taken as a schema for extending the model to varieties of cued recall that are not obviously analogous to categorization. A good example is presented by the studies of sentence memory reported by Anderson and Bower (1972, 1973). In a typical design, subjects were allowed to study a list of short sentences, each having a subject, a verb, and an object, then on test trials were presented with one or two of the first two elements (subject or verb or both) and asked to recall the object. For example, the study sentences might be

> The child hit the landlord.
> The minister praised the landlord.

An interesting, and to most people counterintuitive finding known as the *crossover effect* arises when some subjects are tested with "child hit" and others with "child praised" and it is found that the latter group, for which the recall cues come from different study sentences, exhibits a higher probability of recalling "landlord."

To analyze this experiment in terms of the assumptions of the array model, I will use an abbreviated notation for the subject, verb, and object in terms of their first letters and consider a simplified design in which the study list is just the two sentences given above plus two others. (Generalizing our results to longer lists would be a trivial exercise.) If, following study of the list

> CHL
> MPL
> DNQ
> FOQ

a test is given with CH as the cue, we compute the similarity of the combinations CHL and CHQ to the memory array. Assuming that the similarity, σ, between L and Q (which correspond to category labels in a categorization design) is 0 whereas mismatches between the other elements are represented by similarity s, we obtain

$$\text{Sim(CHL)} = 1+s^2 \qquad (6.43)$$

$$\text{Sim(CHQ)} = 2s^2, \qquad (6.44)$$

and, for probability of recalling the object, L

$$P(\text{L}) = (1+s^2)/(1+3s^2). \qquad (6.45)$$

For a test of the "crossover" cue CP, we obtain

$$\text{Sim(CPL)} = 2s \qquad (6.46)$$

$$\text{Sim(CPQ)} = 2s^2, \qquad (67.47)$$

and, for probability of recalling the object, L

$$P(\text{L}) = 2s/(2s+2s^2) = 1/(1+s). \qquad (6.48)$$

It is easy to show that these expressions predict the crossover effect, with the magnitude depending on the value of s. The difference between $P(\text{L})$ for the intact cue CH and $P(\text{L})$ for the crossover cue CP is 0 when s is equal to 0 or 1, but is positive for all other values of s; examples are,

s	Recall CH	Cue CP
0	1	1
0.1	0.981	0.909
0.5	0.714	0.667
0.8	0.562	0.556
1	0.500	0.500

The differences are not large, even for small values of s, but are in line with the differences reported by Anderson and Bower (1972, 1973). It should be remarked that Anderson and Bower found a crossover effect only when learning occurred under standard "intentional learning" conditions, that is, with subjects instructed before presentation of the study list that it would be followed by a test of memory. In later experiments conducted with an "incidental learning" procedure, that is, with subjects misled about the purpose of the study trials, the effect did not appear. The reason may be that only with the intentional procedure did the subjects attend to the verbatim sentences closely enough so that the effective inter-item similarities would be small.*

6.3.4 Recall without response cueing

A conspicuous question about recall not touched on above is whether the array model can address the common situation in which the individual does not have available, in advance of a test, a set of candidate responses (including the correct one) that can be combined with the stimulus or contextual cue for computations of similarity to the memory array. For brevity, I will refer to this case as *direct* recall, in contrast to the cases

---

* In earlier studies of categorization in the framework of the exemplar model, it has been assumed that effective similarity between attribute values is a function of the degree of selective attention to those attributes during learning (Medin and Schaffer 1978; Nosofsky 1984).

discussed above in which a recall task is, in effect, reduced to forced-choice recognition. A very common example is free or cued recall with words as responses. Suppose, for example, that a learner of German has seen the German word *schön* paired with the English word beautiful. Can the model predict that on a later test with *schön* alone as the stimulus, the learner would tend to respond "beautiful"? The idea that the interpretation could be the same as in the cases discussed previously in this section seems implausible. The number of candidate English words is very large, and there is no evidence that all of those in a person's vocabulary could be retrieved and employed in similarity computations during the short time involved in a recall test. My assumption, supported by a large literature on "articulatory suppression" in short-term recall (reviewed by Baddeley 1986) and rehearsal in both short- and long-term memory, is that direct recall depends on a representation of the evocation of the response in the presence of the stimulus ("beautiful" in the presence of *schön* in the example) having been stored in the memory trace that will be the basis for similarity computations at the time of recall. This condition is commonly met by explicit evocation of the response term of a paired associate item on a learning trial (conspicuously missing in "incidental" learning situations), vocalization of the names of items presented in short-term, ordered recall situations, or by rehearsal of responses during or immediately following learning trials. When the condition is met, then application of the model is straightforward. For a bare-bones illustration, suppose that the paired-associate items

Face 1	Name 1
Face 2	Name 2

have been presented to a learner and the names rehearsed in the presence of the stimuli, so that the memory array includes traces both of the stimuli and of the response evocations:

	Response	
Stimulus	Name 1	Name 2
Face 1	1	0
Face 2	0	1

For a later test with face 1 presented alone, we compute the similarity of face 1 to the array, obtaining (with s as the stimulus similarity parameter and response similarity assumed equal to zero), a similarity of 1 to the name 1 column and a similarity s to the name 2 column, and for probability of name 1 as the response,

$$P(\text{name 1}) = 1/(1+s), \tag{6.49}$$

which depends on s just as in the analogous case of categorization and approaches unity as s tends to zero.

6.3.5 A comment on direct recall

It might seem unreasonable at first thought that people should be able to achieve direct recall effectively only under certain conditions. It may be, however, that having a memory system with this constraint is quite adaptive. It could be quite disruptive to most everyday activities if an individual automatically generated overt recall whenever he or she encountered a stimulus that had been experienced together with some response label in the past. As the memory system appears to be constructed, whenever one anticipates the need for later recall, one can prepare for by generating or rehearsing an appropriate response at the time of original learning. It is often observed that politicians or others who are skilled at remembering people's names take care to use the name of a newly introduced person one or more times while still in the person's presence, thus laying the basis for later direct recall when the person is again encountered. When there has not been occasion to rehearse a response, as in typical experiments on incidental learning or in study when one is passively reading material, later recall may still be achievable if the learner has some way of restricting the candidate set of admissible responses to a number that makes it feasible to generate recall by the forced-choice route,

6.4 On the extendability of the exemplar-similarity model

In Chapters 5 and 6, we have seen numerous examples of the ease of adapting the exemplar model to new research problems and its value in the analysis of situations often very different from those involved in the development of the model. One might ask why the network model has not been treated similarly. Perhaps the key point is that there is typically one direct and natural interpretation of a new situation in terms of the exemplar model whereas interpretation in terms of a network requires many more decisions. Another factor is that over several years of research experience, I have found that when a study involves only structural relationships, which is the case for all of the research examples discussed in these chapters, it is rarely possible to improve on the exemplar model's account of the data by going to a network formalism. When, however, graded values of a quantitative variable, e.g., time or stimulus intensity, enter into a problem, a network interpretation sometimes proves advantageous. We will encounter illustrations of this point in the next chapter in connection with the interpretation of recognition.

Appendix 6.1 Similarity computations for application of the array model to causal inference problems

I will illustrate the similarity computation in terms of the Low level problem of Experiment 1. The design, repeated from Table 5.6 is

Event	*Outcome*
h	B
r	−B
fh	B
a	−B

Hypothesis: d>B.

The key to the computation is to interpret the problem representation as the analog of a categorization problem with the events h, r, fh, and h corresponding to exemplars and the outcomes B and −B to category labels. The event specified in the hypothesis is treated as a probe stimulus, which is compared to the exemplar-category list, similarities being computed via processing assumptions 1–3 and the intersection rule for probe-memory comparisons. Analogously to the preload assumption of the augmented exemplar model (Chapter 3), it is assumed that at the start of each problem the learner has some background information in memory, similarity to the problem events being denoted s_0. Also, it is presumed that the learner has an initial bias to expect that the outcome will not occur if no causal event is present. For simplicity the between-category similarity is set equal to zero.

To obtain the probability that the causal event, d, specified in the hypothesis to be evaluated belongs to the set of situations having B as the outcome, we compute the similarities of the combinations d,B and d,−B to each event-outcome combination listed. The similarity of d,B to the combination in the first row is s since d is not present; similarity to the second row is 0 since B and −B do not match, and so on. Total similarities of d,B and d,−B to the array are 2s and $2s+s_0$, respectively, and the probability of outcome B in the presence of d is

$$P_d(B) = 2s/(4s+s_0); \tag{6.A1}$$

entering the values 0.2 for s and 1 for s_0 yields the value 0.22, the upper right-hand entry in Table 5.8, for the outcome probability.

7   Categorization and recognition

7.1 Recognition: a window to memory?

In this chapter, I depart from the primary focus on classification and broaden the scope of the theory developed in Chapters 1–6 to embrace many of the phenomena traditionally treated in memory research and theory. I start with what is commonly thought to be the most nearly basic index of memory, that is, recognition, and take up the idea presented by an eminent psychologist of a much earlier period that a close study of recognition may yield dividends in helping us to understand apparently more complex forms of memory:

A closer study of recognition than has been made heretofore will probably contribute much to our knowledge of other processes as well.
(Hollingworth 1913)

7.1.1 Experimental paradigms

In ordinary life, we speak of recognition in two principal senses, which may be termed absolute recognition and recognition in context. The former sense applies when you are asked whether you recognize a particular person, that is, whether you remember ever encountering the person before. The latter sense applies if you are asked, instead, whether you recognize a person as one of those who were present at a meeting, or if you recognize a word or phrase as having occurred in a speech. In part for reasons of convenience, research on recognition deals almost universally with recognition in context. An experimental subject is allowed to study a list of words, a set of pictures, or the like, then is tested for recognition, the question being, not whether a test word or picture has ever been encountered, but whether it was included in the studied material. Conclusions from such research are rarely qualified with respect to type of recognition, but probably little harm is done, since there is little reason to doubt that, for the most part, the same processes underlie both types. Occasionally, however, the distinction becomes important and a theory or model needs some representation of the relativity of recognition to a specific context. In this chapter, I will follow the customary practice of discussing research and models without reference to context except in one section where context plays an important role.

The experimental procedures used to test for recognition fall into two main categories, termed old/new and forced choice. After studying a set or series of stimuli of some kind, a subject in the old/new procedure is presented with a test item and responds "old" or "new" (or "yes" or "no"), signifying that the item is or is not recognized as a member of the studied set. In the forced-choice method, the subject is presented, instead, with two or more test items (only one of which was in the studied set) and indicates recognition by choosing one of the test items. The old/new method is the more commonly seen, perhaps in part because it appears to correspond to more everyday life situations and in part because it is associated with the continuous recognition procedure introduced in a very influential study by Shepard and Teghtsoonian (1961). A problem with the old/new method is that performance may be significantly influenced by subjects' biases, that is, strict or lax criteria for the degree of familiarity of a test item required to justify an "old" response. The forced-choice test avoids this susceptibility to bias, but has the drawback that the standard measure of recognition, percentage of correct responses, may be contaminated by random guessing.

The importance of these problems of interpretation of recognition measures first came forcefully to the attention of researchers in connection with the issue of whether recall or recognition provides the more direct or valid indicator of memory. In the classic summary of work on recognition that graduate students of my generation cut their teeth on, given in Woodworth's *Experimental Psychology*, a case was made for the relative simplicity of recognition, viz.

The recognitive processes differ functionally from those of recall in that recognition starts with the object given where recall has to find the object. . . . It would seem that recognition is the simpler process. (Woodworth 1938, p. 47)

To document the idea that recognition is much simpler than recall, Woodworth cited data on memorization of several types of material reported early in the century by Achilles (1920), who obtained recall and recognition scores, and found much higher scores for recognition, as may be seen in Table 7.1. This result might be taken to mean that recognition is a more sensitive indicator than recall and provides more direct evidence about the state of an item in memory. However, that conclusion needs critical

Table 7.1 Comparison of recognition and recall (data from Achilles 1920)

	Percentage correct*		
	Syllables	Words	Proverbs
Recall	12	39	22
Recognition	42	65	67

*Recognition scores corrected for guessing

scrutiny. Even in 1920 it was realized that one cannot usefully compare raw scores from recognition and recall tests directly. Whereas under most circumstances correct recall of an item is good evidence that it has been remembered, simply saying "yes, I recognize the item" on a recognition test is little evidence for anything: the individual being tested may simply have a strategy of saying "yes" to all of the test questions, thus making his responses uninformative about his state of memory. Recognition scores have to be interpreted by a comparison of the individual's responses to truly old items that should be recognized and to actually new items that should be rejected. The method employed by Achilles was evidently the familiar guessing correction that is commonly used in multiple-choice examinations (essentially, subtracting errors from correct responses). This procedure is satisfactory for many practical purposes, but it has been largely superseded in theoretical work by methods based on signal detectability theory. The reason, in brief, is that the guessing correction is based on the premise that errors result from random guessing, an assumption that has been recognized to be an oversimplification since the epoch-making analysis by Tanner and Swets (1954). I will review the use of signal detectability measures in a later section, but first it is in order to sketch briefly the principal theoretical approaches to recognition.

7.1.2 Aspects of recognition theory

Current theoretical approaches differ on several dimensions: (1) specific versus general orientation; (2) strength versus multiple-trace conceptions; and (3) local versus global comparisons of perception and memory.

1. In the earlier literature, recognition and recall were presumed to be different forms of memory and a major theoretical problem was finding the relationship between them. It was natural, then, to develop specific models for recall and specific models for recognition. In contrast, the new trend is to seek more general models that treat recognition as simply one aspect of a memory system that also underlies recall and other cognitive processes (Murdock 1982; Gillund and Shiffrin 1984; Hintzman 1988; Nosofsky 1988*b*).

2. In all recognition theories, it is assumed that experience with an object or event (henceforth, for brevity, simply an *item*) results in the laying down of a memory trace. In the oldest version of trace theory, quite clearly articulated by Hollingworth (1913), the trace of an item is established on its first occurrence and is characterized by a strength, or familiarity value, that increases with repetitions of the item and decreases as a function of time since the last occurrence (Brown 1958; Wickelgren and Norman 1966; Morton 1970). On a test for recognition, the individual compares the strength of the trace activated by a test item with a threshold, or criterion, value and recognizes the item (judges it to have been previously experienced)

if the strength exceeds the criterion. The concept of trace strength in some form is an ingredient of all models of recognition; what has changed over the years is the degree to which it is modified or augmented by other assumptions. One important augmentation is the assumption that recognition depends not only on a judgment of familiarity but also on reinstatement, or recall, of the context in which an item occurred (Hollingworth 1913; Anderson and Bower 1972; Atkinson and Juola 1973). A major modification is the idea that repetition of an item may exert its effects, not by strengthening a unitary trace, but by storing multiple traces and thus making it easier for a new presentation of the item to find a match in memory (Bernbach 1970; Hintzman 1988). Multiple-trace models have not been as fully elaborated as strength models, but they cannot be ignored, because there is relatively direct evidence for the formation of multiple traces (Hintzman, Block, and Summers 1973).

3. In theories of memory developed up to the 1980s, recognition was assumed to depend primarily, or even exclusively, on comparison of a test item to the trace or traces of the given item in memory. That idea seems intuitively natural, but for reasons that will be brought out in the following sections, it is no longer tenable. Thus the influential theories of the present period (including those of Anderson 1973; Ratcliff 1978; Murdock 1982; and Gillund and Shiffrin 1984) all assume that recognition depends on a global comparison of the test item with the current contents of memory. It will become clear as we proceed that what appears to be an important advance in theory has a cost in that we can no longer expect a recognition test (or indeed any kind of behavioral test) to provide direct access to the state of any individual item in memory.

This thumbnail sketch of the present state of theory sets the stage for the task of this chapter, which is to discuss the potentialities of the array-similarity framework for providing a unified interpretation of recognition, recall, and other memory processes. The approach is general in that all of these processes are treated as instances of a general theory of classification. Prime objectives are to show that both the strength and the multiple-trace conceptions and both global and local processing can be accommodated within a common framework.

7.2 Recognition in the array framework

7.2.1 Forced-choice recognition

The forced-choice task is especially convenient for a first look at adapting the core array-similarity model to recognition, interpreted essentially as a particular case of categorization involving only a single category. Suppose that a list of items—I_1, I_2, I_3, I_4—is presented to a learner, then a test is given on which one of the "old" items, say I_1, is presented together with a new item, I_N, and the learner indicates which of the two he recognizes, that is, which occurred during the list presentation. Following the same approach as that of the exemplar model for categorization, we assume that the learner's response will be based on the relative similarities of I_1 and I_N to the items of the list. Letting s be the average similarity between any two non-identical items, the total similarity to memory for I_1 is $1+3s$ and for I_N it is $4s$, and therefore the probability of correctly judging I_1 to be the "old" item is

$$P(C) = (1+3s)/(1+7s). \tag{7.1}$$

More generally, if there are n items in the list, the similarities to memory are $1+(n-1)s$ and ns for Old and New test items, respectively, and probability of a correct response is

$$P(C) = (1+(n-1)s)/(1+(n-1)s+ns)$$
$$= (1+(n-1)s)/(1+(2n-1)s). \tag{7.2}$$

Several predictions follow directly from Equation 7.2. If s is equal to 1, that is, the items are indistinguishable, $P(C)$ is equal to $1/2$; and if s is equal to 0, that is, items are highly dissimilar, $P(C)$ is equal to 1. Between these extremes, recognition probability, $P(C)$, increases monotonically as item similarity decreases—a relationship long familiar in the empirical literature (Woodworth 1938).

Another implication of Equation 7.2 bears on a very well-established phenomenon in the psychology of memory. It is well known to laymen as well as experimenters that one of the chief sources of difficulty for people in achieving correct recognition is the size of the body of relevant material already in memory. Recognizing a student one has seen previously in a seminar of six people is a trivial task compared to recognizing a student from a lecture section of 500. Similarly, in experiments the probability of a subject's recognizing any given item from a list is a much easier task if the list is short than if the list is long (Strong 1912; Bowles and Glanzer 1983; Gillund and Shiffrin 1984; Hintzman 1988; Ratcliff, Clark, and Shiffrin 1990). To see at an intuitive level how the model accounts for this phenomenon, let us continue with the example of recognizing a student from a class. If one is confronted with two students, O who was in the class and N who was not, and asked which of them was in the class, the task is accomplished, in terms of the model, by comparing the featural description of each student with one's memory array for all students in the class and summing the similarity values. The summed similarity is higher for O only because the comparison between O himself and O's representation in the array has the maximal similarity value of unity, whereas for N, not represented in the array, no comparison involves a similarity of unity. Obviously, the advantage for O may be large if the class is small but becomes negligible if the class is very large; and for any given class size, the advantage for O will be greatest if the average similarity, s, between non-identical

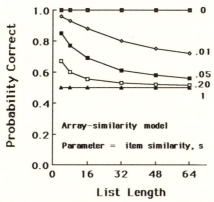

Fig. 7.1 Forced-choice recognition as a function of list length. Predictions of array model for different values of the similarity parameter, *s*.

students is much smaller than unity. This analysis, subsumed in Equation 7.2, implies that forced-choice recognition in a list-length experiment should depend jointly on the number of items in the list and inter-item similarity, in the manner illustrated in Fig. 7.1. It is a well supported empirical generalization that recognizability of an item depends inversely on list length and inter-item similarity in the manner depicted.

When studying similarity effects, one needs to be specific about just what similarities are being manipulated. The critical similarity in the array model is similarity between a test item and the stored mental representations of list items. It has evidently been assumed by many investigators that similarity between the old and new items of a forced-choice test pair should also be important, but Tulving (1981) reviewed the findings of a half dozen relevant previously reported experiments and found virtually no effect of this variable. Seeking an interpretation of this apparently surprising result, Tulving proposed a distinction between the *perceptual* similarity of the old and new item presented on a forced-choice recognition test and what he termed the *ecphoric* similarity between either of these and the item representations stored in memory. These distinctions can readily be implemented in the array model. In the first of two experiments designed by Tulving to separate the two kinds of similarity, subjects were presented with a list of items (pictures), then given forced-choice tests of three types: In type I-I′, an old item, I, was paired with a new item, I′, highly similar to it but not to any of the other items; in type I-J′, old item I was paired with a new item, J′, that was highly similar to some other item, J, in the list; and in type I-X, item I was paired with a new item, X, dissimilar to it and to all other items in the list. Tulving's test data yielded correct recognition probabilities of 0.74, 0.68, and 0.87 for the three test types, respectively, suggesting that the critical factor is not similarity of the new test item to the old test item but, rather, total similarity of the new test item to the members of the stored list.

For a simplified analysis of this experiment, assume that items I_1, I_2, I_3, and I_4 have been presented, then I_1 is tested together with one of the three types of new items. We have no measure of the specific similarities involved in Tulving's experiment, but for illustrative purposes I will choose 0.40 and 0.05 for the high and low similarity values. Computing similarities in the usual way, we find for the summed similarities of the various test items to the list representation,

$$
\begin{array}{ll}
\text{I :} & 1+3(0.05) \\
\text{I':} & 0.4+3(0.05) \\
\text{J':} & 0.4+3(0.05) \\
\text{X:} & 4(0.05),
\end{array}
$$

and

and for predicted recognition probabilities

$$
\begin{array}{lll}
\text{I-I':} & (1+3(0.05))/(1+3(0.05)+0.40+3(0.05)) & = 0.68 \\
\text{I-J':} & (1+3(0.05))/(1+3(0.05)+0.40+3(0.05)) & = 0.68 \\
\text{I-X:} & (1+3(0.05))/(1+3(0.05)+4(0.05)) & = 0.85,
\end{array}
$$

and

quite well in line with the pattern of Tulving's result.*

Another variable that one would expect to be of prime importance for recognition is strength of the memory trace, commonly manipulated by varying either the number of repetitions of the item or the study time allotted to the item on each occurrence. One would intuitively expect recognizability of the item to depend directly on its strength, and, when other factors are equal, this expectation has usually been borne out in experiments (Loftus 1974; Yoselinas, Hockley, and Murdock 1992). Other factors often are not equal, however, in particular, the strengths of other items in a list. Accounting for the joint effects of strength of a target item and strengths of other items in the list has been a central problem for contemporary models of recognition (Ratcliff, Clark, and Shiffrin 1990; Shiffrin, Ratcliff, and Clark 1990; Murdock 1991; Murnane and Shiffrin 1991).

---

* In Tulving's (1981) experiment, the difference between the I-I' and I-J' tests, though not large, appeared to be significant. The source of the difference may lie in the fact that in Tulving's study, the members of a test pair of the type I-I' were two halves of an original picture, which was a photograph of a complex scene. If on these tests, the subjects tended to focus attention on the features that differentiated I and I', then the similarity of I', as perceived, to the representation of I in memory might be reduced relative to the similarity between test item J' and its counterpart, J, in the memory array. Using the values 0.25 and 0.40 for these similarities, rather than 0.40 for both, and recomputing the similarities, we obtain 0.74, 0.68, and 0.85 for the I-I', I-J', and I-X tests.

What these investigators term a *list-strength effect* can be illustrated as follows. Imagine two scenarios, both having to do with the opening day of a school year. In one, an instructor meets N students for the first time in course A and N different students for the first time in course B. The other scenario differs only in that the instructor meets the N students from course B again in course C on the same day. Each scenario continues with the instructor happening to encounter some students from the opening day classes outside of the classroom building a day later, scattered randomly among strangers. One might expect intuitively that, other things equal, recognition of a student from course A should be poorer in the second scenario than in the first. In the first case, students from courses A and B would all seem more familiar than strangers to about the same degree. But in the second case, students from course A would seem less familiar than those from courses B and C, and therefore closer, on a relative scale, to the strangers. Translating this example into the terms of a typical recognition experiment, the first scenario corresponds to presenting subjects with a list of items each of which occurs once (a "pure weak" list), and the second scenario to presenting the same list of items but with half of the items occurring once and half twice (a "mixed" list). A "list-strength" effect would be said to occur if a once-presented item from the mixed list were less well recognized than a once-presented item from the pure list.

A number of our foremost theorists in the field of recognition, including Bennett Murdock, Roger Ratcliff, and Richard Shiffrin, have noted that nearly all recognition models agree with intuition in predicting a list-strength effect and have devoted considerable effort to a search for empirical confirmation. A typical experiment designed to simulate the illustrative situation sketched above uses three lists of stimuli, usually common words. Subjects study one of the lists, then are tested for recognition of a target item. In one case all items in the study list have received a single, usually brief, presentation; in a second case, all items have received a single presentation with an extended duration (or, in some studies, a larger number of presentations at the brief duration); in the third case, half of the items in the study list are of each type. Surprisingly from the standpoint of most extant theory, a large number of experiments conducted with this design have failed to reveal a list strength effect for recognition (Ratcliff, Clark, and Shiffrin 1990; Murnane and Shiffrin 1991; Shiffrin and Murnane 1991, Yonelinas, Hockley, and Murdock 1992), although comparable experiments have uniformly yielded substantial list strength effects for free recall.

Although most of the relevant studies have used old/new recognition tests, it will be convenient to start an analysis of the list-strength problem in terms of the forced-choice version of the array model, for which list-length predictions were shown in Fig. 7.1. The implications of the model for the combined effects of item strength and list strength will first be developed for the experimental design shown at the top of Table 7.2. We suppose that four

Table 7.2 Illustrative array-model analysis of forced-choice recognition

Design

Item	List Type*		
	W	S	M
1	1	2	1
2	1	2	1
3	1	2	2
4	1	2	2

Test Item	Similarity to memory			Probability correct		
	W	S	M	W	S	M
Predictions with $s = 0.1$, $s_0 = 0$						
New	0.4	0.8	0.6			
Old Weak	1.3		1.5	0.76		0.71
Old Strong		2.6	2.4		0.76	0.80
Predictions with $s = 0.1$, $s_0 = 0.25$						
New	0.65	1.05	0.85			
Old Weak	1.55		1.75	0.70		0.67
Old Strong		2.85	2.65		0.73	0.76

* Cell entries are presentation frequencies of items in pure weak (W), pure strong (S), and mixed (M) lists.

items are presented to subjects for study. In the pure weak (W) condition, each is presented once; in the pure strong (S) condition, each is presented twice; and in the mixed (M) condition, two items are presented once and two are presented twice. In the W and S conditions, a test following this presentation offers a choice between a list item, say I_1, and a new item, I_N; in the M condition, the test offers a choice between either a weak or a strong list item, e.g., I_1 or I_3, and the new item, I_N. A list-strength effect would be signified by lower recognition for I_1 in the M than in the W list and higher recognition for I_3 in the M than in the S list, indicating that recognition of a target item is impaired by the presence of strong traces of other items and facilitated by the presence of weak traces of other items.

Predictions for this design depend, of course, on relations between the total similarities of new and old test items to the set of stored item representations (henceforth, for brevity, just "item memory") for each list type. With a value of 0.1 assumed for the inter-item similarity parameter, s, total similarities to memory for each type of test item are as given in the middle panel of Table 7.2. For the pure weak list , similarity to memory is $1+0.3 = 1.3$ for any list item (Old on the test), and 0.4 for a new test item; therefore, on a forced-choice test involving these two items, probability of correct recognition is $1.3/(1.3+0.4) = 0.76$, as shown on the right side of the middle panel of Table 7.2. The other entries in this panel are computed similarly. The recognition probabilities exhibit a list strength effect in that a weak item is better recognized in the pure weak than in the mixed list, whereas a strong item is better recognized in the mixed list. However, comparing pure weak with pure strong, we observe a prediction of no effect of item strength. This surprising result, which holds for all values of s, is contrary to empirical evidence and calls for further analysis.

This last implication of the model is bothersome, but, recalling the failure of the core exemplar model to predict an effect of exemplar repetition in category learning (Chapter 2), we may suspect that a similar remedy might serve here. In developing the recognition model, we have again started with the perhaps oversimplified assumption that the learner begins an experiment with an empty memory array, that is, with no stored information relevant to the task. Actually, however, the instructions and task setting of any experiment convey some information to the subject about the kind of stimulus materials that will be encountered. As in the case of categorization, perhaps we should augment the recognition model by assuming that there is a background memory load, the stored information having some average similarity s_0 to each of the items presented during the experiment. With this extension, the memory array corresponding to the design at the top of Table 7.2 becomes

	Item	Weak	Strong	Mixed
Background	I_0	1	1	1
List	I_1	1	2	1
	I_2	1	2	1
	I_3	1	2	2
	I_4	1	2	2

where I_0 denotes the background load. This quantity may be regarded simply as background noise, as the term is used in signal detection theory, since it does not reflect the learner's experience with the items presented during the study series.The effect of this extension is seen at the bottom of Table 7.2, where the quantities shown in the middle panel have been recomputed with s_0 set equal to 0.25. We now observe an item strength effect in the W versus S comparison, and again a list strength effect, though reduced from that seen in the middle panel.

To include list length, also, in our comparisons, the same parameter values used for the bottom panel of Table 7.2 have been applied to an analogous

Table 7.3 Predictions of the augmented array-similarity model for list-length and list-strength effects on forced-choice recognition

	List type			
	Pure		Mixed	
List length	Weak	Strong	Weak	Strong
Probability correct				
4	0.70	0.73	0.67	0.76
8	0.65	0.66	0.62	0.69
d'				
4	0.76	0.86	0.63	0.99
8	0.54	0.61	0.43	0.71

Note: Computed with $s = 0.1$, $s_0 = 0.25$.

design with a list length of 8 items, and the results for both list lengths are assembled in Table 7.3. A list-length effect is predicted, recognition probability dropping from length four to length eight in all conditions, and an item strength effect is again manifest, though its magnitude decreases with increasing list length. With the background parameter included, the model predicts effects of all three variables represented—list length, item strength, and list strength. The first two of these predictions are certainly correct, qualitatively at least, and the third one will be discussed in a later section.

7.2.2 Old/new recognition

In what is termed a continuous old/new recognition experiment, a series of stimulus patterns is presented to the learner with some patterns recurring at various points in the series. In some studies (e.g., Shepard and Teghtsoonian 1961), each pattern recurs exactly once, in others (e.g., Estes 1986*b*) the patterns are randomly sampled from a master set with no restriction on recurrences. In the other popular design (termed study-test), the learner views a list of items, then is tested with a mixture of old and new items. On each trial in the continuous procedure and on each test trial in the study-test procedure, the learner views the pattern presented and judges whether it is "old" or "new." Ordinarily the learner receives no informative feedback about correctness of the response, and I shall assume this procedure in the following development of the models.

We view this situation as a special case of categorization in which Old and New are the categories to which test items are assigned by the learner. As in the forced-choice case, the predictions of the array model about old/new recognition are based on an analysis of the similarities of test items to memory in the various conditions of interest. The approach is similar to that of Nosovsky (1988*b*,1991*a*) but differs in some specific assumptions.

It will again be convenient to start our analysis with a hypothetical experiment in which a sequence of four all-different items, I_1–I_4, is presented for study; however, in this case, the sequence is followed by an old/new test on either an old item, e.g., I_1, or a new item, I_N. We assume that after presentation of the four items, a representation of each item is stored in the Old category. Also, as in the forced-choice case, we need to allow for the possibility that when the categories are defined for a learner, some information about the kinds of items to be presented (possibly including their anticipated relative frequencies) is stored in the otherwise initially empty memory array along with the category labels, yielding a memory array of the form

Category

Item	*Old*	*New*
I_0	1	0
I_0'	0	1
I_1	1	0
I_2	1	0
I_3	1	0
I_4	1	0

where I_0 and I_0', representing background information (or "noise") are defined analogously to I_0 in the forced-choice analysis.

For purposes of illustrative calculations, we will assume a single value s for similarity between any two item representations and values s_0 and s_N for the similarity of any item to I_0 and I_0', respectively. The values of s_0 and s_N will determine the bias for Old or New responses prior to the input of the study list. For simplicity, s_0 will be assumed equal to 0 in the first examples to be presented.

On a test of an old item following presentation of the 4-item list, the total similarity of the item, say I_1, to the Old category is $1+3s$ and to the New category is s_N, yielding for the probability of an Old response

$$P_O(O) = (1+3s)/(1+3s+s_N). \tag{7.3}$$

On a test with a new item, I_N, the similarities are $4s$ and s_N, and probability of an Old response is

$$P_N(O) = 4s/(4s+s_N). \tag{7.4}$$

---

* It is quite possible the I_0 and I_0' would be the same, but for generality, we allow for the possibility that in some situations they may be different.

More generally, for a list of n distinct items, these expressions become

$$P_O(O) = (1+(n-1)s)/(1+(n-1)s+s_N).$$ (7.5)

and

$$P_N(O) = ns/(ns+s_N).$$ (7.6)

Several properties of these functions are illustrated in Fig. 7.2 with smaller and larger values of s_N in the upper and lower panels, respectively, and two values of the similarity parameter, s, in each panel.

The most salient aspect of the figure is the uniform increase with list length for both correct recognitions, that is, percentages of Old responses to list items, labelled h (hits), and percentages of Old responses to new items, labelled fa (false alarms). These trends can be expected to hold regardless of

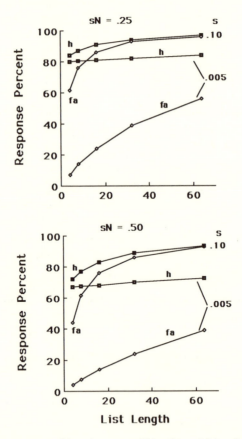

Fig. 7.2 Old/new recognition, in terms of hits (h) and false alarms (fa) in relation to list length and similarity. Predictions of the array model with parameter values discussed in the text.

parameter values (except *s* values of 1 or 0) since both measures depend directly on the total similarity of the test item, whether old or new, to the members of the list representation in memory, and the number of representations will grow with list length.

The increasing functions shown in Fig. 7.2 do not, of course, imply that accuracy of recognition is increasing with list length. One might surmise the opposite, since the functions for false alarms grow more rapidly with list length than do those for hits. The surmise is correct, as may be seen in Fig. 7.3, in which each pair of functions for hits and false alarms in Fig. 7.2 has been transformed into a single function for the *d'* measure of signal detectability theory (Appendix 7.1). This measure takes account of the fact that a subject can vary at will his or her criterion for the degree of familiarity of a test item (corresponding to total similarity to memory in the model) required to warrant a judgment of old. Other things equal, a stricter criterion will lower and a more lax criterion will raise the probabilities of both hits and false alarms. However, it is the difference between these probabilities that indexes accuracy of recognition, and *d'* is essentially this difference expressed in standard deviation units (Swets 1964; McNicol 1972; Murdock 1974; MacMillan and Creelman 1990).

The *d'* values in Fig. 7.3 decrease with list length and vary inversely with similarity as would be expected either on intuitive grounds or on the basis of the large research literature. Most interestingly, variation in the background parameter, s_N, which had appreciable effects on the hit and false alarm functions (Fig. 7.2), exerts almost no effect on *d'* values, thus playing a role analogous to variation of the criterion in a signal detectability model.

It is straightforward to apply the model to an experiment in which we examine the effects of list length, item strength, and list strength on old/new

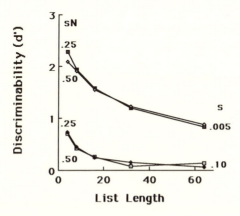

Fig. 7.3 Old/new recognition accuracy (*d'*) in relation to list length and similarity, computed from the h (filled symbols) and fa (open symbols) functions of Fig. 7.2.

recognition with the same design as the one for which forced-choice predictions are given in Table 7.3. In such an experiment (conducted in my laboratory with random consonant triads as stimuli), we found that the data required a very small value of s and a nonzero value of s_0 (about 1/4 the magnitude of s_N) so I have chosen the values $s = 0.001$, $s_0 = 0.10$, and $s_N = 0.40$ for illustrative computations. To include both s_0 and s_N in the computation, Equations 7.5 and 7.6 become

$$P_O(O) = (1+(n-1)s+s_0)/(1+(n-1)s+s_0+s_N). \qquad (7.7)$$

and

$$P_N(O) = (ns+s_0)/(ns+s_0+s_N), \qquad (7.8)$$

respectively. The derivations follow closely those given above in conjunction with Table 7.2 for the forced-choice case except that for old/new recognition the similarities of old and new test items to memory are entered in two separate probability expressions: for either type of test item, the probability of Old has similarity of the item to the old array as the numerator and that quantity plus s_N, similarity of the item to the New array, as the denominator. Equations 7.7 and 7.8 are applicable only to the pure, weak condition in this design; modifications to accommodate the pure, strong and the mixed conditions are straightforward and are given in Appendix 7.2.

With the pairs of old and new recognition probabilities computed for the various conditions from Equations 7.7 and 7.8 and their variants transformed to d', we obtain the predictions shown in Table 7.4. The pattern of predicted effects agrees closely with that reported in a number of published studies (Ratcliff, Clark, and Shiffrin 1990; Murnane and Shiffrin 1991; Shiffrin and Murnane 1991; Yonelinas, Hockley, and Murdock 1992). As expected from the analysis above, recognition decreases with list length in all conditions, but only slightly, not surprising in view of the short list lengths, and increases with item strength in both the pure and the mixed conditions. List strength effects are predicted to be negligible, recognition of both weak and strong items being virtually equal in the pure and mixed lists. This result

Table 7.4　Predictions of the array-similarity model (d' values) for list-length and list-strength effects on old/new recognition

	List Type			
	Pure		Mixed	
List length	Weak	Strong	Weak	Strong
4	1.44	1.80	1.42	1.80
8	1.43	1.74	1.40	1.76

Note: Computed with $s = 0.001$, $s_0 = 0.10$, $s_N = 0.40$

for list strength is of special interest in view of the failure of many current recognition models to accommodate the null effect (Ratcliff, Clark, and Shiffrin 1990; Yonelinas, Hockley, and Murdock 1992). We should not overstate the result, however: the array model does not unconditionally predict the absence of a list strength effect; the prediction holds only when experimental conditions (e.g., type of items, range of list lengths) lead to an estimated value for s_N substantially higher than that for s_0, coupled with a small value of the similarity parameter, s, that is, an initial bias toward "new" responses and highly discriminable items.

7.2.3 The role of memory load in recognition

Although it is a longstanding tradition in psychology to speak in terms of "effects," such as list-length effects, it is important to be aware that the empirical relationships referred to are always complex and in need of finer analysis before we can expect real generality to emerge. Recognition of an item that has previously appeared in a list is usually found to decrease with length of the list, but only if other relevant factors are controlled. For example, it is necessarily the case that, as list length increases, so also does the average interval between the occurrence of an item during list presentation and the occurrence of the item on a subsequent test. And it is well known that recognition is a function not only of length of the study list but of position of the item in the study list and in the test series (Murdock and Anderson 1975). To move toward real generality, we need to go from the level of these empirical effects to the more abstract level of variables that actually determine performance at the point of a recognition test. This step must of course be aided by a suitable model. In the array model family, the critical variable is the size and makeup of the set of item representations to which the test item is compared—in brief, the current relevant memory load.

To show how the effects of memory load are handled by the array-similarity model, I will briefly summarize an experiment conducted in my laboratory. (Details of the design and procedure are given in Appendix 7.3.) The purpose was to see how the different memory arrays built up during the first phase of the experiment would affect recognition performance in the second phase. In Phase 1 (preliminary training), different groups had similar series, either short (24 trials) or long (72 trials), and with either building descriptions (Bldg) or digit strings (Digit) as stimuli. In Phase 2 (the test phase), all subjects were given a 24-trial continuous, old/new recognition series with Bldg stimuli.

Before we look at the full set of predictions and results, let us see how a priori predictions can be derived from the array-similarity model by examining a hypothetical mini-experiment of essentially the same design but using only a single type of stimuli, as illustrated in Table 7.5. The problem

Table 7.5   Illustration of effect of memory load on old/new recognition

Study		Test item	Probability "Old"
Phase 1	Phase 2		
No preload			
	I_1 I_2	I_1	$(1+s)/(1+s+s_0) = 0.71$
		I_3	$2s/(2s+s_0) = 0.50$
Preload			
I_5 I_6	I_1 I_2	I_1	$(1+3s)/(1+3s+s_0) = 0.78$
		I_3	$4s/(4s+s_0) = 0.67$

Note: $s = 0.25$, $s_0 = 0.50$

is to predict recognition of a target item, I_1, in two conditions that are equated with respect to the interval and the event occurrences intervening between its study presentation and the test but that differ with respect to the number of memory representations that the item must be compared to on the test—two in the No preload and four in the Preload condition. The numerator of the expression for probability of an old response to I_1 (a hit) is, of course, the total similarity of I_1 to the relevant current memory contents (including the background constant, I_0), and is seen to increase from $1+s$ in the No Preload to $1+3s$ in the Preload condition. However, the total similarity of the new test item, I_3 to memory, increases more rapidly (from $2s$ to $4s$), and therefore the probability of an Old response to I_3 (a false alarm) increases faster than the probability of a hit. Consequently, when the response probabilities computed with the parameter values shown in Table 7.5 are transformed to d's, the value for No preload is 0.56, for Preload 0.33. The pattern seen in this example is predicted regardless of particular values of the s and s_0 parameters: Probabilities of Old responses to both Old and New items should increase but d' should decrease with the size of the preload.

In our experiment, recognition was not significantly affected by the difference between short and long Phase 1 series, so data for both are pooled over this factor in the summary given in Table 7.6, where observed percentages of hits and false alarms are compared to predictions from the array model. From the analysis of the example in Table 7.5, we expect that the effect of having had Bldg stimuli in Phase 1 will be a small increase in hits and a larger increase in false alarms in the test series, and this effect is apparent in both the data and the numerical predictions of the array model given in Table 7.6. The memory load built up during Phase 1 was large enough so that no significant change in these values from the first to the second test block is predicted, and none is observed. Following Digit

Table 7.6 Data* of memory load experiment with predictions from array model

Phase 1 Item type	Test block			
	1		2	
	Old	New	Old	New
Data				
Bldg	76	36	77	31
Digits	63	14	68	28
Model				
Bldg	74	46	74	46
Digits	72	15	70	21

*Percentages of Old responses in test series with Bldg items.

presentations in Phase 1, the frequency of false alarms is predicted to increase somewhat over test blocks, and this trend is seen in the data. From the pattern of hits and false alarms, it is apparent that recognition accuracy in the test series, as indexed by d' values both for the data and for the model predictions, is reduced by experience with Bldg stimuli in Phase 1 but that this disadvantage for the Bldg preload condition decreases somewhat over the test series.

The designs both of the hypothetical experiment of Table 7.5 and the Bldg/Digit study are of the type familiar under the label *proactive inhibition* in the literature on interference in memory (Woodworth 1938; Murdock 1974). With the simplified version of the array model considered in this section, we would have to predict that in our study, the results would be the same if Phase 1 and Phase 2 had been interchanged, yielding what is known as a *retroactive inhibition*, or, *retroactive interference*, design (Woodworth 1938; Murdock 1974). This symmetry might not obtain if we allowed for possible decay of stored representations over time by including in the array model the decay parameter introduced in Chapter 4 in connection with categorization. The general point to be made is that within the array framework, all such effects are assumed to be the outcome of the interplay of a limited number of factors, the most central always being the memory load at the point of recognition testing.

7.2.4 Effects of item repetition

Repetition of an item would seem intuitively to be a sure way of increasing its recognizability, and empirical studies have yielded results in agreement with intuition (Kintsch 1965; Gillund and Shiffrin 1984; Murdock and

Lamon 1988). Curiously, however, accounting for repetition effects has proved to be troublesome for some currently influential models (Murdock and Lamon 1988). Analysis of the problem in the framework of the array model will show that there can be no universal "repetition effect," for the influence of repetition depends on the levels of other factors. And, although repetition should generally be facilitating, conditions can be specified under which some measures of recognition do not increase with repetition.

We can conveniently start the analysis in terms of the simple hypothetical experiment represented in Table 7.7. In a list of constant length, a target item, I_1 (shown in bold in the table) occurs once, twice, or four times, then recognition is tested for the target item or for a new item, I_N. In the lower part of the table are shown the results of computing total similarities of I_1 and I_N to the memory arrays and entering these in the usual expressions for

Table 7.7   Illustrative predictions of array model for repetition effect in yes/no recognition

Occurrences of critical item (I_1)		
1	2	4
I_2	I_2	$\mathbf{I_1}$
I_3	I_3	$\mathbf{I_1}$
I_4	$\mathbf{I_1}$	$\mathbf{I_1}$
$\mathbf{I_1}$	$\mathbf{I_1}$	$\mathbf{I_1}$
I_5	I_5	I_5
I_6	I_6	I_6
I_7	I_7	I_7
I_8	I_8	I_8

Test with I_1

$$P(O) = \frac{1+7s}{1+7s+s_0} \qquad \frac{2+6s}{2+6s+s_0} \qquad \frac{4+4s}{4+4s+s_0}$$

With $s = 0.25$, $s_0 = 1$,

$P(O) = 0.733$ 0.778   0.833

Test with I_N (New)

$$P(O) = \frac{8s}{8s+s_0} \qquad \frac{8s}{8s+s_0} \qquad \frac{8s}{8s+s_0}$$

$\quad\quad = 0.670$ 0.670   0.670

$d' = 0.18$ 0.33   0.52

probability of an Old response. With the parameter values $s=0.25$ and $s_0=1$, these probabilities yield the d' measures in the bottom row of the table. The increase in d' with repetitions is as anticipated, but the form of the function cannot be assumed to be general, even for these parameter values. Rather than holding list length constant, for example, the design might have held the number of non-repeated items constant, the items I_5, I_6, I_7, and I_8 being combined with one, two, or four occurrences of I_1. Then similar computations would yield the d' values 0.29, 0.42, and 0.51 for one, two , or four occurrences of I_1. Fig. 7.4 illustrates different forms of the function relating d' to number of repetitions of a single target item embedded in lists of different constant length (upper panel) or in lists with different constant numbers of non-repeated items (lower panel).

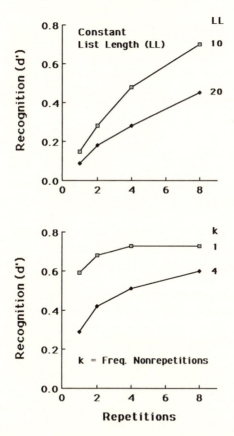

Fig. 7.4 Predictions of Array Model (d' values) for old/new recognition as a function of number of repetitions of a target item: in the upper panel frequency of repetition varies while list length is held constant; in the lower panel, frequency (Freq.) of repetition varies while number of non-repeated items in the list is held constant.

The crux of the matter is that, as discussed earlier, the critical variable is the memory load at the point of a test, measured by the total similarity between old or new test items and the memory array. In the class of experiments involving a repeated target item together with varying numbers of non-repeated items, the numerator of the expression for probability of an Old response to the target item is $n+ks$, where n is the number of occurrences of the target item, k the number of non-repeated items, and s the similarity parameter. Thus, for any given value of s, the recognition probability is the same for all combinations of n and k that yield the same value of $n+ks$. (For example, with s equal to 0.25, the combination $n=4$ and $k=4$ and the combination $n=2$ and $k=12$ both yield $n+ks$ equal to 5). If we know or can estimate the value of s for an empirical situation, we can, therefore, predict conditions under which recognition probability will be invariant over number of repetitions.

The situation is similar with respect to the similarity-to-memory term $(n+k)s$ that appears in the numerator of the expression for probability of an Old response to a new item: All combinations of n and k that yield the same value for this quantity imply the same response probability. But here we can make a stronger prediction than could be done for a test on the target item: Constant values of $n+k$ imply constant response probabilities for any value of s, so we can test the prediction without having to know the value of s. Unfortunately, I know of no published data appropriate to test this prediction.

More generally, data available in the literature are not entirely adequate for the purpose of testing predictions of models concerning effects of item repetition on recognition. One problem is that the number of repetitions has usually been limited to one or two. More important, conditions have not been arranged to allow satisfactory estimates of accuracy of recognition. The standard measure of accuracy, the d' index of signal detectability, requires for its computation matched values of $P_O(\text{Old})$ and $P_N(\text{Old})$, the probabilities of giving positive recognition responses (i. e., saying "old") to actually old (repeated) and actually new stimuli, respectively. In the usual design, different stimuli in a list are repeated different numbers of times during a study series; then the proportions of Old responses to stimuli that have been repeated 1, 2, or more times are paired with a single average value of the proportion of Old responses to new stimuli to enable the estimate of d' at each number of repetitions. The weakness in this procedure is that the trials yielding the data used to compute $P_N(\text{Old})$ for the estimation of d' after any given number of repetitions do not occur at the same points in the study series as the trials yielding the data for computation of $P_O(\text{Old})$.

An unpublished experiment conducted in my laboratory, described in Appendix 7.4, was designed to test the implication of the array model that the effect of item repetition depends on the current state of memory. A continuous old/new recognition procedure was used with a range of one to

Table 7.8 Design of repetition study in terms of stimulus lists shown in study blocks

Group	Item type	Block						
		1	2	3	4	5	6	7
No shift	Repeated	s_1	s_1	s_1	s_1	s_1	s_1	s_1
	Novel	s_7	s_2	s_3	s_4	s_5	s_6	s_8
Shift	Repeated	s_1	s_1	s_1	s_1	s_1	s_1	s_7
	Novel	s_2	s_3	s_4	s_5	s_6	s_7	s_8

six repetitions of target items. The design matches, on the average, the trials in the series that yield estimates of $P_O(\text{Old})$ and $P_N(\text{Old})$ at each number of repetitions, and also allows an assessment of the way repetition effects depend on the current memory load. Further, the stimuli were constructed so as to facilitate analyses of the data in terms of the array and similarity-network models. The design is summarized in Table 7.8. For the no shift group, a set of target items, labeled s_1, occurred in each of seven successive blocks of old/new recognition trials, and in each block was randomly intermixed with a new set of never-repeated items. Percentages of correct recognitions of the target items, or d' values obtained by pairing these with the percentages of Old responses to New stimuli in each block, provide the primary measures of the effect of target repetition. However, in the light of the preceding analyses, we recognize that the percentages of Old responses to the repeated items might be expected to increase from block to block merely because of the steadily increasing total memory load. Thus, we included the shift group, treated just as the no shift group on the first six blocks, but with the set of new items from block 6, denoted s_7 in the table, repeated in block 7. Any effect of repetitions of the target items above that due to the increasing total memory load can be measured in block 7, in terms of the difference between recognition of target set s_1 by the no shift group and recognition of target set s_7 by the shift group.

The results, in terms of the changes in percentages of hits and false alarms over blocks for the two groups are shown in Fig. 7.5. Considering first the no shift group, the principal trend is, as expected, a continuous increase in both functions over blocks. What might not have been anticipated is the closely parallel trend over the last six blocks, raising the question whether the trend for old patterns actually reflects an effect of repetition or only the concurrently increasing total memory load. The question is answered by the functions for the shift group, showing a sharp drop in the percentage of hits in block 7, where the score is based on responses to patterns that had occurred only once previously. Clearly, when the total number of representations in

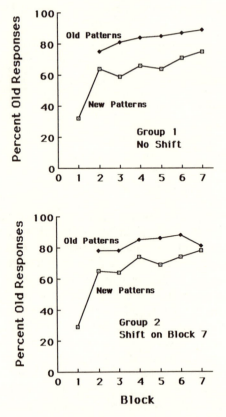

Fig. 7.5   Array model predictions of hit and false alarm percentages for repetition experiment.

the memory array is controlled, hit rate on a repeated item still depends directly on the number of representations of that item in memory.

To show how accuracy of recognition, as distinguished from hit rate, varies with repetition, the hit and false alarm percentages have been transformed to d' values. The d' functions, presented in Fig. 7.6, are somewhat irregular (the d' values being less stable than the percentages on which they are based), but exhibit a generally increasing trend over blocks and the expected drop on block 7 for the shift group. The d' vauess computed for the array model, also included in Fig. 7.6, underestimate the overall increase somewhat but nicely predict the shift effect.

This experiment has simulated conditions that may often arise outside the laboratory when a target item is repeated occasionally over a period of time and the learner is concurrently exposed to samples of new but similar items. The probability of correct recognition of the target item increases with repetition, but the probability of false recognition of new but similar items

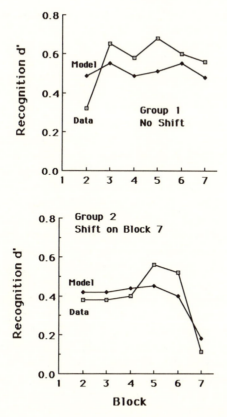

Fig. 7.6 Values of *d'* corresponding to the functions of Fig. 7.5.

grows in parallel, as a consequence of the expanding memory array to which both old and new test items must be compared. Accuracy of recognition, measured in terms of *d'* or the equivalent, may nonetheless increase over the period, as in this study, but conditions could obtain (high similarity between target and non-target items and high relative frequency of non-targets) under which accuracy of recognition would not increase with repetition.

7.2.5 Word-frequency and the "mirror effect"

A phenomenon termed the word-frequency effect in recognition has been a popular research topic for some 25 years, doubtless because of its counterintuitive character. The gist of the effect is better recognition of rare than of common words when these are used as stimuli in any of the standard recognition tasks, contrasting with the universal finding of better recall of common than of rare words. Early studies demonstrated the effect for both forced-choice and old/new recognition (Shepard 1967, and Schulman 1967, respectively), and I am not aware of any failure to replicate in a long series of follow-ups. The effect could not have been predicted by any of the standard theories of recognition and was first given a plausible theoretical interpretation by Glanzer and Bowles (1976) in terms of a model that combined the decision mechanism of signal detection theory with a stimulus sampling process.

Analysis of this phenomenon in terms of the array model is straightforward, and can be conveniently illustrated in terms of the simplified hypothetical example shown in Table 7.9. We consider four words that have occurred in everyday life with high (4) or low (1) frequencies. Two of these, W_1 and W_2 are presented in a study list, then all four are presented on old/new recognition tests, the subjects understanding that a word is to be called old only if it is recognized to be a member of the study list. The correct response category is, of course, Old for W_1 and W_2 and New for W_3 and W_4. The only modification we make in the array model as previously applied to other recognition tasks is to assume that the representation in memory of each word in the study list includes a contextual feature, f_x, identical for all words in the list and unique to the experimental study-test situation. Thus, prior to the list presentation, each of the four words has a representation in memory, but these representations do not include feature f_x. During list presentation, new representations of W_1 and W_2 are stored, each including f_x. The effect is that on a test given immediately in the same situation, each test word will be accompanied by feature f_x, and on this account will be more similar to memory representations that include this feature than to representations that do not. For computational purposes, the similarity between presence and absence of f_x is denoted σ.

Table 7.9 The Word-Frequency Effect in Recognition

Prior Experience		Experiment		
Item	Frequency	Study	Test	Category
W_1	High (4)	W_1	W_1	Old
W_2	Low (1)	W_2	W_2	Old
W_3	High (4)		W_3	New
W_4	Low (1)		W_4	New

	Sim(Old)	Sim(New)
Test W_1	$1+s+s(4+6s)$	s_0
Test W_2	$1+s+s(1+9s)$	s_0'
Test W_3	$2s+s(4+6s)$	s_0
Test W_4	$2s+s(1+9s)$	s_0'

$$P(\text{Old}) = \text{Sim(Old)}/(\text{Sim(Old)}+\text{Sim(New)})$$

Taking account of both inter-item similarity, s, and contextual similarity, σ, in the usual way, total similarities of test items to the Old and New memory arrays are computed as shown at the bottom of Table 7.9. On a test of W_1, for example, total similarity to the representations of the study list is $1+s$ and to the pre-experimental representations is $4+6s$, but the latter component is multiplied by σ to take account of the difference in context. Total similarities for the other test words are computed similarly, and each test word has a similarity to the New category, denoted s_0 or s_0' in the table. Taking s equal to 0, σ equal to 0.02, and s_0 and s_0' both equal to 0.24, we obtain values of 0.82, 0.81, 0.25, and 0.08 for probabilities of responding Old to words W_1, W_2, W_3, and W_4, respectively. These parameter values were chosen so as to put the predictions in roughly the same range as the empirical Old proportions, 0.82, 0.88, 0.16, and 0.12 reported by MacCormack and Swenson (1972) for a study conducted with essentially the same design. The correspondence is not unencouraging, with the false alarm rate being both observed and predicted to be higher for high frequency words, which would yield higher measures of recognition in terms of d' for the low frequency words—the classic word-frequency effect.

However, there is a small disparity between the predicted and observed patterns in that the observed hit rate is higher for low (0.88) than high (0.82) test words from the study list, whereas the model predicts a small inequality in the wrong direction (0.81 versus 0.82). The combination of both higher hit rates and lower false alarm rates on low frequency than on high frequency words constitutes what Glanzer and his associates (Glanzer and Adams 1990; Glanzer, Adams, and Iverson 1991) term the "mirror effect." The failure of the array model to predict the mirror effect is a consequence of our assuming the same value of s_0 for all test words (i.e., $s_0 = s_0'$ in Table 7.9), but that assumption is not necessary and may not be appropriate. We would expect words with high frequencies in everyday life to have higher total similarities than low frequency words to the background information associated with the New category and reflected in the value of s_0.[*] When we allow for this difference by assuming s_0 to be larger for the high than for the low frequency words (accomplished in Table 7.9 by setting $s_0=0.30$ and $s_0'=0.18$), we obtain $P(O)$ values of 0.78, 0.85, 0.17, and 0.10 for the W_1, W_2, W_3, and W_4 tests of Table 7.9, now reflecting in all respects the pattern observed by MacCormack and Swenson (1972).

7.3 Recognition in the similarity-network model

In 1991, when I presented the substance of this volume in the Fitts Lectures at the University of Michigan, it appeared that the array-similarity model

---

[*] The reasoning is that background information about kinds of words to be expected in the experimental situation would be more likely to reflect properties of common than rare words.

could not handle some important aspects of recognition. It seemed, in particular, that to predict effects of variations in item strength, it would be necessary to go to a network model. As will be apparent from the preceding sections of this chapter, subsequent work changed that picture. However, it is still of interest to apply a network model to the same set of recognition phenomena that we have examined in connection with the array model. By choosing for this purpose the same model we applied to categorization in preceding chapters, a similarity-network that differs from the array model primarily in its learning assumptions, we may gain some indication of whether a competitive learning process is implicated in recognition tasks.

Application of the similarity-network model to recognition is straightforward and closely parallels the formulation just given for the array-similarity model. We assume that on presentation of a sequence of items in a recognition experiment, a pattern node is created in the network for each item, together with a connection to a category node (representing the category "old items"), and that on each occurrence of an item the weight (denoted w_i for item i) on its connection to the category node is increased by the same learning function previously defined in connection with binary categorization (Chapter 3, Equation 3.10).

Starting again with a simplified situation in which a learner studies a sequence of four items, I_1, I_2, I_3, I_4, and then is tested for recognition with an old or a new item, the memory array at the point of the test is assumed to have the same form in the similarity-network model as in the array-similarity model except that the strengths of item representations are the weights on the connections between item and category nodes rather than the frequencies of item presentations. That is, the array-model representation

	Category	
Item	Old	New
I_0	0	1
I_1	1	0
I_2	1	0
I_3	1	0
I_4	1	0

becomes

	Category	
Item	Old	New
I_0	0	w_0
I_1	w_1	0
I_2	w_2	0
I_3	w_3	0
I_4	w_4	0

Table 7.10 Predictions of the similarity-network model for list-length and list-strength effects on forced-choice recognition

	List type				
	Pure			Mixed	
List length	Weak	Strong		Weak	Strong
% correct					
4	0.73	0.80		0.74	0.80
8	0.72	0.75		0.72	0.76
d'					
4	0.86	1.19		0.90	1.19
8	0.82	0.95		0.82	0.97

Note: Computed with $b = 0.25$, $c = 4$, $s = 0.25$.

Computation of forced-choice recognition probabilities for the network proceeds just as for the array model, with weights substituted for frequencies. Thus, for the four-item list shown above, the output weight for a test on old item I_1 is $w_1 + s(w_2 + w_3 + w_4)$; the output weight for new item I_N is $s(w_1 + w_2 + w_3 + w_4)$; and the recognition probability* on a forced-choice test between I_1 and I_N is

$$P(C) = (w_1 + s(w_2 + w_3 + w_4))/(w_1 + s(w_1 + 2w_2 + 2w_3 + 2w_4)), \qquad (7.9)$$

which reduces to Equation 7.1 if all of the w_i are set equal to 1. Computing the network weights for strong and weak items with the network model parameters set to the values 0.25 for β (the learning rate), 4 for c (the scaling constant), and 0.25 for s, we obtain the predicted recognition probabilities for the list strength experiment displayed in Table 7.10 in the same format as that of Table 7.3. Like the array-similarity model, the network model predicts virtually no list strength effect (seen in comparisons of W with W(M) and S with S(M) in Tables 7.3 for the array and Table 7.10 for the network model). The data pattern implied by the models agrees qualitatively in all respects with that reported by Yonelinas, Hockley, and Murdock (1992) for an experiment of analogous design: a positive effect of item strength, a negative effect of list length, and virtually no effect of list strength. Quantitatively, it appears that the network model mirrors the data pattern a little more closely (the item-strength effect being somewhat larger and the list-strength effect more nearly equal to zero).

---

* This expression for recognition probability could be applied without modification, but for technical reasons, it is usual to subject each of the outputs to an exponential transformation, e.g., $w_1 + s(w_2 + w_3 + w_4)$ becoming $e^{c(w_1 + s(w_2 + w_3 + w_4))}$, before entering it into the expression for probability. This practice is followed in the examples given here.

The computation of recognition probability for an Old/New test proceeds similarly to the forced-choice case. For a test with old item I_1, the output to the Old category node is $w_1+s(w_2+w_3+w_4)$, the output to the New category node is w_0, and probability of calling the item old (again neglecting the exponential transformation) is

$$P_O(O) = (w_1+s(w_2+w_3+w_4))/(w_1+s(w_2+w_3+w_4)+w_0), \quad (7.10)$$

and the probability of calling a new item old is

$$P_N(O) = s(w_1+w_2+w_3+w_4)/(s(w_1+w_2+w_3+w_4)+w_0). \quad (7.11)$$

Computing values of these functions (with the learning and scaling parameters, β and c, set equal to 0.6 and 2) and converting the recognition probabilities to d' values yields the illustrative list-length functions shown in Fig. 7.7.

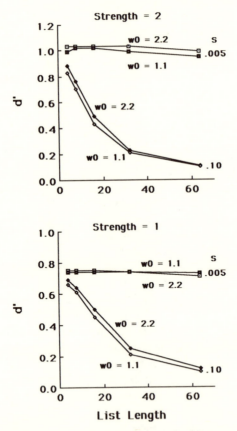

Fig. 7.7 Similarity-network predictions of old/new recognition (d' values) in relation to list length, item similarity (s) and new category weight (w_0) at two levels of item strength.

Little can be said about how well the trends seen in this figure are borne out empirically. Few studies in the literature have varied list length over a reasonable range and none, to my knowledge have done so with control of correlated factors (such as retention interval) and variation in parameters related to item strength and similarity. The specific forms of the theoretical list-length functions depend, of course, on the parameter values. However, several predictions are quite general, namely, that steepness of the functions is strongly related to the value of the item similarity parameter, s, and that the level of the functions is raised by increasing item strength. The initial weight parameter, w_0, has almost no effect on the functions plotted in terms of d', indicating that it corresponds closely to the criterion parameter of signal detectability theory, as was true of the background "noise" parameter s_N of the array-similarity model (Fig. 7.3).

Turning to the joint effects of list length, item strength, and list strength on old/new recognition (shown for forced-choice recognition in Table 7.10), we obtain the d' values shown in Table 7.11. The upper and lower two rows of the table represent different levels of item strength, $w,s=1,2$ signifying strengths of 1 and 2 , and $w,s=4,8$ strengths of 4 and 8 for weak and strong items, respectively. Except for items of strength 1, recognition decreases with list length, and under all conditions recognition increases with item strength. In contrast, list strength effects (seen in comparisons of corresponding cells of the table for pure and mixed lists) are uniformly very small.

We can understand better why the network model predicts negligible list strength effects by looking at the weights computed for items in pure and mixed lists. Consider, for example, the case of list length 4 and $w,s=4,8$ in Table 7.11. The weight computed for a weak item in the pure list is 0.640 and

Table 7.11   Predictions of the similarity-network model (d' values) for list-length and list-strength effects on old/new recognition

| | List type | | | |
| | Pure | | Mixed | |
List length	Weak	Strong	Weak	Strong
W,S = 1,2				
4	0.63	1.02	0.66	0.99
8	0.69	0.94	0.72	0.96
W,S = 4,8				
4	1.34	1.51	1.26	1.56
8	1.07	1.10	1.02	1.17

Note: Computed with $b = 0.25$, $c = 4$, $s = 0.1$, $w_0 = 0.25$.

in the mixed list 0.619. However, this drop is almost exactly compensated by an increase in the weight of a strong item from 0.748 in the pure to 0.777 in the mixed list. When an item is presented for test, it activates not only its own node in the network but also the nodes for all of the other list items, to a degree determined by their similarities. Thus, for a test of a weak item from the pure list in this example, the total output is

$$0.640+0.1(0.640+0.640+0.640) = 0.832;$$

and the output for a weak item from the mixed list is

$$0.619+0.1(0.619+0.777+0.777) = 0.836,$$

so the difference is very small.

On the whole, the predicted pattern of effects for the network model corresponds closely to that reported in numerous experiments (Ratcliff, Clark, and Shiffrin 1990; Murnane and Shiffrin 1991; Yonelinas, Hockley, and Murdock 1992). It appears from the analyses shown here that the interaction of strength of a target (to-be-recognized) item with strength of its competitors in the memory array is handled somewhat better by the interactive learning process of the network model than by the non-interactive process assumed in the array-similarity model, but any general conclusion waits on actual fitting of the two models to appropriate data.

7.4 Short-term memory search

On the basis of our discussion of categorization in short- and long-term memory in Chapter 4, there is reason to believe that only a few items can be simultaneously maintained in a chronologically ordered array on which a sequential search is possible. Among familiar recognition tasks, perhaps only the short-term recognition task introduced by Sternberg (1966) obviously meets this qualification. In this task, a subject views a list of items, commonly random digits, letters, or words, presented sequentially, then is tested by presentation of an old or new item for a speeded recognition test. The list is short enough, usually 1–6 items, so that errors are rare, and the data of main interest are reaction times.

The finding that reaction time increases approximately linearly with size of the memory set (i.e., list length) has been taken to support the assumption that the task is accomplished by a search process, that is, a sequential comparison of the test item with the members of the ordered memory array. Further, the fact that the slope of the set-size function, that is, the function relating reaction time to list length, for old test items often proves to be about one-half the slope of the function for new items suggests that the comparison process is self-terminating—ending when a match between the test item and a member of the memory array is encountered. The linearity of the set-size function does not necessarily imply sequential processing; the array model, as applied to list-length functions earlier in this chapter, is compatible with linearity if a constant unit time is required for each computation of similarity between a test item and a member of the memory array.* However, the evidence concerning reaction times in short-term categorization tasks discussed in Chapter 4 indicated that, within distinct limits, processing may be both sequential and self-terminating.

For the Sternberg paradigm I will assume that, once a list of k items of information has been stored in memory, the option is open to the individual whether to base responding on comparison of a probe with the stored array by the global process, or, instead, to compare the probe with the stored items one at a time, deciding at each step whether to make a recognition response or to continue the sequential search. In the sequential process, the individual would first compare the test item I_x with the last item presented, I_k, and compute their similarity, $\mathrm{Sim}xk$, then compute a choice probability

$$P = \mathrm{Sim}xk/(\mathrm{Sim}xk + \mathrm{Sim}xB), \qquad (7.12)$$

where B is background noise, and with that probability respond immediately, "Yes, this item was in the memory set." With probability $1-P$, the individual would withhold the response and continue by comparing the test item to the next to last item in the array, and so on.† In what might be called a pure sequential model, if the process goes to the end of the list without evocation of a positive response, then, a New response is made and the trial is over. In what may be termed a combined sequential/global model the search process is identical, operating on the same memory array; all that is different is that if the process grinds through to the end and there has been no positive response, the individual then shifts to the global process, and outputs a response based on the similarity of the probe to the full memory array. It is not necessary to assume that the sequential and global computations are successive. It may well be that they begin together upon presentation of the test item and proceed in parallel, but that the output of the global computation is accepted as the basis for responding only if the sequential process fails.

To illustrate the application of the array model to the Sternberg task, functions predicted by the pure sequential form of the model are presented in Fig. 7.8, in terms of reaction times to Old (+) and New (−) test items in

---

* That a linear set-size function may be predicted even if all comparisons are made in parallel is now well-established (Townsend 1990), though the fact was not generally understood at the time of Sternberg's first publications on short-term search.

† Two additional parameters are defined in the general form of the model. First, it is assumed that at each step of the sequential search, if an old response is not evoked, the search terminates with probability a and continues with probability $1 - a$. Second, it is assumed that the time required for a single comparison in the global computation is equal to the time required for one step in the search multiplied by a constant, d.

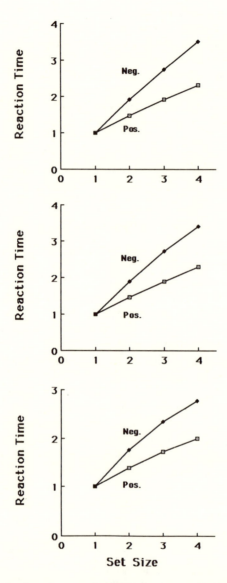

Fig. 7.8 Set-size functions predicted by the sequential version of the array model in terms of reaction times on positive (Pos.) and negative (Neg.) trials (old and new test items, respectively). In the upper two panels, inter-item similarity is very low, in the bottom panel, somewhat increased. Parameter values for the top panel were $s_0=0.05$, $s=0.001$, $B=0.025$; $a=0.05$, and $d=0.5$; for the middle panel, B was reduced to 0.02, and for the bottom panel, s was increased to 0.005.

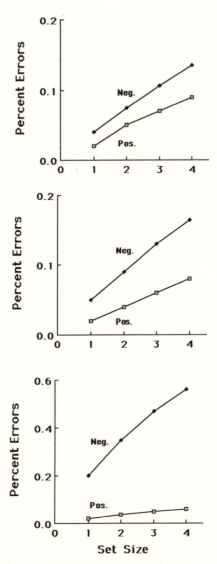

Fig. 7.9 Set-size functions of Fig. 7.8 converted to error percentages.

relation to set size, and in Fig. 7.9 for percentages of errors to each type of test item.

The patterns displayed for reaction time look very much like those reported in many relevant studies (e.g., Schneider and Shiffrin 1977). When inter-item similarity is very low (the upper two panels), set-size functions for both positive and negative trials are close to linear and show the approximately 2:1 ratio of negative to positive slopes that signifies self-termination. Increasing inter-item similarity (bottom panel of Fig. 7.8) shortens reaction times on both positive and negative tests, owing to the increase in global similarities of test items to the memory array, and produces some curvature in the set-size functions. In Fig. 7.9, we see that set-size functions for errors exhibit relations between slopes for positive and negative tests roughly similar to those for reaction times. Increasing inter-item similarity produces a much more conspicuous effect on error functions than on reaction time functions, errors on negative tests being greatly increased but errors on positive tests greatly decreased. These predictions seem not implausible, but relevant empirical data seem to be unavailable in the literature because investigators in the Sternberg tradition have uniformly tried to hold error frequencies to very low levels.

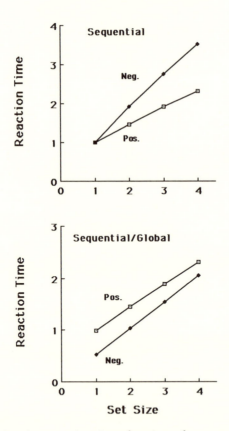

Fig. 7.10 Set-size, reaction-time functions for sequential (upper panel) and sequential/global (lower panel) versions of array model, computed with the same parameter values.

The set-size functions for the sequential model shown in the top panels of Figs. 7.8 and 7.9 are reproduced in Figs. 7.10 and 7.11 for convenience in comparing them with functions computed for the sequential/global model with the same parameter values and shown in the lower panels. The slopes of the reaction time functions are little affected by the addition of the global component; and the drop from the upper to the lower panel of Fig. 7.10 in overall level of reaction times for negative tests may be peculiar to the particular assumption that times for single comparisons in the global process are only half those for the sequential process. The relationships shown for error functions in Fig. 7.11 do not depend on this special assumption and thus may have more generality. Because the response probabilities generated by the global process are based on much larger similarities than those generated by the sequential process, the probability of an Old response is

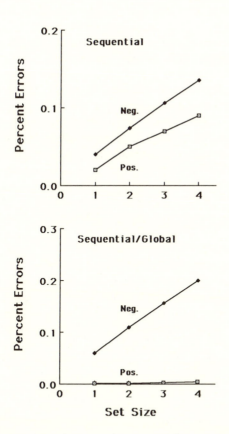

Fig. 7.11 Set-size, error functions for sequential (upper panel) and sequential/global (lower panel) versions of array model, computed with the same parameter values.

larger at each set size for the sequential/global model, yielding lower probabilities of errors on positive tests (misses) but higher probabilities of errors on negative trials (false alarms)

A substantial effort will be needed to assess the empirical adequacy of the various versions of the array model for the Sternberg task and to determine whether subjects tend to shift from pure sequential to sequential/global processing when it would be adaptive (for example, when there is a premium for a high hit rate). The main point of interest in the presentation given here is that, unlike most other theoretical approaches to the Sternberg paradigm, the array model requires no special assumptions about relationships between reaction times and error frequencies in order to yield predictions regarding both types of data.

7.5 On recognition as a measure of memory

Referring back to the opening passage of this chapter, we conclude that recognition does not, in general, provide a direct window to memory. Except in very short-term memory, a recognition test does not yield direct access to the memory representation of the tested item. Rather, computation of the global similarity of the item to the current contents of the memory array yields evidence as to whether the item has, in fact, been stored on some previous occasion. Further, the judgment as to whether a test item is old or new is a relative one, based on the relative similarities of the old and new items presented on a forced-choice test or the relative similarities of a test item to the Old and New arrays in an old/new test. Recognition may often provide the best available basis for estimating memory storage, but only if interpretations of data are guided by appropriate models.

Appendix 7.1 Application of signal detectability theory to recognition

A common problem in sensory psychology is to determine a person's ability to detect a signal in a noisy background, for example, a word transmitted on an intercom or an image of an airplane on a cluttered radar screen. The critical question is whether a response of "yes" to a display including a signal signifies that the observer detected the signal or only that the observer had a bias for saying yes. The standard way of dealing with this problem, adapted from analogous problems in engineering, is based on signal detectability theory, available to psychologists in numerous sources (e.g., Swets 1964; McNicol 1972). The essentials of the theory for our purposes are illustrated in Fig. A7.1.1. Populations of trials on which an observer is presented with noise alone or with the signal in noise are assumed to generate the distributions of internal states represented by the two normal distribution curves shown in the figure. The problem for the observer is that

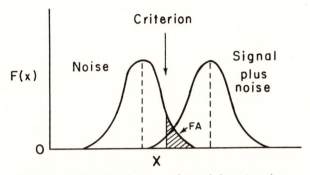

Fig. 7.A1   Signal and noise distributions of signal detection theory.

the internal state generated by a stimulus corresponding to any particular point on the x axis might have come from either distribution. The observer's solution is assumed to be to set a criterion above which all stimuli will be reported as signals and below which all stimuli will be reported as noise. Moving the criterion to the left will increase the frequencies of both correct detections and incorrect yes responses, *hits* (H) and *false alarms* (FA), respectively, in the terminology of the theory; moving the criterion to the right will decrease false alarms at the expense of also decreasing the frequency of hits. The degree of separation of the means of the signal and noise distributions (denoted by d' in the theory) is the basic measure of accuracy of detection, and the computational machinery of the theory enables one to estimate d' from observed frequencies of hits and false alarms.

Following the introduction of detectability theory into psychology by Tanner and Swets (1954), it became the standard basis for distinguishing discriminability from response bias in perception and psychophysics, and the possibility of applying the theory also to recognition memory was seized on by Murdock (1965), among others.

The analogy between experiments on sensory detection and on recognition memory hinges on the correspondence between the yes and no responses to a recognition test and the yes and no responses to a test of sensory detection. The data of either a detection or an old/new recognition experiment can be summarized in a fourfold table, as in Table 7.A1. The problem for the investigator in the recognition case is to decide whether an Old response reflects the presence of a trace of the test stimulus in memory or only of a response bias. A simple and useful tactic is to convert the observed response proportions to the measure labeled d in the table—the difference between the proportions of hits and false alarms. Applying signal detectability theory, the same response proportions are converted to an

Table 7.A1   The fourfold table for old/new recognition

Stimulus	Response		Probability
	"Old"	"New"	
Old	Hit	Miss	$P_O(O)$
New	False alarm	Correct rejection	$P_N(O)$

Indices of discriminability
$$d = P_O(O) - P_N(O)$$
$$d' = f\{P_O(O), P_N(O)\}$$

Numerical example

Old	0.60	0.40	0.60
New	0.50	0.50	0.50

Indices of discriminability
$$d = 0.10$$
$$d' = 0.26$$

estimate, denoted d', of the difference between the two distributions shown in Fig. 7.A1. Among its desirable properties, d' is expressed in standard deviation units, familar to psychologists in innumerable contexts, so one immediately recognizes a d' of 0 as indicating no discrimination between signal and noise, or between presence and absence of a memory trace, and a d' of 2 or 3 as indicating a high degree of discrimination. I will not go into the mathematics of deriving d' or the problems of determining whether the assumptions that need to be made about the noise and signal plus noise distributions are justified in specific applications.* Like many investigators in cognitive psychology, I use the d' measure as a convenient index of discriminability that facilitates comparisons of results across studies, without much concern about the interpretation in terms of normal distribution curves, and look up the d' values for empirically obtained hit and false alarm frequencies in the tables published in Swets (1964).

Appendix 7.2   Array-model computations for list-length/list-strength design in old/new recognition

For convenience, we start by reproducing Equations 7.7 and 7.8 from the text. These give probabilities of hits and false alarm as a function of list length, n, item similarity, s, and old and new category preload parameters, s_0

---

* The derivations are presented at an elementary level by McNicol (1972).

and s_N for the pure weak condition (each item in the study list has a single presentation),

$$P_O(O) = (1+(n-1)s+s_0)/(1+(n-1)s+s_0+s_N) \tag{7.A1}$$

and

$$P_N(O) = (ns+s_0)/(ns+s_0+s_N). \tag{7.A2}$$

For the Pure Strong condition (each item in the study list has two presentations), these become

$$P_O(O) = (2+2(n-1)s+s_0)/(2+2(n-1)s+s_0+s_N) \tag{7.A3}$$

and

$$P_N(O) = (2ns+s_0)/(2ns+s_0+s_N). \tag{7.A4}$$

The conversion merely requires doubling the summed similarity of an old or new test item to the items stored in the Old category of the memory array. For the mixed condition, we need to distinguish on an old test whether the tested item was weak or strong (presented once or twice). For a weak item, hit probability is

$$P_O(O) = (1+(n_1-1)s+2n_1s+s_0)/(1+(n_1-1)s+2n_1s+s_0+s_N) \tag{7.A5}$$

and for a strong item

$$P_O(O) = (2+2(n_1-1)s+n_1s+s_0)/(2+2(n_1-1)s+n_1s+s_0+s_N), \tag{7.A6}$$

where $n_1 = n/2$. Finally, probability of a false alarm on a test of a new item is

$$P_N(O) = (n_1s+2n_1s+s_0)/(n_1s+2n_1s+s_0+s_N). \tag{7.A7}$$

Appendix 7.3 Summary of study of memory load in old/new recognition: Experiment 7.1

The purpose of the experiment was to assess the effects of different memory preloads on old/new recognition. The different preloads were produced by giving subjects preliminary experience (Phase 1) with sequences of stimuli that were entirely distinct from those used in the subsequent recognition test but of either the same or a different type. The data of main interest were obtained in Phase 2 where subjects in all conditions were engaged in a 24-trial old/new recognition test in which 12 items (brief descriptions of buildings) each occurred twice. The question at issue was how recognition during this test series would be affected by the memory load that had been generated by the immediately preceding experience with either very similar or very dissimilar items.

Table 7.A2   Design of memory load study

Condition	Phase 1 Trials			Phase 2 Trials	
	1–24	25–48	49–72	1–12	13–24
1			Bldg1	Bldg2	Bldg2
2	Bldg1	Bldg1	Bldg1	Bldg2	Bldg2
3			Digits	Bldg2	Bldg2
4	Digits	Digits	Digits	Bldg2	Bldg2

Note: Bldg1 and Bldg2 denote samples from sets 1 and 2, described in the text.

Method

The subjects were 48 Harvard undergraduates, 12 in each of the four conditions of the experiment, who were paid for their service. Stimuli were presented on a microcomputer screen and responses entered on the keyboard.

The stimuli for which recognition was tested in Phase 2 were descriptions of buildings (denoted Bldg), each constituting a triad of features (e.g., stone, Victorian, landscaped) drawn from a set of eight. The other type of stimuli used were digit triads (denoted Digit) drawn without replacement from the range 101–999.

The design is summarized in Table 7.A2. During Phase 1, subjects in conditions 1 and 2 viewed sequences of 24 or 72 Bldg stimuli drawn from a set of 12, denoted Set 1; each stimulus occurred twice within each block of 24 trials. Subjects in conditions 3 and 4 viewed sequences of 24 or 72 Digit stimuli, triads with the same constraints on repetition. In all conditions, subjects responded to the stimuli as described below for the test trials.

During Phase 2, subjects in all conditions were tested on the same set of Bldg stimuli, Set 2, which was entirely distinct from Set 1, although the stimuli in the two sets were of course highly similar, being formed from the same list of eight features. The test comprised a series of 24 trials during which 12 stimuli each occurred twice, and on each trial subjects made an estimate of the probability that the test stimulus was "old."

Results

The data of primary interest are the percentages of old responses to old and new stimuli in the test series and the d' scores derived from these. Mean response percentages are presented separately for the first and second 12 trials of the test series in Table 7.A3. Analyses of variance were computed on the response percentages and d' values over the full test series. In the analysis

Table 7.A3 Percentages of old responses to old and new test stimuli in memory load study

		Test trials			
		1–12		13–24	
Condition	Preload	New	Old	New	Old
1	24 Bldg	40	80	40	72
2	72 Bldg	33	73	22	82
3	24 Digits	10	51	28	69
4	72 Digits	17	75	28	66

Note: Computed with $s = 0.1$, $s_0 = 0.25$.

of response percentages, the main effect of Bldg vs. Digit preload was significant for responses to new stimuli ($F(1,40) = 56.9$, $p<0.001$) but non-significant for old stimuli. The main effect of new vs. old stimuli and the interaction of this factor with type of preload were both significant ($F(1,40) = 268.8$ and 15.75, respectively, $p<0.001$). The difference between Bldg preload and no preload (using the first 24 trials of Phase 1 in conditions 1 and 2 for the no preload data) was significant for responses to new stimuli ($F(1,20) = 45.9$, $p<0.001$) but not significant for responses to old stimuli. The effect of Digit preload vs. no preload was not significant for either old or new stimuli. Analyses on the d' measures showed a significant effect of Bldg preload vs. no preload ($F(1,20) = 18.73$), $p<0.001$) and Bldg vs. Digit preload ($F(1,20) = 13.49$, $p<0.001$) but nonsignificance for Digit preload vs. no preload.*

Appendix 7.4 Summary of repetition study: Experiment 7.2

Method

Design

The stimuli were a set of pronounceable pseudowords comprising all of the 64 patterns that could be constructed by choosing one member of the pair of letters assigned to each of six positions. The letters, in their serial positions, were:

c   a   s   p   e   h

w   u   n   f   i   d

---

* It should be noted that the tests for preload vs. no preload were less sensitive than any of the other comparisons because they were based on data from different stimulus sets as well as different subject groups.

yielding the stimulus pseudowords caspeh, canfid, wanpeh, and so on. The 64 patterns were randomly partitioned into eight subsets of eight patterns each, henceforth denoted s1, s2, . . . ,s8. Pairs of subsets were combined, with the elements randomly intermixed, to form the 16-stimulus lists presented in study blocks. The assignments of subsets to lists are shown in Table 6.10 for each of two groups, denoted Shift and No shift. For the No shift group, subset s1 was included in the study list for each block, hence constituting repeated items in blocks 2–7, and was combined with a different subset of novel items in each block. The shift group had essentially the same arrangement on blocks 1–6, but the repeated items in block 7 came from the subset that was novel in block 6.

The 32 subjects were divided into two groups of 16, and, within each group, four subjects were assigned to each of four random partitionings of the 64-item stimulus set.

Procedure

The subjects were Harvard undergraduates or other student-age individuals from the Harvard community. They were instructed that they would see a series on nonsense words on a Macintosh computer screen, some of which might be repeated, and were to decide for each display how confident they were that the nonsense word was old or new, that is, had or had not appeared previously in the series. A confidence judgment was made by typing a number from 1 to 100 on the computer keyboard, 100 indicating highest confidence that the item was old and 1 indicating highest confidence that the item was new. After seeing a sample display of a letter string not included in

Table 7.A4   Data from repetition study

	Block		
	2	6	7
% *Old	Old*			
No shift	75	87	89
Shift	77	87	81
% *Old	New*			
No shift	64	71	75
Shift	65	74	78
d'			
No shift	0.28	0.53	0.63
Shift	0.39	0.55	0.17

the experimental set, the subjects ran through the 112 experimental trials in continuous sequence, with no indication of breaks between blocks.

Results

Data of prime interest for statistical analysis are the percentages of correct recognitions (Old|old), false alarms (Old|new), and the corresponding d' values for blocks 2, 6, and 7, summarized for the no shift and shift groups in Table 7.A4. An ANOVA on the percentage correct scores yielded a highly significant repetition effect, blocks: $F(2,48) = 16.1, p<0.001$ and a marginally significant interaction of blocks with groups, $F(2,48) = 3.5, p<0.05$. The increase in Old|new over blocks was similarly significant, $F(2,48) = 9.2$, $p<0.001$, but the interaction with blocks was nonsignificant. For the d' values, only the decrease from block 6 to block 7 in the shift group was significant, $t(15) = 2.9, p = 0.01$. The comparison of d' values for the two groups on block 7 enables us to conclude that there is a significant effect of number of repetitions when the point in the series at which the test occurs (and therefore the total memory load at the point of the test) is controlled.

8   Categorization and cognition: reprise

Presenting a picture of the state of research and theory in a rapidly moving field poses special challenges. In the short time since I began preparing the lectures that led to this book, my view of the field of categorization research and the family relationships among models has changed in some conspicuous respects. Even the centrality of classification in the domain of cognition appears now in a somewhat different light. Although classification is indeed implicated in many, perhaps all, forms of cognitive performance, the unifying theme we have seen emerging from the works reviewed is not commonality in aspects of performance, but rather the pervasive importance of the concepts of memory representation in terms of attributes and of access to memory by similarity computations. In this chapter, with the benefit of a new theoretical perspective, we will take a second look at some pivotal, often controversial, concepts and distinctions that were taken up without thorough analysis in earlier chapters.

8.1 The basis of classification in memory

8.1.1 The new faces of instance memory

The central role of instance memory in cognitive research and theory comes as a late chapter in a Horatio Alger "rags-to-riches" story. What is now termed episodic, or instance, memory was long relegated to the lowliest class of cognitive functions, associated with rote memorization, mnemonic stunts, and the like. But two distinct, though related, lines of theoretical development beginning in the 1970s have led to the casting of this concept in a radically different light. One line is a growing appreciation of the range of cognitive activities in which instance memory is significantly implicated. First, an early study of the learning of artificial grammars by Reber (1967) yielded the suggestion that, under some conditions, the learning might proceed by passive storage of memories of specific examples rather than by a process of abstraction, an idea that was later documented and extended by Brooks (1978). Next, instance memory appeared as a basic ingredient of the dynamic, episodic memory system in Schank's artificial intelligence program for language processing and thinking (Schank 1982; Schank, Collins, and Hunter 1986). Proceeding toward the present, the trend has continued with demonstrations of a role of instance memory in knowledge acquisition by Whittlesea (1987), in the perception and recognition of letters and words by

Whittlesea and Brooks (1988), in the development of automatization of performance by Logan (1988), and, still further afield, in phenomena of social influence and imitation by Kvadsheim (1992).

Indeed, instance memory is in the air. However, no number of demonstrations that it is implicated in various phenomena adds up to an advance in theory. Progress toward supplying the missing ingredient, an understanding of the mechanisms that bring instance memory to bear on performance, has come from developments in the broader sphere of models of memory (reviewed by Estes 1991*a*). The perhaps most conspicuous trend over the past two decades has been from a conception of item storage and retrieval (characteristic of the models assembled in Norman 1972) to one of global computation on composite memories (Hinton and Anderson 1981; Murdock 1982; Rumelhart and McClelland 1986; Estes, in press). The continuation of this trend in the present volume is marked by the simplicity and tractability of the process assumed for accessing a composite "instance memory" by similarity computations based on the product rule. The power of the concept of instance memory as a vehicle of thought is now seen to lie in the potentiality for bringing the whole weight of accumulated memory to bear on current judgments and decisions, rather than in the uncertain and relatively rare retrieval of specific memories of past episodes.

8.1.2 Summary of the assumptions of the array-similarity model

Because my presentation of the core array-similarity model has unfolded incrementally over several chapters of this book, it may useful to bring the principal assumptions together in compact form for ease of reference.

(a) Learning

At the end of an experimental trial, or other comparable learning episode, a featural representation of the stimulus pattern perceived, including a category label if one has been presented, is stored in the memory array. In general, pattern storage is assumed to be probabilistic rather than deterministic, with a parameter, p, representing the probability that the pattern presented on a trial is effectively stored in memory. For simplicity, p is assumed equal to unity unless otherwise specified.

(b) Decay in availability of stored representations

With some probability, any stored pattern suffers decay (i.e., becomes less available for comparisons with newly perceived patterns) during any trial following storage. For mathematical convenience, the decay probability is denoted $1-a$, where a has a value between 0 and 1; thus, a is the probability that no decay occurs on a trial.

(c) The product rule

The similarity between any two patterns each described by N binary-valued attributes or on/off features is given by the expression s^{N-k}, where k denotes the number of matches between the two patterns and s is a similarity parameter with a value between 0 and 1. In the case of continuous-valued attributes, the value of s for the ith attribute, denoted s_i, is given by the exponential function

$$s_i = e^{-cd_i}, \tag{8.1}$$

where d_i is the distance between the patterns on the ith attribute, and c is a constant; the similarity between the patterns is given by the product of the s_i over all N attributes.

(d) Initial memory load

At the outset of any categorization task, some background information about types of materials to be encountered is assumed to be stored in the memory array. A parameter s_0, denoting the average similarity of any exemplar pattern to this background information, is added to the sum whenever the similarity of a test pattern to the array is computed.

(e) Category similarity

Category labels are assumed to have the same properties as the features or attributes of the stimulus patterns that serve as category exemplars. If, in a category structure, the category exemplars are defined in terms of N attributes, then a memory representation of the occurrence of an exemplar plus a category label is defined on $N+1$ attributes, one of which may be termed a categorical attribute. The similarity between any two different category labels (i.e., values on the categorical attribute) is represented by a parameter σ having the same properties as the parameter s, which represents similarity between two different stimulus features.

(f) Computation of exemplar-to-category similarities and categorization probabilities

When a stimulus pattern Π is presented for categorization with, for example, A and B as the alternative categories, the features of Π are combined with those of the category labels to form two vectors (feature lists), which may be denoted Π,A and Π,B. The summed similarity of each of these to the current contents of the full memory array, denoted Sim(Π,A) and Sim(Π,B), respectively, is then computed by means of the product rule (applied as specified in Chapter 6, p.158). The ratio of these summed similarities determines the categorization probability according to an expression of the form

$$P(\text{A}) = \text{Sim}(\Pi,\text{A})/(\text{Sim}(\Pi,\text{A})+\text{Sim}(\Pi,\text{B})). \tag{8.2}$$

8.2 Concepts and categories

It did not seem fruitful to dwell on the distinction between the key terms concept and category at the start of this book, because meanings are usually better grasped through experiencing terms in use than by pursuing precise definitions. However, it may be useful at this point to look at the distinction in the light of the many applications of the terms in the preceding chapters. For a standard definition of *concept*, we find in the American Heritage Dictionary "a general idea or understanding, especially one derived from specific instances." This characterization seems quite satisfactory as far as it goes, but we need also some clarification of what it means to have a concept—that is, in what observable respects does an individual who grasps a particular concept differ from an individual who does not? Our review of research on concepts and categories suggests an answer: the dictionary definition should continue ". . . and taking the form of a knowledge structure that enables or mediates categorizations." The mark of having mastered a concept is the ability to categorize objects or events of a domain in ways that could not be accomplished in the absence of the concept.

So far, so good, but now we need some sharpening of the everyday notion of categorization. Starting again with the dictionary, we find for category: "a specific division in a system of classification; class." The key term here is "system." Not all ways of classifying a collection of objects satisfy our intuitive notion of categorization. As expressed by Murphy and Medin (1985), members of a category must have a property termed *coherence*. If we numbered the trees we encountered in a walk through a woods, we could define the classes "odd trees" and "even trees," but these classes would entirely lack coherence because knowledge of the class membership of a tree would convey no other information about it. In contrast, classes defined on the basis of properties of bark and shapes of leaves would be seen as sensible and coherent. The body of research discussed in the preceding chapters enables us to go further toward sharpening the notions of category and coherence: a category is a knowledge structure relating information about instances to category labels and allowing both prediction from attributes of instances to category assignments and inference from category labels to attributes of instances. In the example of the trees, perceiving the shape of a leaf may enable us to say with confidence that a particular tree is an oak; and knowing that a tree is an oak will enable us to predict that its seeds will be acorns.

My conclusion that category coherence is at bottom a consequence of similarity relationships may seem at odds with the argument of Murphy and Medin (1985) that coherence derives from the organization of concepts by background knowledge and informal theories. However, I think the differences in interpretations are resolvable. I will comment separately on the roles of similarity and background knowledge.

Murphy and Medin make the point that similarity does not explain why, in people's everyday experience, some possible categories are formed and some are not. On this issue, I would say, first, that similarity relationships among objects or events are crucial determiners of what categories can be formed in a domain (in general agreement with Smith 1990). Second, similarity plays a critical role in determining the functional, or adaptive, value of categorizations by virtue of being basic to the computational algorithms that enable us to extract information from representations of categories in the memory system. The question of how a learner in a natural environment selects the categories to be formed from among all those that could be formed is beyond the scope of the theories developed or reviewed in this book. A number of theorists have contributed insights concerning the properties of categories that determine their usefulness in natural environments (Anderson 1991; Ahn and Medin 1992; Corter and Gluck 1992), but, except for an exploratory effort by Ahn and Medin (1992), nothing has been accomplished toward modelling the process of category formation.

The role of background knowledge in categorization has not been discussed hitherto in this volume because the task I undertook was to explicate the mental machinery that enables us to form and use concepts and categories, and our understanding of this machinery comes largely from laboratory studies carried out under highly simplified conditions. In most of the studies, the information made available to experimental subjects is confined to observation of category exemplars, defined almost exclusively in terms of simple, perceptual features. Doubtless the learning that occurs is often influenced to some degree by background knowledge, including informal theories or "mental models," that subjects bring to the experimental situation. But merely recognizing the relevance of prior knowledge does not do much to advance theory. What is the form of representation of background knowledge in memory, and what mental operations bring the knowledge to bear on a specific task? In trying to attack these questions, I proceed on the working hypothesis that knowledge brought by subjects to category learning experiments may be represented in the same array format as information gained from observations of instances and may be processed by the same similarity-based computational procedures. I will illustrate this idea in terms of an example that expands on the medical diagnosis paradigm used in many experimental studies.

Let us imagine that our ability to diagnose the presence or absence of a disease, M, evolves through two stages. In the first stage, we have opportunities to learn the frequencies with which certain observable symptoms occur in people who do or do not have the disease. We would expect this experience to give rise to a memory array taking the form

Symptoms	M	M−
a	0.3	0.2
cd	0.1	0.4
d	0.2	0.3
ad	0.4	0.1

the lower-case letters denoting individual symptoms, M and M- the presence and absence of the disease, and the cell entries illustrative of relative frequencies with which the symptoms, alone or in combination, might have been observed in the categories. We can compute from the exemplar model the probability of assigning each symptom pattern to each category in the usual way. The overall probability of correct categorization depends on the exemplar frequencies, but assuming all to be equally frequent, we determine, skipping details, that the maximum probability correct is about 0.72 (obtaining when the similarity parameter, s, is equal to 0).

Now, suppose that a genetic defect is discovered in the absence of which disease M cannot occur, although some people with the defect may not manifest the disease. How can we represent this knowledge in the array framework so that we can predict the effect of the knowledge on diagnostic judgments? The straightforward approach is to define features g and g− to denote presence and absence of the defect, respectively, these features having the same formal properties as the perceptible symptoms a, b, c, and d. Our knowledge about the relation between the defect and the disease can then be represented in the form

Feature	M	M−
g	1	0.4
g−	0	0.6

The numerical values in the M− column are again purely illustrative, of course. In an actual research situation, estimates of these values would be based on empirical data.

The next question is how this information would be used by a diagnostician. One possibility is simply to add the features g and g− to the other symptoms and form a new array in which entries in the column of exemplars (symptom patterns) would be ag, ag−, cdg, and so on., and compute similarities on this array in the standard manner. However, one might feel (in line with the thesis of Murphy and Medin 1985) that the features g and g− should have a special status because of the causal relation between these and the disease. To provide this potentiality, I propose that for an individual who has the special knowledge about the genetic defect and also has observed the symptom-disease occurrences, both memory arrays are formed, and that the individual has the option of using either as the basis for categorization. When the g,g− array is used, similarity computations for the example yield for probability of correct categorization

$$P(C) = \alpha\left[1/(1.4+0.6s)\right] + (1-\alpha)\left[(0.6+0.4s)/(0.6+1.4s)\right], \qquad (8.3)$$

where α denotes the probability of occurrence of g. When s is equal to 0, $P(C)$ takes on its maximal value

$$P(C) = \alpha(1/1.4) + (1-\alpha)(1), \qquad (8.4)$$

which could be as small as 0.7 in the implausible event that α was equal to 1, but would be much higher for moderate to small values of α (e. g., 0.85 for $\alpha=0.5$ and 0.97 for $\alpha=0.1$).

Development of a submodel for the process whereby the individual chooses which array to consult at the point of making a categorization judgment is the objective of current research that it would be premature to bring up here. The main thrust of this discussion is to make the point that acknowledgment of the importance of background knowledge does not imply that we need throw up our hands and put aside the theory we have built up to deal with memory arrays generated in simplified laboratory situations. It seems more fruitful to proceed on the assumption that the same basic machinery will continue to serve—specifically, that background knowledge and theories can be represented in an individual's memory system and processed in the same way as information gained from observation of category instances.

8.3 The place of rules in a memory-based theory

With a grasp of the scope and power of array-similarity models, we may be able to do something toward clarifying the role of rules and heuristics in concept formation. As brought out in Chapter 1, there has traditionally been a sharp opposition between approaches to categorization and induction centered on the discovery and use of rules and approaches based on processes of learning and memory. Over several decades since the early work on concept formation, these approaches have diverged, as witness the debates between proponents of connectionist and rule-based treatments of language acquisition and processing (Lachter and Bever 1988; Pinker and Prince 1988; Seidenberg and McClelland 1989) and reasoning (Holland, Holyoak, Nisbett, and Thagand 1986; Smith, Langston, and Nisbett 1992), and the efforts to choose between interpretations of concept formation and categorization based on instance memory and those based on rules and hypothesis testing (Nosofsky, Clark, and Shin 1989).

Critiques of connectionist approaches to cognition typically start by arguing, no doubt correctly, that no model in that category has been able to account for all forms of performance in a cognitive domain, including, for example, language acquisition, categorization, and reasoning. They continue then with a claim that all performance can be interpreted in terms of the possession and use of rules. The interpretations have an unsatisfying character, however, for it is clear a priori that once we know what performance occurs in any situation, we can describe it in terms of rules. Recall, for example, the XOR classification task discussed in Chapter 2, p. 48, with the design

Exemplar	Category	
	A	B
11	1	0
12	0	1
21	0	1
22	1	0

where the two columns under Exemplar represent two features, each of which has a value of either 1 or 2, and the entries under Category indicate that in a block of four trials exemplars 11 and 22 each occur once in Category A, and exemplars 12 and 21 each once in Category B. If a learner masters this task, we can say (gratuitously) that he or she has adopted a rule to the effect that patterns with the same value on both attributes should be assigned to Category A and the other patterns to Category B. But what does describing the observed performance as rule governed add to our understanding? We would like to have a theory that could address such questions as how learning would be affected if pattern 22 never occurred or if the entries under Category in the design table were changed in some specific way. To be able to deal with such questions, we need a theory that specifies how rules are represented in the memory system and how the representations are processed in response to task demands. As with the role of background knowledge, my suggestion is that classification by means of rules can be accommodated within a theory based on conceptions of memory and memory processing.

The currently standard way of representing rules in cognitive theory is the apparatus of production systems (Anderson 1983; Holland, Holyoak, Nisbett, and Thagard 1986; Newell 1973). A production is a condition-action pair; an example from the XOR task discussed in Chapter 2 (p. 48) is "if the exemplar pattern is 11 or 22, then assign it to Category A." A production system is a set of productions that accomplishes a given task. However, for the interpretation of classification, the production system may be regarded as just a specialization of the array model. For the XOR problem, the array representation (Chapter 2, Table 2.12) generates probabilities for assigning each exemplar pattern to Categories A and B; in the special case when the probabilities are all 1 or 0, the array model functions exactly like a production system. The array model is not limited to this special case and is richer in its implications, providing straightforward answers to questions like those raised above. For example, if the probabilities of exemplars in categories in the array above are changed from 1 and 0 to 0.9 and 0.1, the probability of Category A in the presence of exemplar 11 is readily computed to be $(0.9+0.1s)/(1+s)$, which varies in value from 0.5 to 0.9 depending on the value of s.

Since any object or event that can enter into the condition of a production can be described in terms of attributes, it seems clear that any rule can be expressed in an array representation. In special cases, like the simple XOR problem, the rule for correct categorization may be equivalent to the array representation of the problem. More generally, the representation of a rule must be abstracted from the full array representation. Suppose, for example, that a third, "noise," attribute were added to the exemplar patterns in the XOR task, yielding the representation

Exemplar	Category	
	A	B
111	1	0
112	1	0
121	0	1
122	0	1
211	0	1
212	0	1
221	1	0
222	1	0

the third feature being described as "noise" because each of its values occurs with equal frequency in Categories A and B. Now the array model could solve the problem, i.e., yield uniformly correct categorizations, only if the similarity parameter, s, were equal to 0. The rule for correct categorization would be the same as before, but stated in terms of only the first two attributes of each pattern. One way in which the array-similarity model can cope with situations that call for attending to relevant and ignoring irrelevant cues or attributes was discussed in Chapter 1, p. 26, and the mechanism suggested there in connection with the "twin problem" could be adapted to the three-feature XOR problem, thus possibly eliminating the need to distinguish memory-based from rule-based decisions.

However, if we wish to evaluate an approach closer to that of traditional hypothesis-testing models, that also can be done within the array framework. We might, for example, assume that, as a consequence of instructions or prior learning, a learner in the three-feature XOR situation starts with some probability of ignoring some one of the attributes and therefore forming a reduced memory array. If the third attribute were ignored, the reduced array would be the two-attribute array shown above, and responding on the basis of this array (which could be described as rule-based responding) would be uniformly correct. If the first or second attribute were ignored, the reduced array generated would not yield uniformly correct responding, and one might speak of an incorrect or inadequate rule. It would seem reasonably straightforward to construct an adaptive network model to account for the way in which an individual might learn by trial and error to select the best available reduced array as the basis for responding, but I will not pursue the details here. I wish only to make the point that rules need not be viewed as differing qualitatively from the memory representations of the array framework and that interpretations of categorization in terms of rules and interpretations in terms of memory processing may converge as increased attention is directed to the problems of how rules are represented in the human memory system and what cognitive operations bring rules into operation in specific tasks.

8.4 Representation and structure

In the array framework, classification is viewed as a special, though signally important, case of cognitive activity based on a memory system characterized by several general properties: traces of perceived items are coded and recorded in terms of attributes; the encoded traces are accessed by computing the similarity of a probe item, not just to the representation of that item, but to the whole current memory array. Accessibility of an item depends on the number of repetitions of the item, but generally even more strongly on the similarity of the item to others stored in the array and to the total size of the array.

The core array model comprises these concepts, all deriving, in essentials, from Medin and Schaffer (1978), together with the augmented processing assumptions regarding the computation of similarities between perceived items and memory arrays presented in Chapters 3 and 6. In this volume, I have been mainly concerned with testing and extending the capability of the core model to yield a priori predictions about phenomena of categorization and memory. The variety of new applications of the core model presented in the preceding chapters, together with the many detailed accounts of categorization data reported for the closely related "general context model" of Nosofsky (1984, 1986, 1992a), raise the question whether the framework of this model family is a sufficient basis for theories of classification and memory. Suggestions that the answer is negative have emerged on two fronts.

8.4.1 The issue of independence of attributes

Goldstone, Medin, and Gentner (1991) question the basic idea that representations of objects and events are encoded in memory in terms of independent attributes. In the array framework, we assume that attributes are independent; new features or attributes may be formed that involve relations among simpler or more primitive ones, but this process of "unitization" is assumed to result from a slower form of learning than the much faster process responsible for the acquisition of categorizations. For the most part, relational information emerges from computations based on the product rule when memory is tested. Goldstone, Medin, and Gentner propose, in contrast, that relational information is encoded in memory by means of a special class of features that are processed differently than independent attributes. At this juncture, almost nothing can be done to evaluate the claim for a need to assume different modes of similarity computation for independent and relational features. Data reported by Goldstone, et al appear supportive of their position. However, the interpretations are based on intuitive suppositions about the way their stimulus displays are encoded by their experimental subjects. In one of their experiments, displays took the form

Type A	T	S	C
	T	S	C

Type B	T	S	C
	T	S	C
	S	S	S

where T, S, and C denote outline drawings of identical triangles, squares, and circles, respectively. For each type of display, subjects were asked to judge whether the stimulus (column of drawings) at the left was more similar to the stimulus in the center or the stimulus at the right. The result was a strong preference for center in Type A and right in Type B displays. On the assumption that T, S, and C are the features in terms of which subjects encode the stimuli, Goldstone, Medin, and Gentner argue that the result violates feature independence because it is incompatible with the contrast model of similarity. Obviously, on the same assumption, the result is also incompatible with the product rule. However, the supposition that subjects encode the stimuli solely in terms of T, S, and C as features needs justification. To disconfirm either the contrast model or the product rule, one would have to show that no reasonable assumption about the features used allows the model to predict the result. By "reasonable," I mean, not just that an assumption is intuitively plausible, but, further, that independent support for it can be adduced by standard methods, as, for example, feature listings by subjects or multidimensional scaling analyses. Models are not sources of new insights about the nature of attributes; rather, they are tools of analysis that can aid in the evaluation of assumptions or hypotheses about the nature of attributes (Dienes 1992). The findings of Goldstone, Medin, and Gentner pose an interesting challenge for array and network models, but much more spadework is needed to determine whether the findings can or cannot be accommodated within this model family.

8.4.2 Array versus network representations

Models of the array family, in particular the core model and the general context model, have been shown to account for many aspects of categorization, mainly static relationships between learning and transfer. But in earlier versions, they lacked specific assumptions as to how stimuli are processed in real time in the course of accessing memory and generating a categorization response. New results presented in this volume provide evidence that different modes of processing may be associated with different stages in the learning of a categorization. In the initial stage, representations of perceived category exemplars are stored in a chronologically ordered array, and these items can be retrieved by a process of sequential search. But as learning continues and the number of stored items becomes large, order information is lost, so that at a later stage, the accumulated memory is best interpreted as a canonical array, containing only featural information about exemplar patterns and their associated category labels.

The distinction between a chronological and a canonical memory array was introduced earlier without discussion (Chapter 4, pp. 106–8; also, Estes, in press). Now it needs closer examination. The terms "chronological" and "canonical" convey the spirit of the desired distinction, but have the drawback that they seem to imply a proliferation of types of arrays, as occurred with types of memory "stores" in an earlier period (Craik and Levy 1976; Roediger 1980). Actually, I think it is sufficient to think in terms of a single memory array. Under some conditions, sets of items in the array can be described, somewhat metaphorically as being chronologically organized and accessible by sequential search, but the relevant conditions may lie in similarity relations between the stored items and potential memory probes. Consider, for example, a typical short-term recognition experiment of the kind initiated by Sternberg (1966). On any experimental trial, a list of items (most often digits or words) is presented sequentially to the subject, and we assume that the sequence is encoded in the memory array in terms of perceptual features of the items together with contextual features. The latter represent characteristics of the background in which the items are perceived, including temporal positions within the trial. Thus, a memory representation of a three-item list presented on a typical trial would take the form

$$I_1 x$$
$$I_2 x$$
$$I_3 x$$

where I_i denotes item i defined in terms of its perceptual features , and x the features of the background context common to all items on the list. We assume that when some item from the list (termed a positive probe) is presented on an immediate recognition test, the background is unchanged and therefore the features of the list background, x, accompany the probe item. Thus for a test on item 2, the representation of the probe would be $I_2 x$ and its similarity to the list array would be $1+2s$, where s is the average perceptual similarity between items. If the same list had been presented earlier in the experimental session, the total memory array would contain representations deriving from both the earlier and the current trial,

$$I_1 x'$$
$$I_2 x'$$
$$I_3 x'$$
$$I_1 x$$
$$I_2 x$$
$$I_3 x$$
$$.$$
$$. \, ,$$

where x' denotes a list context different from x. Analyses of short-term memory studies in terms of the model indicate that the similarity between x and x' for lists presented in the same experimental session is often large enough to cause appreciable numbers of confusion errors between lists but that this similarity approaches zero for lists experienced in different situations or at much longer intervals (Estes 1991*b*). When the similarity between present and earlier contexts is zero or negligibly different from zero, a test item from the list with context x has virtually zero probability of activating any item from the earlier list, and we customarily drop the x terms from both the array and the probe representations, leaving just

$$I_1$$
$$I_2$$
$$I_3$$

for the array and I_2 for the probe in the example.

When lists of items are short, and especially when the task calls for ordered recall or recognition of items in their positions, we may expect information about the relative positions of items within a list to be included in the memory representation, e.g.,

$$I_1 x p_1$$
$$I_2 x p_2$$
$$I_3 x p_3$$

where p_i denotes the representation of list position for item i, and we speak, for convenience, of a chronologically ordered array. If a test item, for example, "item 1 in position 1," includes positional information, then the similarities between different p_i enter into the computation of item-to-category similarities and response probabilities. If a test item, e.g., $I_1 x$, does not include positional information, then we customarily drop the p_i terms from the array representation, since the positional similarities will not enter into similarity computations.

The point to be emphasized is that a chronologically ordered array is not a distinct type of memory structure; it is simply an array that includes positional information about item occurrences. Possibly some positional information is always included in a memory array; however, we take it into account only if test conditions make it relevant to similarity computations. The canonical form in which memory arrays have been written throughout most of this volume is a convenient shorthand portrayal of arrays formed in situations where neither positional nor contextual information needs to be taken into account. Thus, for example, the memory array for a list I_1 A, I_2 B, I_1 B, I_3 B, I_2 A, I_1 A, I_4 B presented in a categorization task can be portrayed alternatively in the format denoted "chronological,"

Item	Category
I_1	A
I_2	B
I_1	B
I_3	B
I_2	A
I_1	A
I_4	B

or in the format termed "canonical,"

Item	Category	
	A	B
I_1	2	1
I_2	1	1
I_3	0	1
I_4	0	1

Augmented by specific assumptions about similarity computations (spelled out in Chapter 6), the array-similarity model yields promising accounts of details of category learning and new applications to phenomena of inductive thinking (Chapter 6) and recognition and recall (Chapter 7).* It appears that this model will have enduring value for many purposes, but at the same time one may question whether it can provide a sufficient basis for interpreting all aspects of classification.

Among the phenomena that at this juncture seem to overtax the resources of the array-similarity model are some aspects of category-to-feature inference (discussed in Chapter 5), inverse base-rate effects (Medin and Edelson 1988), and relearning after reversals or other shifts of category assignments (Hurwitz 1990; Kruschke 1992b). An alternative approach to the modelling of categorization, deriving from connectionist theory, offers some promise of overcoming these limitations. The first exploration of this approach (Gluck and Bower 1988b) produced an adaptive network model that appeared to handle details of category learning more effectively than exemplar models (Estes, Campbell, Hatsopoulis, and Hurwitz 1989). However, the first comparisons were carried out on a very limited data base, and it soon became apparent that the network model had to be augmented with a means of handling nonlinear similarity relations, as done in my similarity-network model or in the closely related configural-cue model (Gluck and Bower 1988a; Gluck, Bower, and Hee 1989; Gluck 1991)† to produce a viable competitor to the exemplar model. Work discussed in Chapters 4 and 5 of this volume shows that the similarity-network and the augmented exemplar model are difficult to distinguish in their ability to handle most phenomena of classification. The network model does prove superior to the exemplar model at interpreting category-to-feature inference. The competitive learning mechanism of the network model enables it to generate the non-monotonic trends that have been observed for this type of inference over a learning series, an accomplishment beyond the scope of the exemplar model. And, as brought out in Chapter 7, the similarity-network model appears superior at interpreting some aspects of recognition, in particular, those having to do with manipulations of strength of memory traces. Further elaboration of the network architecture by addition of a layer of "hidden units" seems to be essential to progress on the shift phenomena (Hurwitz 1990; Kruschke 1992b).

---

* See also Medin and Florian (1992).

† Handling similarity in a different way, namely by adding some assumptions of stimulus sampling theory to the network formalism, has yielded a promising account of inverse base-rate effects (Gluck 1992); however, this version of the network model has not yet been extensively tested.

Over the last few years, research bearing on array and network model families has focussed largely on attempts to mount evidence differentially favoring the connectionist approach. The story of those attempts has been a series of "chapters" each starting with a new demonstration of superiority of a network model and concluding with some relatively minor revision or augmentation of the array model that redresses the balance. However, there has also been interest in constructing a model that could combine the special advantages of the array-similarity framework and the adaptive network. Efforts in that direction have produced the similarity-network model (Estes 1988; this volume, Chapter 3) and the much more elaborate ALCOVE model of Kruschke (1992*a*).

When I was preparing the lectures that eventuated in this volume, I thought that unification of the array-similarity and connectionist network formalisms was obviously the best available strategy. However, more recent research, discussed in Chapters 4 and 5, suggests possible advantages to a modular architecture within which models of these two types coexist, operating in parallel and competing for control of output channels, with one module being dominant early in learning, or in tasks restricted to short-term memory, and the other later in learning, or in tasks relying heavily on long-term memory. It would be premature to speculate about related brain mechanisms, but there are interesting parallels between this notion of parallel, though asynchronous, modules at the cognitive level and the kind of neural system suggested by research on hippocampal function (Squire 1992) and related neural modelling (McNaughton and Nadel 1990; Gluck and Myers 1992). Squire suggests that the ability to remember after a learning experience that an object was present in a particular context and later to retrieve the memory of the object depends on a hippocampal system that "binds together" the results of processing that occurs at different cortical sites during learning. However, this system is not essential to the functioning of long-term memory.

As the result of processes that are still poorly understood, the organization of memory storage is slowly transformed as time passes after learning. This transformation could involve rehearsal, additional retrieval opportunities, or acquisition of related material, or it could be largely endogenous. In any case, with time, the role of the hippocampal system diminishes until it is no longer necessary for either the maintenance of memory in storage or its retrieval. Concurrently the sites of storage in neocortex undergo two related kinds of changes. First, forgetting occurs. ... Second, the distributed networks that together constitute a whole memory develop greater coherence. (Squire 1992, p. 224)

I anticipate that an active line of research in the near future will focus on the problem of specifying a control structure that could accommodate concurrent array-similarity and network modules and a transition over time in the dominance of one or the other as the basis for cognitive performance.

8.5 Alternative theoretical approaches

8.5.1 The ACT framework

In this section, I will remark on a few currently active approaches to categorization and memory that differ in various respects from the one presented in the preceding chapters.* Among these, the "adaptive character of thought" (ACT) model of Anderson (1983) is by far the broadest in scope, with applications ranging from short-term recognition to complex forms of reasoning and language processing. Anderson's general "cognitive architecture" is much more elaborate than the array framework, so I will limit comparisons to the specialized version of ACT that has been applied to categorization by Anderson, Kline, and Beasley (1979) and Elio and Anderson (1981). The representational assumptions of ACT are very general, information about category exemplars being stored in memory in the form of propositions. However, attribute descriptions can be cast in propositional form, so one could regard the array representation as a possible special case of propositional representation. One important difference is that ACT does not employ the product rule, or any comparable algorithm, for computation of similarities, and consequently similarity does not play a central role in memory access in the ACT model. Another difference is that, in ACT, processes of generalization and differentiation cause the memory for a sequence of category exemplars to include not only representations of the perceived patterns but also derived, or "abstract," patterns that include only what is common to successively perceived exemplars of a given category. As a consequence, predictions from ACT resemble those from the exemplar model in many respects but also are sensitive to the way in which similar patterns are blocked during a sequence of learning trials, a property for which Elio and Anderson (1981) report some support. On the output side, ACT generates categorization responses on the basis of exemplar information by means of production systems. On the surface, the production formalism appears quite different from the computation of response probabilities in the array model, but, as mentioned earlier in this chapter, the properties of a production system are quite similar to those of an exemplar-by-category array coupled with computation of response probabilities via the product rule.

The two approaches diverge more widely in their treatments of other phenomena of memory, such as recognition and recall. In ACT, recognition is based on finding a match between a perceived stimulus pattern and a representation of the pattern in memory rather than on the global similarity between the perceived pattern and a whole memory array. Here the array approach is much closer to that of most other contemporary models of

---

* An instructive discussion of relations among some of these approaches is given by Cohen and Massaro (1992).

memory (Ratcliff 1978; Murdock 1982; Shiffrin, Ratcliff, and Clark 1990; Shiffrin and Raaijmakers 1992).

In some recent work, Anderson has departed somewhat from the ACT framework to pursue what he terms a "rational model" of categorization and memory (Anderson 1990,1991). The guiding idea in this development is that by studying the environment in which people carry out cognitive activities and the information systems that technology has produced, one should be able to discover the properties that must characterize an optimal information-processing system, and should then find that human memory has evolved so as to realize just these properties. Progress toward this goal is difficult to evaluate, but Anderson has augmented his "rational" assumptions with some of the machinery of ACT and finds that this composite model can account for many phenomena of categorization. In particular, it overcomes the inability of ACT to deal with probabilistic categorizations. As work goes on in an active field, it becomes difficult to produce a genuinely novel approach, so it does not come as a surprise that Nosofsky (1991a) has been able to show a close relationship between Anderson's "rational" model and his general context model. The two models in fact prove to be formally identical in some applications.

8.5.2 Hintzman's Minerva model

Another theoretical effort having many commonalities with those of Medin, Nosofsky, and myself is that of Hintzman (1986, 1988). Starting from experimental demonstrations that repetitions of an event in varied contexts produce distinct representations in memory, Hintzman developed a multiple-trace theory, dubbed Minerva, in which the representational assumptions are essentially the same as those of the array framework, and the only notable difference in processing assumptions is that Hintzman does not employ the product rule for similarity computations. The model has evolved through a series of versions, all implemented as computer simulations, and, in its present form, yields interpretations of categorization and recognition generally similar to those of array models. Like the array models, Hintzman's model has led to a number of new experimental findings; but the focus in the two approaches has been on different phenomena (Hintzman, for example, being much more concerned with frequency judgments and spacing effects) so there has been little interest in formal comparisons between them.

8.5.3 The general recognition model

The approach to categorization and recognition of Ashby and his associates, (Ashby and Perrin 1988; Ashby and Lee 1991,1992; Ashby 1992; Ashby and

Maddox, in press) is perhaps the one most distinctively different from that of the array family, especially in its representational assumptions. Rather than storing representations of perceived category exemplars in memory, the learner forms a representation of a multidimensional cognitive space appropriate to the task at hand and develops decision criteria in the form of curves that partition the space into regions that correspond to categories. The learning processes responsible for forming the representation and partitioning the space have not been dealt with in detail, attention being focussed mainly on the decision process. Categorization performance is a matter of assigning stimuli to appropriate regions. A perceived stimulus generates, not a single point in the cognitive space, as assumed by Nosofsky (1984, 1986, 1992a), but a distribution of points. The distribution is assumed to be multivariate normal in form, and the decision process is basically a generalization of classical signal detection theory.

Ashby's general recognition model has been developed in conjunction with a program of research on categorization and recognition utilizing very simple stimuli that vary on continuous sensory dimensions, and in this domain, it generates impressive quantitative accounts of performance. Comparisons between the general recognition model and the general context model in application to this domain have yielded results interpreted as favorable to each model by different investigators (Ashby and Lee 1991; Maddox and Ashby 1993; Nosofsky and Smith 1992).

8.5.4 Multilayer connectionist networks

A severe limitation of the models I have discussed in both the array and network families, is that interpretation of any situation has to start with intuitive judgments about the attributes or features of stimuli that require representation in the model. More complex models have been developed, for example, multilayer networks including "hidden units," that can address the problem of how a learner may discover the features or patterns relevant to a task in the course of category learning (see, for example, Hinton and Anderson 1981), but the implementation of this approach in relation to research on classification has hardly begun. I suspect that intensive exploration of the potentialities of hidden-unit models may be the next wave of theoretical effort in this area. For a straw in the wind, see Taraban and Palacios (in press).

8.5.5 On differential tests of models

Comparing two models in terms of their ability to fit a particular data set can be instructive, particularly to the investigators concerned, but, for the following reason, I doubt that they can be of much value in relative evaluation or choice between alternative approaches. A very common scenario in psychological research has two investigators (or groups), X and Y, each developing a model in close interaction with a program of research that aids in the testing and refining of successive versions of the model. The models are intended to apply to the same psychological domain, but the research programs employ almost non-overlapping materials and designs. At some point, either X or Y decides to apply the latest version of each model to experimental results generated in his research situation and finds his model to be superior. Impartial observers are likely to think that the exercise has merely yielded a foregone conclusion. A "fair," or really instructive comparison could take either of two forms. Ideally, the models should be compared with respect to their ability to handle the combined results of the two research programs. Unfortunately, the stage is not often set for this kind of comparison, and certainly it is not in the case of general recognition versus array models. More often it is feasible at a given time only to compare the two models in one of the research situations; but in such cases some preparatory work needs to be done. If, say, Y's data are to be used, then X, or someone thoroughly versed in X's approach, should adapt X's model to the situation in the same way that Y has done for Y's model, so that the comparison will involve the most appropriate representative of each approach.

An additional thought I will offer on comparisons is that differential tests of alternative models or approaches are best viewed as exercises that can yield information of value in the continuing development of each alternative, not as a game that should result in one alternative winning (being selected) and the other losing (being discarded). The "game" orientation presupposes that a clear-cut decision is always achievable, but the history of science presents many cases in which competing theories (e.g., the particle and wave theories of light) continue to coexist indefinitely. In the case of general recognition theory versus the array approach, I suspect that comparisons by means of fitting models to particular data sets are of limited value at this juncture because the ground on which comparisons are made is shifting rapidly. In the work reported in this volume, we have seen many indications that both modes of processing and the nature of memory representations may shift markedly from early to late in learning and from short-term to long-term memory domains. It is possible that similar shifts may be found in the tasks relied on by the developers of general recognition theory and that comparisons of the models may yield different results depending on stage of learning and temporal constraints on memory.

All of the approaches to classification and memory that I have touched on have produced models that gain support by virtue of their impressive accounts of data in selected experimental situations. The result may well be that constituents of apparently quite distinct models will appear in new combinations in the next wave of theory development. Differential evaluation of models is a multivalued enterprise and will certainly continue. However, I suspect that the center of most exciting action may be shifting toward efforts to develop a picture of the way in which different types of representations and decision mechanisms may coexist in the human cognitive system and how they relate to concepts emerging from neuroscience.

References

Achilles, E. M. (1920). Experimental studies in recall and recognition. *Archives of Psychology*, **27**, 1–80.

Ahn, W. and Medin, D. L. (1992). A two-stage model of category construction. *Cognitive Science*, **16**, 81–121.

Anderson, J. A. (1973). A theory for the recognition of items from short memorized lists. *Psychological Review*, **80**, 417–38.

Anderson, J. R. (1976). *Language, memory and thought*. Erlbaum, Hillsdale, NJ.

—— (1983). *The architecture of cognition*. Harvard University Press, Cambridge, MA.

—— (1990). *The adaptive character of thought*. Erlbaum, Hillsdale, NJ.

—— (1991). The adaptive character of human categorization. *Psychological Review*, **98**, 409–29.

—— and Bower, G. H. (1972). Configural properties in sentence memory. *Journal of Verbal Learning and Verbal Behavior*, **11**, 594–605.

—— and —— (1973). *Human associative memory*. Winston, Washington, D.C.

——, Kline, P. J. and Beasley, C. M. (1979). A general learning theory and its application to schema abstraction. In *The psychology of learning and motivation*, Vol. 13, (ed. G. H. Bower), pp. 277–318. Academic Press, New York.

Ashby, F. G. (1992). Multidimensional models of categorization. In *Multidimensional models of perception and cognition* (ed. F. G. Ashby), pp. 449–483. Erlbaum, Hillsdale, N.J.

—— and Lee, W. W. (1991). Predicting similarity and categorization from identification. *Journal of Experimental Psychology:General*, **120**, 150–72.

—— and —— (1992). On the relationship among identification, similarity and categorization: Reply to Nosofsky and Smith (1992). *Journal of Experimental Psychology: General*, **121**, 385–93.

—— and Maddox, W. T. (in press). Relations between prototype, exemplar and decision bound models of categorization. *Journal of Mathematical Psychology*.

—— and Perrin, N. A. (1988). Toward a unified theory of similarity and recognition. *Psychological Review*, **95**, 124–50.

Atkinson, R. C., Bower, G. H. and Crothers, E. J. (1965). *An introduction to mathematical learning theory*. Wiley, New York.

—— and Estes, W. K. (1963). Stimulus sampling theory. In *Handbook of Mathematical Psychology*, Vol. 2, (ed. R. D. Luce, R. R. Bush and E. Galanter), pp. 121–268). Wiley, New York.

—— and Juola, J. F. (1973). Factors influencing speed and accuracy of word recognition. In *Attention and performance. IV* (ed. S. Kornblum), pp. 583–612. Academic Press, New York.

—— and Shiffrin, R. (1968). Human memory: A proposed system and its control processes. In *The psychology of learning and motivation: advances in research and theory*, Vol. 2 (ed. K. W. Spence and J. T. Spence), pp. 89–195. Academic Press, New York.

Attneave, F. (1957). Transfer of experience with class-schemata to identification-learning of patterns and shapes. *Journal of Experimental Psychology*, **54**, 81–8.

Baddeley, A. D. (1976). *The psychology of memory*. Basic Books, New York.

—— (1986). *Working memory*. Oxford University Press, Oxford.

Bamber, D. (1969). Reaction times and error rates for "same"–"different" judgments of multidimensional stimuli. *Perception & Psychophysics*, **6**, 169–74.

Berkeley, G. (1710/1947). Treatise concerning the principles of human knowledge. In *The world's great thinkers. Man and spirit: the speculative philosophers*, (ed. S. Commins and R. N. Linscott). Random House, New York.

Bernbach, H. A. (1970). A multiple-copy model for postperceptual memory. In *Models of human memory*, (ed. D. A. Norman), pp. 103–16. Academic Press, New York.

Bjork, E. L. and Healy, A. F. (1974). Short-term order and item retention. *Journal of Verbal Learning and Verbal Behavior*, **13**, 80–97.

Bordage, G. and Zacks, R. (1984). The structure of medical knowledge in the memories of medical students and practitioners. *Medical Education*, **18**, 406–16.

Bourne, L. E. and Restle, F. (1959). A mathematical theory of concept identification. *Psychological Review*, **66**, 278–96.

Bower, G. H. (1961). Application of a model to paired-associate learning. *Psychometrika*, **26**, 255–80.

—— (1967). A multicomponent theory of the memory trace. In *The psychology of learning and motivation: advances in research and theory*, Vol. 1, (ed. K. W. Spence and J. T. Spence), pp. 230–327. Academic Press, New York.

Bowles, N. L. and Glanzer, M. (1983). An analysis of interference in memory. *Memory and cognition*, **11**, 307–15.

Breen, T. J. and Schvaneveldt, R. W. (1986). Classification of empirically derived prototypes as a function of category experience. *Memory & cognition*, **14**, 313–20.

Brooks, L. R. (1978). Non-analytic concept formation and memory for instances. In *Cognition and concepts*, (ed. E. Rosch and B. LLoyd), pp. 169–211. Erlbaum, Hillsdale, NJ.

——, Norman, G. R. and Allen, S. W. (1991). Role of specific similarity in a medical diagnostic task. *Journal of Experimental Psychology: General*, **120**, 278–87.

Brown, J. (1958). Some tests of the decay theory of immediate memory. *Quarterly Journal of Experimental Psychology*, **10**, 12–21.

Bruner, J. S., Goodnow, J. J. and Austin, G. A. (1956). *A study of thinking*. Wiley, New York.

Busemeyer, J. R., Dewey, G. I. and Medin, D. L. (1984). Evaluation of exemplar-based generalization and the abstraction of categorical information. *Journal of Experimental Psychology: Learning, Memory and Cognition*, **10**, 638–48.

—— and Myung, J. (1988). A new method for investigating prototype learning. *Journal of Experimental Psychology: Learning, Memory and Cognition*, **14**, 3–11.

Bush, R. R. and Mosteller, F. (1951). A mathematical model for simple learning. *Psychological Review*, **58**, 313–23.

Carr, H. A. (1931). The laws of association. *Psychological Review*, **38**, 212–28.

Carroll, J. D. and Wish, M. (1974). Multidimensional perceptual models and measurement methods. In *Handbook of perception*, Vol. II, (ed. E. C. Carterette and M. P. Friedman), pp. 391–447. Academic Press, New York.

Cobos, P. L., Rando, M. A. and Lopez Gutierrez, F. J. (1992). *A connectionist approach to biases in probability judgements*. Paper presented at the *XXV International Congress of Psychology*, Brussels.

Cohen, M. M. and Massaro, D. W. (1992). On the similarity of categorization models. In *Multidimensional models of perception and cognition* (ed. F. G. Ashby), pp. 395–447. Erlbaum, Hillsdale, N.J.

Collins, A. M. and Loftus, E. F. (1975). A spreading-activation theory of semantic processing. *Psychological Review*, **82**, 407–28.

——, Brown, J. Seely and Newman, S. E. (1989). Cognitive apprenticeship: Teaching the crafts of reading, writing and mathematics. In *Knowing, learning and instruction: Essays in honor of Robert Glaser*, (ed. L. B. Resnick), pp. 453–94. Erlbaum, Hillsdale, NJ.

Conrad, R. (1964). Acoustic confusions in immediate memory. *British Journal of Psychology*, **55**, 75–84.

—— (1967). Interference or decay over short retention intervals? *Journal of Verbal Learning and Verbal Behavior*, **6**, 49–54.

Corter, J. E. and Gluck, M. A. (1992). Explaining basic categories: Feature predictability and information. *Psychological Bulletin*, **111**, 291–303.

——, —— and Bower, G. H. (1988). Basic levels in hierarchically structured categories. *Proceedings of the Tenth Annual Conference of the Cognitive Science Society*. Erlbaum, Hillsdale, NJ.

Craik, F. I. M. and Levy, B. A. (1976). The concept of primary memory. In *Handbook of learning and cognitive processes*, Vol. 4, (ed. W. K. Estes), pp. 133–75. Erlbaum, Hillsdale, NJ.

D'Andrade, R. G. (1989). Cultural cognition. In *Foundations of cognitive science*, (ed. M. I. Posner), pp. 795–830. MIT Press, Cambridge, MA.

Dell, G. S. (1985). Positive feedback in hierarchical connectionist models: Applications to language production. *Cognitive Science*, **9**, 3–23.

Dienes, Z. (1992). Connectionist and memory-array models of artificial grammar learning. *Cognitive Science*, **16**, 41–79.

Elio, R. and Anderson, J. R. (1981). The effects of category generalizations and instance similarity on schema abstraction. *Journal of Experimental Psychology: Human Learning and Memory*, **7**, 397–417.

Elstein, A. S., Shulman, L. S. and Sprafka, S. A. (1990). Medical problem solving: A ten-year retrospective. *Evaluation and the Health Professions*, **13**, 5–36.

Estes, W. K. (1950). Toward a statistical theory of learning. *Psychological Review*, **57**, 94–107.

—— (1958). Stimulus-response theory of drive. In *Nebraska symposium on motivation*, Vol. 6 (ed. M. R. Jones), pp. 35–69). Nebraska University Press, Lincoln, Nebraska.

—— (1972). An associative basis for coding and organization in memory. In *Coding processes in human memory* (ed. A. W. Melton and E. Martin), pp. 161–90). Winston, Washington, D. C.

—— (1973). Memory and conditioning. In *Contemporary approaches to conditioning and learning* (ed. F. J. McGuigan and D. B. Lumsden), pp. 265–86. Winston,

Washington, D. C.

—— (1976). The cognitive side of probability learning. *Psychological Review*, **83**, 37–64.

—— (1986*a*). Array models for category learning. *Cognitive Psychology*, **18**, 500–49.

—— (1986*b*). Storage and retrieval processes in category learning. *Journal of Experimental Psychology: General*, **115**, 155–74.

—— (1988). Toward a framework for combining connectionist and symbol-processing models. *Journal of Memory and Language*, **27**, 196–212.

—— (1989*a*). Early and late memory processing in models for category learning. In *Current issues in cognitive processes: The Tulane Flowerree Symposium on Cognition* (ed. C. Izawa), pp. 11–24. Erlbaum, Hillsdale, NJ.

—— (1989*b*). Human learning and memory. In *Stevens' handbook of experimental psychology*, Vol. 2, *Learning and Cognition* (ed. R. C. Atkinson, R. J. Herrnstein, G. Lindzey and R. D. Luce), pp. 351–416. Wiley, New York.

—— (1991*a*). Cognitive architectures from the standpoint of an experimental psychologist. In *Annual review of psychology* Vol. 42, (ed. M. R. Rosenzweig and L. W. Porter), pp. 1–28. Annual Reviews, Inc., Palo Alto, CA.

—— (1991*b*). On types of item coding and sources of recall in short-term memory. In *Relating theory and data: essays in honor of Bennet B. Murdock* (ed. W. E. Hockley and S. Lewandowsky), pp. 155–73). Erlbaum, Hillsdale, NJ.

—— (1991c). *Statistical models in behavioral research*. Erlbaum, Hillsdale, NJ.

—— (1992). Mental psychophysics of categorization and decision. In *cognition, information processing and psychophysics: basic issues* (ed. H.-G. Geissler, S. W. Link and J. T. Townsend), pp. 123–39. Erlbaum, Hillsdale, NJ:

—— (in press). Models of categorization and category learning. In *The psychology of learning and motivation*, Vol. 29, *Categorization by humans and machines* (ed. G. V. Nakamura, R. Taraban, J. M. Palacios and D. L. Medin). Academic Press, San Diego.

——, Campbell, J. A., Hatsopoulis, N. and Hurwitz, J. B. (1989). Base-rate effects in category learning: A comparison of parallel network and memory storage-retrieval models. *Journal of Experimental Psychology: Learning, Memory and Cognition*, **15**, 556–71.

—— and Hopkins, B. L. (1961). Acquisition and transfer in pattern-vs.-component discrimination learning. *Journal of Experimental Psychology*, **61**, 322–8.

Fisher, S. C. (1931). A critique of insight in Kohler's Gestalt Psychology. *American Journal of Psychology*, **43**, 131–6.

Fried, L. S. and Holyoak, K. J. (1984). Induction of category distributions: A framework for classification learning. *Journal of Experimental Psychology: Learning, Memory and Cognition*, **10**, 234–57.

Galton, F. (1878). Composite portraits. *Nature*, **18**, 97–100.

Garner, W. R. (1974). *The processing of information and structure*. Erlbaum, Hillsdale, NJ.

—— (1976). Interaction of stimulus dimensions in concept and choice processes. *Cognitive Psychology*, **8**, 98–123.

Gillund, G. and Shiffrin, R. M. (1984). A retrieval model for both recognition and recall. *Psychological Review*, **91**, 1–67.

Glanzer, M. and Adams, J. K. (1990). The mirror effect in recognition memory.

Journal of Experimental Psychology: Learning, Memory and Cognition, **16**, 5–16.

——, —— and Iverson, G. (1991). Forgetting and the mirror effect in recognition memory: Concentering of underlying distributions. *Journal of Experimental Psychology: Learning, Memory and Cognition*, **17**, 81–93.

—— and Bowles, N. (1976). Analysis of the word-frequency effect in recognition memory. *Journal of Experimental Psychology: Human Learning and Memory*, **2**, 21–31.

Gluck, M. A. (1984). Category learning and judgment: from features to categories and back again. (Unpublished manuscript).

—— (1991). Stimulus generalization and representation in adaptive network models of category learning. *Psychological Science*, **2**, 50–5.

—— (1992). Stimulus sampling and distributed representations in adaptive network theories of learning. In *From learning theory to connectionist theory: essays in honor of William K. Estes* (ed. A. Healy, S. M. Kosslyn and R. M. Shiffrin), pp. 169–99. Erlbaum, Hillsdale, NJ.

—— and Bower, G. H. (1988*a*). Evaluating an adaptive network model for human learning. *Journal of Memory and Language*, **27**, 166–95.

—— and —— (1988*b*). From conditioning to category learning: An adaptive network model. *Journal of Experimental Psychology: General*, **117**, 225–44.

——, —— and Hee, M. R. (1989). A configural-cue network model of animal and human associative learning. *Proceedings of the Eleventh Annual Conference of the Cognitive Science Society*. Erlbaum, Hillsdale, NJ.

—— and Myers, C. E. (1992). Hippocampal-system function in representation and generalization: A computational theory. *Proceedings of the Eleventh Annual Conference of the Cognitive Science Society*, pp. 390–5. Erlbaum, Hillsdale, NJ.

Goldstone, R. L. and Medin, D. L. (in press). Interactive activation, similarity and mapping. In *Advances in connectionist and neural computation theory*, Vol. 2: *Connectionist approaches to analogy, metaphor and case-based reasoning* (ed. J. K. Holyoak and J. Barnden). ABLEX, Norwood, NJ.

——, —— and Gentner, D. (1991). Relational similarity and the nonindependence of features in similarity judgments. *Cognitive Psychology*, **23**, 222–62.

Gynther, M. D. (1957). Differential eyelid conditioning as a function of stimulus similarity and strength of response to the CS. *Journal of Experimental Psychology*, **53**, 408–16.

Hamilton, W. (1859). *Lectures on metaphysics and logic*. Blackwood, Edinburgh.

Hampton, J. A. (1988). Overextension of conjunctive concepts: evidence for a unitary model of concept typicality and class inclusion. *Journal of Experimental Psychology: Learning, Memory and Cognition*, **14**, 12–32.

Hayes-Roth, B. and Hayes-Roth, F. (1977). Concept learning and the recognition and classification of exemplars. *Journal of Verbal Learning and Verbal Behavior*, **16**, 321–38.

Healy, A. F. (1974). Separating item from order information in short-term memory. *Journal of Verbal Learning and Verbal Behavior*, **13**, 644–55.

Hebb, D. O. (1949). *Organization of behavior: a neurophysiological theory*. Wiley, New York.

Heidbreder, E. (1924). An experimental study of thinking. *Archives of Psychology*, **11** (#73)

Heit, E. (1992). Categorization using chains of examples. *Cognitive Psychology*, **24**, 341–80.

Hinton, G. E. and Anderson, J. A. (1981). *Parallel models of associative memory.* Erlbaum, Hillsdale, NJ.

Hintzman, D. L. (1986). "Schema abstraction" in a multiple tract model. *Psychological Review*, **93**, 411–28.

—— (1988). Judgments of frequency and recognition memory in a multiple-trace memory. *Psychological Review*, **95**, 528–51.

——, Block, R. A. and Summers, J. J. (1973). Modality tags and memory for repetitions: locus of the spacing effect. *Journal of Verbal Learning and Verbal Behavior*, **12**, 229–38.

Holland, J. H., Holyoak, K. J., Nisbett, R. E. and Thagard, P. R. (1986). *Induction: processes of inference, learning and discovery.*MIT Press, Cambridge, MA.

Hollingworth, H. L. (1913). Characteristic differences between recall and recognition. *American Journal of Psychology*, **24**, 532–44.

—— (1928). General laws of redintegration. *Journal of General Psychology*, **1**, 79–90.

Homa, D., Sterling, S. and Trepel, L. (1981). Limitations of exemplar-based generalization and the abstraction of categorical information. *Journal of Experimental Psychology: Learning, Memory and Cognition*, **7**, 418–39.

—— and Vosburgh, R. (1976). Category breadth and the abstraction of prototypical information. *Journal of Experimental Psychology; Human Learning and Memory*, **2**, 322–30.

Hubel, D. H. and Wiesel, T. N. (1962). Receptive fields, binocular interaction and functional architecture in the cat's visual cortex. *Journal of Physiology*, **160**, 106–54.

Hull, C. L. (1920). Quantitative aspects of the evolution of concepts. *Psychological Monographs*, **28**(#123).

—— (1943). *Principles of behavior.* Appleton-Century-Crofts, New York.

Hume, D. (1748/1947). An enquiry concerning human understanding. In *The world's great thinkers. Man and spirit: the speculative philosophers* (ed. S. Commins and R. N. Linscott), pp. 341–420). Random House, New York.

Hunt, E. (1989). Cognitive science: Definition, status and questions. *Annual review of psychology* Vol. 40, pp. 603–29. Annual Reviews, Inc, Palo Alto, CA.

——, Marin, J. and Stone, P. (1966). *Experiments in induction.* Academic Press, New York.

Hurwitz, J. B. (1990). *A hidden-pattern unit model of category learning.* Ph.D., Harvard University.

Izawa, C. (1967). Function of test trials in paired-associate learning. *Journal of Experimental Psychology*, **75**, 194–209.

—— (1985). A test of the differences between anticipation and study-test methods of paired-associate learning. *Journal of Experimental Psychology: Learning, Memory and Cognition*, **11**, 165–84.

Jacoby, L. L. and Brooks, L. R. (1984). Nonanalytic cognition: memory, perception and concept formation. In *The psychology of learning and motivation: advances in research and theory* Vol. 18, (ed. G. H. Bower), pp. 1–47. Academic Press, New York.

Jakobson, R., Fant, C. G. M. and Halle, M. (1952). *Preliminaries to speech analysis:the distinctive features and their correlates*. MIT Press, Cambridge, MA.

Jolicoeur, P., Gluck, M. and Kosslyn, S. M. (1984). Pictures and names: making the connection. *Cognitive Psychology*, **16**, 243–75.

Kintsch, W. (1965). The effects of repetition on the short-term memory function. *Psychonomic Science*, **2**, 149–50.

Knapp, A. G. and Anderson, J. A. (1984). Theory of categorization based on distributed memory storage. *Journal of Experimental Psychology: Learning, Memory and Cognition*, **10**, 616–37.

Konorski, J. (1967). *Integrative activity of the brain*. University of Chicago Press, Chicago.

Krueger, L. E. (1978). A theory of perceptual matching. *Psychological Review*, **85**, 278–304.

Kruschke, J. K. (1990). *A connectionist model of category learning*. Ph. D. dissertation, University of California, Berkeley.

—— (1992*a*). ALCOVE: An exemplar-based connectionist model of category learning. *Psychological Review*, **99**, 22–44.

—— (1992*b*). *Dimensional relevance shifts in category learning*. Technical report no.79, Indiana University, Bloomington, IN.

Kuhl, P. K., Williams, K. A., Lacerda, F., Stevens, K. N. and Lindblom, B. (1992). Linguistic experience alters phonetic perception in infants by 6 months of age. *Science*, **255**, 606–8.

Kvadsheim, R. (1992). *The intelligent imitator: towards an exemplar theory of behavioral choice*. North-Holland, Amsterdam.

LaBerge, D. L. (1959). A model with neutral elements. In *Studies in mathematical learning theory* (ed. R. R. Bush and W. K. Estes), pp. 53–64. Stanford University Press, Stanford, CA.

Lachter, J. and Bever, T. G. (1988). The relation between linguistic structure and the associative theories of language learning: a constructive critique of some common learning models. *Cognition*, **28**, 195–247.

Lee, C. L. (1992). The perturbation model of short-term memory: A review and some further developments. In *From learning processes to cognitive processes: essays in honor of William K. Estes*, (ed. A. Healy, S. M. Kosslyn and R. M. Shiffrin), pp. 119–41. Erlbaum, Hillsdale, NJ.

—— and Estes, W. K. (1977). Order and position in primary memory for letter strings. *Journal of Verbal Learning and Verbal Behavior*, **16**, 395–418.

—— and —— (1981). Item and order information in short-term memory: evidence for multilevel perturbation processes. *Journal of Experimental Psychology: Learning, Memory and Cognition*, **7**, 149–69.

Lesgold, A. M., Rubinson, H., Feltovich, P., Klopfer, D., Glaser, R. and Wang, Y. (1988). Expertise in a complex skill. In *The nature of expertise*, (ed. M. T. H. Chi, R. Glaser and M. Farr), pp. 322–51. Erlbaum, Hillsdale, NJ.

Levine, M. (1967). The size of the hypothesis set during discrimination learning. *Psychological Review*, **74**, 428–30.

—— (1971). Hypothesis theory and nonlearning despite ideal S-R reinforcement contingencies. *Psychological Review*, **78**, 130–40.

Levine, M. and Shefner, J. M. (1981). *Fundamentals of sensation and perception*. Addison-Wesley, Reading, MA.

Loftus, G., R. (1974). Acquisition of information from rapidly presented verbal and non-verbal stimuli. *Memory and Cognition*, **2**, 545–8.

Logan, G. D. (1988). Toward an instance theory of automatization. *Psychological Review*, **95**, 492–527.

Luce, R. D. (1963). Detection and recognition. In *Handbook of mathematical psychology*. Vol. 1, (ed. R. D. Luce, R. R. Bush and E. Galanter), pp. 103–89. Wiley, New York.

—— and Krumhansl, C. L. (1988). Measurement, scaling and psychophysics. In *Stevens' handbook of experimental psychology*, 2nd edn, (ed. R. C. Atkinson, R. J. Herrnstein, G. Lindzey and R. D. Luce), pp. 3–74. Wiley, New York.

MacCormack, P. D. and Swenson, A. L. (1972). Recognition memory for common and rare words. *Journal of Experimental Psychology*, **95**, 72–7.

MacMillan, J. (1987). *The role of frequency memory in category judgments*. Ph.D., Harvard University.

Macmillan, N. A. and Creelman, C. D. (1990). Response bias: characteristics of detection theory, threshold theory and "nonparametric" indexes. *Psychological Bulletin*, **107**, 401–13.

Maddox, W. T. and Ashby, F. G. (1993). Comparing decision bound and exemplar models of categorization. *Perception and Psychophysics*, **53**, 49–70.

McGeoch, J. A. (1942). *The psychology of human learning*. Longmans, Green, New York.

McNaughton, B. L. and Nadel, L. (1990). Hebb–Marr networks and the neurobiological representation of action in space. In *Neuroscience and connectionist theory* (ed. M. A. Gluck and D. E. Rumelhart), pp. 1–63. Erlbaum, Hillsdale, NJ.

McNicol, D. (1972). *A primer of signal detection theory*. George Allen and Unwin, London.

Medin, D. L. (1975). A theory of context in discrimination learning. In *The psychology of learning and motivation*, Vol. 9. (ed. G. H. Bower), pp. 263–314. Academic Press, New York.

—— (1976). Theories of discrimination learning and learning set. In *Handbook of learning and cognitive processes*, Vol. 2, (ed. W. K. Estes), pp. 131–69).Erlbaum, Hillsdale, NJ.

——, Altom, M. L., Edelson, S. M. and Freko, D. (1982). Correlated symptoms and simulated medical classification. *Journal of Experimental Psychology: Learning, Memory and Cognition*, **8**, 37–50.

——, —— and Murphy, T. D. (1984). Given versus induced category representations: Use of prototype and exemplar information in classification. *Journal of Experimental Psychology: Learning, Memory and Cognition*, **10**, 333–52.

——, Dewey, G. I. and Murphy, T. D. (1983). Relationships between item and category learning: evidence that abstraction is not automatic. *Journal of Experimental Psychology: Human Learning and Memory*, **9**, 607–25.

—— and Edelson, S. M. (1988). Problem structure and the use of base rate information from experience. *Journal of Experimental Psychology: General*, **117**, 68–85.

—— and Florian, J. E. (1992). Abstraction and selective coding in exemplar-based models of categorization. In *From learning processes to cognitive processes: essays in honor of William K. Estes* (ed. A. Healy, S. M. Kosslyn and R. M. Shiffrin), pp. 207–34. Erlbaum, Hillsdale, NJ

—— and Schaffer, M. M. (1978). Context theory of classification learning. *Psychological Review*, **85**, 207–38.

—— and Schwanenflugel, P. J. (1981). Linear separability in classification learning. *Journal of Experimental Psychology: Learning, Memory and Cognition*, 7, 355–68.

Minsky, M. L. and Papert, S. A. (1969). *Perceptrons*. MIT Press, Cambridge, MA.

Mordkowitz, E. R. (1990). *The exodus of concrete ideas: adaptive abstraction in a multi-trace categorization architecture*. Ph.D., Harvard University.

Morton, J. (1970). A functional model for memory. In *Models of human memory*, (ed. D. A. Norman), pp. 203–54. Academic Press, New York.

Moyer, R. S. and Landauer, T. K. (1967). Time required for judgments of numerical inequality. *Nature*, **215**, 1519–20.

Murdock, B. B., Jr. (1965). Signal-detection theory and short-term memory. *Journal of Experimental Psychology*, **70**, 443–7.

—— (1974). *Human memory: theory and data*. Erlbaum, Potomac, MD.

—— (1982). A theory for the storage and retrieval of item and associative information. *Psychological Review*, **89**, 609–26.

—— (1991). *The list-strength effect (LSE) and global matching models*. Paper given at the *Meeting of the Psychonomic Society*, San Francisco.

—— and Anderson, R. E. (1975). Encoding, storage and retrieval of item information. In *Information processing and cognition: the loyola symposium*, (ed. R. L. Solso), pp. 145–94. Erlbaum, Hillsdale, NJ.

—— and Lamon, M. (1988). The replacement effect: repeating some items while replacing others. *Memory and Cognition*, **16**, 91–101.

Murnane, K. and Shiffrin, R. M. (1991). Interference and the representation of events in memory. *Journal of Experimental Psychology: Learning, Memory and Cognition*, **17**, 855–74.

Murphy, G. L. and Medin, D. L. (1985). The role of theories in conceptual coherence. *Psychological Review*, **92**, 284–316.

—— and Smith, E. E. (1982). Basic-level superiority in picture categorization. *Journal of Verbal Learning and Verbal Behavior*, **21**, 1–20.

Nelson, T. O. (1976). Reinforcement and human memory. In *Handbook of learning and cognitive processes*, Vol. 3, (ed. W. K. Estes), pp. 207–46. Erlbaum, Hillsdale, NJ.

Newell, A. (1973). Production systems: models of control structures. In *Visual information processing*, (ed. W. G. Chase), pp. 463–526. Academic Press, New York.

Nisbett, R. E., Zukier, H. and Lemley, R. (1981). The dilution effect: Nondiagnostic information weakens the implications of diagnostic information. *Cognitive Psychology*, **13**, 248–77.

Norman, D. A. (1972). *Models of human memory*. Academic Press, New York.

Nosofsky, R. M. (1984). Choice, similarity and the context theory of classification. *Journal of Experimental Psychology: Learning, Memory and Cognition*, **10**, 104–14.

—— (1986). Attention, similarity and the identification-categorization relationship. *Journal of Experimental Psychology: General*, **115**, 39–57.

—— (1987). Attention and learning processes in the identification and categorization of integral stimuli. *Journal of Experimental Psychology: Learning, Memory and*

Cognition, **13,** 87–108.

—— (1988*a*). Exemplar-based acccounts of relations between classification, recognition and typicality. *Journal of Experimental Psychology: Learning, Memory and Cognition,* **14,** 700–8.

—— (1988*b*). Similarity, frequency and category representations. *Journal of Experimental Psychology: Learning, Memory and Cognition,* **14,** 54–65.

—— (1990). Relations between exemplar-similarity and likelihood models of classification. *Journal of Mathematical Psychology,* **34,** 393–418.

—— (1991*a*). Relation between the rational model and the context model of categorization. *Psychological Science,* **3,** 416–21.

—— (1991*b*). Tests of an exemplar model for relating perceptual classification and recognition. *Journal of Experimental Psychology: Human Perception and Performance,* **17,** 3–27.

—— (1992*a*). Exemplars, prototypes and similarity rules. In *From learning theory to connectionist theory: essays in honor of William K. Estes,* (ed. A. Healy, S. M. Kosslyn and R. M. Shiffrin), pp. 149–67. Erlbaum, Hillsdale, NJ.

—— (1992*b*). Similarity scaling and cognitive process models. In *Annual review of psychology.* Vol. 43, (ed. M. R. Rosenzweig and L. W. Porter), pp. 25–53. Annual Reviews, Inc, Palo Alto, CA.

——, Clark, S. E. and Shin, H. J. (1989). Rules and exemplars in categorization, identification and recognition. *Journal of Experimental Psychology: Learning, Memory and Cognition,* **15,** 282–304.

——, Kruschke, J. K. and McKinley, S. (1992). Combining exemplar-based category representations and connectionist learning rules. *Journal of Experimental Psychology: Learning, Memory and Cognition,* **18,** 211–33.

—— and Smith, J. E. K. (1992). Similarity, identification and categorization: comment on Ashby and Lee, 1991. *Journal of Experimental Psychology: General,* **121,** 237–45.

Oden, G. C. (1977). Integration of fuzzy logical information. *Journal of Experimental Psychology: Human Perception and Performance,* **3,** 565–75.

Osherson, D. N. and Smith, E. E. (1981). On the adequacy of prototype theory as a theory of concepts. *Cognition,* **9,** 35–58.

——, ——, Wilkie, O., Lopez, A. and Shafir, E. (1990). Category-based induction. *Psychological Review,* **97,** 185–200.

Pavlov, I. P. (1927). *Conditioned reflexes.* Oxford University Press, London.

Pinker, S. and Prince, A. (1988). On language and connectionism: analysis of a parallel distributed processing model of language acquisition. *Cognition,* **28,** 73–193.

Posner, M. I. (1978). *Chronometric explorations of mind.* Erlbaum, Hillsdale, NJ.

—— and Keele, S. W. (1968). On the genesis of abstract ideas. *Journal of Experimental Psychology,* **77,** 353–63.

—— and —— (1970). Retention of abstract ideas. *Journal of Experimental Psychology,* **83,** 304–8.

Raaijmakers, J. G. W. and Shiffrin, R. M. (1981). Search of associative memory. *Psychological Review,* **88,** 93–134.

Ratcliff, R. (1978). A theory of memory retrieval. *Psychological Review,* **85,** 59–108.

——, Clark, S. E. and Shiffrin, R. M. (1990). The list-strength effect: I. data and discussion. *Journal of Experimental Psychology: Learning, Memory and Cognition*, **16**, 163–78.

Reber, A. S. (1967). Implicit learning of artificial grammars. *Journal of Verbal Learning and Verbal Behavior*, **5**, 855–63.

—— and Millward, R. B. (1968). Event observations in probability learning. *Journal of Experimental Psychology*, **77**, 317–27.

Reed, S. K. (1972). Pattern recognition and classification. *Cognitive Psychology*, **3**, 382–407.

—— (1978). Category vs, item learning: implications for categorization models. *Memory and Cognition*, **6**, 612–621.

Rescorla, R. A. and Wagner, A. R. (1972). A theory of Pavlovian conditioning: variations in the effectiveness of reinforcement and non-reinforcement. In *Classical conditioning II: current research and theory*, (ed. A. H. Black and W. F. Prokasy), pp. 64–99. Appleton-Century-Crofts, New York.

Restle, F. (1955). A theory of discrimination learning. *Psychological Review*, **62**, 11–9.

—— (1961). *Psychology of judgment and choice*. Wiley, New York.

Robbins, D. (1970). Stimulus selection in human discrimination learning and transfer. *Journal of Experimental Psychology*, **84**, 282–90.

Robinson, E. S. (1932). *Association theory today*. Century, New York.

Roediger, H. L., III (1980). Memory metaphors in cognitive psychology. *Memory and Cognition*, **8**, 231–46.

Rosch, E. (1973). On the internal structure of perceptual and semantic categories. In *Cognitive development and the acquisition of language*, (ed. T. E. Moore), pp. 111–44. Academic Press, New York.

—— (1978). Principles of categorization. In *Cognition and categorization*, (ed. E. Rosch and B. B. Lloyd), pp. 27–48. Erlbaum, Hillsdale, NJ.

—— and Mervis, C. B. (1975). Family resemblance studies in the internal structure of categories. *Cognitive Psychology*, **7**, 573–605.

——, ——, Gray, D. and Boyes-Braehm, P. (1976). Basic objects in natural categories. *Cognitive psychology*, **3**, 382–439.

——, Simpson, C. and Miller, R. S. (1976). Structural bases of typicality effects. *Journal of Experimental Psychology: Human Perception and Performance*, **2**, 491–502.

Rudy, J. R. and Wagner, A. R. (1975). Stimulus selection. In *Handbook of learning and cognitive processes*, Vol. 2, (ed. W. K. Estes), pp. 269–303. Erlbaum, Hillsdale, NJ.

Rumelhart, D. E., Lindsay, P. H. and Norman, D. A. (1972). A process model for long term memory. In *Organization of memory*, (ed. E. Tulving and W. Donaldson), pp. 197–246). Academic Press, New York.

—— and McClelland, J. L. (1986). *Parallel distributed processing*, Vol. 1.MIT Press, Cambridge, MA.

Schank, R. C. (1982). *Dynamic memory:a theory of learning in computers and people*. Cambridge, Cambridge University Press.

——, Collins, G. C. and Hunter, L. E. (1986). Transcending inductive category learning. *Behavioral and Brain Sciences*, **9**, 639–86.

Schneider, W. and Shiffrin, R. M. (1977). Controlled and automatic human information processing: I. detection, search and attention. *Psychological Review*,

84, 1–66.

Schulman, A. I. (1967). Word length and rarity in recognition memory. *Psychonomic Science*, **9**, 211–2.

Schustack, M. W. and Sternberg, R. J. (1981). Evaluation of evidence in causal inference. *Journal of Experimental Psychology: General*, **110**, 101–120.

Schyns, P. G. (1991). A modular neural network model of concept acquisition. *Cognitive Science*, **15**, 461–508.

Seidenberg, M. S. and McClelland, J. L. (1989). A distributed, developmental model of word recognition and naming. *Psychological Review*, **96**, 523–68.

Shanks, D. R. (1990). Connectionism and the learning of probabilistic concepts. *Quarterly Journal of Experimental Psychology*, **42A**, 209–37.

Shepard, R. N. (1958). Stimulus and response generalization: deduction of the generalization gradient from a trace model. *Psychological Review*, **65**, 242–56.

—— (1967). Recognition memory for words, sentences and pictures. *Journal of Verbal Learning and Verbal Behavior*, **6**, 156–63.

—— (1974). Representation of structure in similarity data. *Psychometrika*, **39**, 373–421.

— (1987). Toward a universal law of generalization for psychological science. *Science*, **237**, 1317–23.

—— and Chang, J. J. (1963). Stimulus generalization in the learning of classifications. *Journal of Experimental Psychology*, **65**, 94–102.

—— and Cooper, L. A. (1982). *Mental images and their transformations*. MIT Press, Cambridge, MA.

——, Hovland, C. I. and Jenkins, H. M. (1961). Learning and memorization of classifications. *Psychological Monographs*, **75**, 1–41.

——, Romney, A. K. and Nerlove, S. (1972). *Multidimensional scaling: theory and applications in the behavioral sciences*. Academic Press, New York.

—— and Teghtsoonian, M. (1961). Retention of information under conditions approaching a steady state. *Journal of Experimental Psychology*, **62**, 302–9.

Shiffrin, R. M. and Murnane, K. (1991). Composition, distribution and interference in memory. In *Relating theory and data: essays in honor of Bennet B. Murdock*, (ed. W. E. Hockley and S. Lewandowsky), pp. 331–46. Erlbaum, Hillsdale, NJ.

—— and Raaijmakers, J. (1992). The SAM retrieval model: a retrospective and prospective. In *From learning processes to cognitive processes: essays in honor of William K. Estes*, (ed. A. Healy, S. M. Kosslyn and R. M. Shiffrin), pp. 69–86. Erlbaum, Hillsdale, NJ.

——, Ratcliff, R. and Clark, S. E. (1990). The list-strength effect: theoretical mechanisms. *Journal of Experimental Psychology: Learning, Memory and Cognition*, **16**, 179–95.

Shin, H. J. and Nosofsky, R. M. (1991). *Similarity-scaling studies of "dot-pattern" classification and recognition*. Technical report, Indiana University.

Silverman, W. P. (1973). The perception of identity in simultaneously presented complex visual displays. *Memory and Cognition*, **1**, 459–66.

Smith, E. E. (1978). Theories of semantic memory. In *Handbook of learning and cognitive processes*, Vol. 6 (ed. W. K. Estes), pp. 1–56. Erlbaum, Hillsdale, NJ.

—— (1990). Categorization. In *An invitation to cognitive science*, Vol. 3. *Thinking* (ed. D. N. Osherson and E. E. Smith), pp. 33–53. The MIT Press, Cambridge, MA.

——, Langston, C. and Nisbett, R. (1992). The case for rules in reasoning. *Cognitive Science*, **16**, 1–40.

——, Lopez, A. and Osherson, D. N. (1992). Category membership, similarity and naive induction. In *From learning processes to cognitive processes: essays in honor of William K. Estes*, (ed. A. Healy, S. M. Kosslyn and R. M. Shiffrin), pp. 181–206. Erlbaum, Hillsdale, NJ.

—— and Medin, D. L. (1981). *Categories and concepts*. Harvard University Press, Cambridge, MA.

—— and Osherson, D. N. (1984). Conceptual combination with prototype concepts. *Cognitive Science*, **11**, 337–61.

——, ——, Rips, L. J. and Keane, M. (1988). Combining prototypes: a selective modification model. *Cognitive Science*, **12**, 485–527.

——, Shoben, E. J. and Rips, L. J. (1974). Structure and process in semantic memory. *Psychological Review*, **81**, 214–41.

Spear, N. E. (1976). Retrieval of memories: a psychobiological approach. In *Handbook of learning and cognitive processes*, Vol. 4, (ed. W. K. Estes), pp. 17–90. Erlbaum, Hillsdale, NJ.

Spiegelhalter, D. J. and Knill-Jones, R. F. (1984). Statistical and knowledge-based approaches to clinical decision-support systems. *Journal of the Royal Statistical Society*, **147**, 35–77.

Squire, L. R. (1992). Memory and the hippocampus. *Psychological Review*, **99**, 195–231.

Stepanovich, B. P. (1927). An experimental study of the mental processes involved in judgment. *British Journal of Psychology*, **12** (Monograph Supplement), 1–138.

Sternberg, S. (1966). High-speed scanning in human memory. *Science*, **153**, 652–4.

Stone, G. O. (1986). An analysis of the delta rule and the learning of statistical associations. In *Parallel distributed processing*, Vol. I, (ed. D. E. Rumelhart and J. L. McClelland), pp. 444–59. MIT Press, Cambridge, MA.

Strong, E. K. (1912). The effect of length of series upon recognition memory. *Psychological Review*, **19**, 447–462.

Sutherland, N. S. and Mackintosh, N. J. (1971). *Mechanisms of animal discrimination learning*. Academic Press, New York.

Swets, J. A. (1964). *Signal detection and recognition by human observers: contemporary readings*. Wiley, New York.

Tanaka, J. W. and Taylor, M. (1991). Categorization and expertise: is the basic level in the eye of the beholder? *Cognitive Psychology*, **23**, 457–82.

Tanner, W. P., Jr. and Swets, J. A. (1954). A decision-making theory of visual detection. *Psychological Review*, **61**, 401–9.

Taraban, R. and Palacios, J. M. (in press). Exemplar models and weighted cue models in category learning. In *The psychology of learning and motivation*, Vol. 29, *Categorization by humans and machines*, (ed. G. V. Nakamura, R. Taraban and D. L. Medin), Academic Press, San Diego, CA.

Thorndike, E. L. (1913). *Educational psychology*, Vol. II, *The psychology of learning*. Teachers College, Columbia University, New York.

—— (1931). *Human learning*. Century, New York.

Townsend, J. T. (1990). Serial vs. parallel processing. *Psychological Science*, **1**, 46–54.

Trabasso, T. and Bower, G. H. (1968). *Attention in learning*. Wiley, New York.

Tulving, E. (1981). Similarity relations in recognition. *Journal of Verbal Learning and Verbal Behavior*, **20**, 479–96.

Tversky, A. (1977). Features of similarity. *Psychological Review*, **84**, 327–52.

Uhl, C. N. (1964). Effect of overlapping cues upon discrimination learning. *Journal of Experimental Psychology*, **67**, 91–7.

Underwood, B. J. (1969). Attributes of memory. *Psychological Review*, **76**, 559–73.

——, Runquist, W. N. and Schulz, R. W. (1959). Response learning in paired-associate lists as a function of intralist similarity. *Journal of Experimental Psychology*, **58**, 70–78.

Uttal, W. R. (1973). *The psychobiology of sensory coding*. Harper and Row, New York.

Whittlesea, B. W. A. (1987). Preservation of specific experiences in the representation of general knowledge. *Journal of Experimental Psychology: Learning, Memory and Cognition*, **13**, 3–17.

—— and Brooks, L. R. (1988). Critical influence of particular experiences in the perception of letters, words and phrases. *Memory and Cognition*, **16**, 387–99.

Wickelgren, W. A. and Norman, D. A. (1966). Strength models and serial position in short-term recognition memory. *Journal of Mathematical Psychology*, **3**, 316–47.

Wickens, T. D. (1982). *Models for behavior: stochastic processes in psychology*. Freeman, San Francisco.

Woodworth, R. S. (1938). *Experimental psychology*. Holt, New York.

Yonelinas, A. P., Hockley, W. E. and Murdock, B. B. (1992). Tests of the list-strength effect in recognition memory. *Journal of Experimental Psychology: Learning, Memory and Cognition*, **18**, 345–55.

Zeaman, D. and House, B. J. (1963). The role of attention in retardate discrimination learning. In *Handbook of mental deficiency*, (ed. N. R. Ellis), pp. 159–223. McGraw-Hill, New York.

Author index

Subject index